Lawrence Verry Inc.

REVIEW COPY

Boyce, W.B..
Notes on South African Affairs

Africana Collectanea # 39

LIST PRICE

$13.00

Publishers - Distributors - Importers
MYSTIC, CONNECTICUT
06355

AFRICANA COLLECTANEA
VOLUME XXXIX

NOTES ON
SOUTH AFRICAN AFFAIRS

AFRICANA COLLECTANEA SERIES

VOL	I	J. M. Bowker *Speeches, Letters and Selections*
VOL	II	R. Godlonton and E. Irving *Narrative of the Kaffir War 1850–1851–1852*
VOL	III	W. C. Holden *The Past and Future of the Kaffir Races*
VOL	IV	W. C. Holden *History of the Colony of Natal*
VOL	V	S. M. Molema *The Bantu Past and Present*
VOL	VI	Capt. William Cornwallis Harris *The Wild Sports of Southern Africa*
VOL	VII	G. W. Stow *The Native Races of South Africa*
VOL and	VIII IX	Sir Andries Stockenstrom *Autobiography (Vols. I/II)*
VOL	X	J. M. Orpen *Reminiscences of Life in S.A.*
VOL	XI	R. Godlonton *A Narrative of the Irruption of the Kaffir Hordes*
VOL	XII	W. Collins *Free Statia*
VOL	XIII	A. T. Bryant *Olden Times in Zululand and Natal*
VOL and	XIV XV	J. Bird *The Annals of Natal (Vols. I/II)*
VOL	XVI	E. Casalis *The Basutos: or twenty-three years in South Africa.*
VOL and	XVII XVIII	A. Steedman *Wanderings and Adventures in the Interior of Southern Africa. 2 vols.*
VOL	XIX	W. Bird *State of Good Hope in 1822.*
VOL	XX	Th. Pringle *Narrative of a Residence in South Africa*
VOL	XXI	A. F. Gardiner *Narrative of a Journey to the Zoolu Country in South Africa.*

VOL	XXII	Sir James E. Alexander
and	XXIII	*An Expedition of Discovery into the Interior of Africa. Vols. I/II*
VOL	XXIV	C. J. Andersson
		Lake Ngami
VOL	XXV	J. Centlivres Chase
		The Cape of Good Hope and the Eastern Province of Algoa Bay.
VOL	XXVI	W. Ch. Baldwin
		African Hunting and Adventure
VOL	XXVII	T. Arbousset, and F. Daumas
		Narrative of an Exploratory Tour to the North-East of the Colony of the Cape of Good Hope.
VOL	XXVIII	W. H. I. Bleek, and L. C. Lloyd
		Specimens of Bushman Folklore
VOL	XXIX	C. J. Andersson
		The Okavango River
VOL	XXX	J. Centlivres Chase
		The Natal Papers
VOL	XXXI	C. J. Andersson
		Notes of Travel in South Africa
VOL	XXXII	J. C. Voigt
and	XXXIII	*Fifty years of the history of the Republic in South Africa (1795–1845) (Vols. I/II)*
VOL	XXXIV	B. Shaw
		Memorials of South Africa
VOL	XXXV	H. Callaway
		Religious systems of the Amazulu
VOL	XXXVI	J. McKay
		Reminiscences of the last Kaffir War
VOL	XXXVII	J. Tyler
		Forty Years Among the Zulus.
VOL	XXXVIII	E. Casalis
		My Life in Basutoland

Notes on South African Affairs

W. B. BOYCE

Facsimile Reprint

C. STRUIK (PTY) LTD.
CAPE TOWN
1971

C. Struik (Pty) Ltd.
Africana Specialist and Publisher

This edition is limited to 1 000 numbered copies.
Nos. 1 to 50 are specially bound in de luxe style.

THIS IS NUMBER 521

ISBN 0 86977 007 1

W. B. BOYCE

William Binnington Boyce, a Yorkshireman, arrived in South Africa as a missionary assistant to the Rev. William Shaw, superintendent of the Albany Wesleyan Methodist District, in the year 1829. A young man, twenty-seven years old, he was sent by Shaw to found a mission station, named Buntingville, in Pondoland, and was subsequently stationed at Mount Coke, Wesleyville, Newtondale and Grahamstown, all within the mission field on the Eastern Frontier. He returned to England in 1843. In the absence of William Shaw in England during the years 1834–1837, he was the most prominent Wesleyan missionary in this field. He became a trusted adviser to Sir Benjamin D'Urban during the Sixth Kaffir War, 1834–1835, but the part played by Wesleyan missionaries during that war brought them into disfavour in England, and Boyce himself was strongly criticised. Boyce however, has set out his opinions unequivocally in his *Notes on South African Affairs*. He prefaces this volume with an "Advertisement to the Reader" that he cannot spread what he deems sound views on South African Affairs without entering upon discussions of various civil and political questions, which he believes have a close connection with the religious interests of the Colonists and Aborigines. Though he thinks that his opinions generally accord with those held by other Wesleyan missionaries, his publication must in no way compromise them: the author takes sole responsibility for the opinions and reasons stated. His Notes accordingly reflect the part he played in the Sixth Kaffir War and the correspondence with the Governor, Sir Benjamin D'Urban, is illuminative. The coverage of the Notes, as stated by himself, "from 1834–1838, with reference to the civil, political and religious Condition of the Colonists and Aborigines" is widespread, and includes in fact, everything germane to the administration of the frontier. A glance at the titles of the Notes, with their numerous subdivisions, impresses one with the thoroughness of the discussions instituted, and the importance of the volume to the student of history becomes apparent. Criticism is by no means negative but is positively constructive. This is illustrated by Note IV, "Hints for the improvement of the present Border Policy".

Regarding the value of the volume, Theal, the well recognised authority on South African historical matters, comments: "Without agreeing with all the speculative remarks in this book, it must be pronounced most accurate in the facts which it records. It is one of the very best volumes of its time with reference to South Africa, for its author was not only an intelligent, but a fearlessly outspoken and honest man, who tried to tell the truth of white people and black."

Lesser authorities are agreed upon its factual accuracy and objectivity. Sir Harry Smith referring to his personal relations with Boyce described him as "a most excellent man of business, honest frank and energetic" and also "a man of comprehensive knowledge generally, and especially of the Kaffir character: he may be firmly relied upon, and is inflexible of purpose and candid in his opinions". Finally, it should not be overlooked as recorded in his Notes, that Boyce and his fellow missionaries, Shepstone and Palmer, in 1835, undertook to negotiate peace between the Governor and the chiefs Maqomo and Tyali, who were then in the Amatola mountains.

Boyce's lasting claim to fame, however, rests upon his discovery of the Euphonic Concord in Xhosa.

When missionaries were first stationed amongst the African races of southern Africa it was to find that there was a complete absence of any literature in the vernacular languages. Accordingly in addition to propagating the Gospel they studied closely the local dialects with the hope that they would soon have available the printed Bible, hymn books and books of instruction, for the educational uplift and spiritual direction of the heathen. Very great progress had been made in their knowledge of the dialects spoken in various parts and translations of many portions of the Scriptures and of Prayers had been made into Xhosa, and simple hymns composed; although their best work there was a feeling that it was all subject to revision in the light of a grammatical rule which, despite their efforts to find it, remained undiscovered.

Boyce had been sent to South Africa in the hope that his previous linguistic and other studies would enable him to master the Kaffir language. Between him and William Shaw, under whom he was stationed, sprang up an intimate and lifelong friendship and later Boyce, as "His Oldest Surviving

Friend" wrote his *Memoir of the Rev. William Shaw* in 1874.

Shaw records that during "some months" when Boyce was his guest they frequently entered into long and detailed explanations regarding their existing knowledge of the language and "especially the nature of the difficulty which had hitherto baffled all our efforts". Briefly stated, the missionaries observed in the Kaffir language a peculiar contrivance, apparently for the purpose of securing euphony in what was frequently an extended species of alliteration. Despite detailed and prolonged studies which led to the formation of various theories, all was brought to a deadlock and the incomplete knowledge of the rules continued.

As fully briefed by Shaw as was possible he sent Boyce off to found the Buntingville mission station in Pondoland. He was earnestly exhorted by Shaw to give himself "wholly to this study". Shaw arranged for young Theophilus Shepstone, a thoroughly fluent Xhosa linguist, to live at the mission so that Boyce might "try out" his theories and general information acquired by the hard way of study on Theophilus and, later, Mr. J. C. Warner, a catechist, joined them, also a fluent linguist. Boyce adopted the inductive method, and collected a large number of words and sentences. "These were written down, and afterwards tabulated". Shaw states "that Boyce possessed a remarkably quick perception, with great aptitude and powers for analysis and generalisation", and applying these insights to the material collected by him he saw that the whole was governed by fixed and invariable rules. Then in the light of the knowledge he had acquired, at a glance, the whole scheme was revealed to him, and "thus was the only serious difficulty regarding the structure of the language finally conquered". The importance of the discovery can hardly be too highly estimated when it is considered that the Euphonic Concord, as Boyce designated it, runs through and regulates almost the entire grammatical structure of the Kaffir language, and also the widespread family of Bantu languages, including those spoken along the eastern side of the African continent.

Various traditional accounts are recorded of Boyce's moment of discovery of the rule for which he had so ardently studied but that given by the Rev. H. H. Dugmore, a lifelong friend of

Boyce, may safely be accepted. "Passing backwards and forwards one evening in front of his house, the rule for the general application of the Euphonic Concord flashed suddenly upon him, like a ray of light from heaven. With the almost literal Eureka of Archimedes, he rushed into the house exclaiming 'I've got it, I've got it'. And taking the application of the rule by following it through endless varieties of construction through a sleepless three days and nights, he established the correctness of his principle with a success triumphant and complete."

Boyce had indeed leaped into prominence, as he was to do in other fields, for it seems that his discovery was made after only two years study, when in his official reports, the term euphonic or alliteral concord was first coined.

Briefly stated, "what Boyce discovered was that in the Kafir sentences the noun was the governing element and that all the other parts of speech were thrown immediately into an alliterative or euphonic concord with the subject noun". The foundation of all future study of the Bantu family of languages was well and truly laid. Simple illustrations are:

    *Z*onke i*z*into e*z*ilungileyo *z*ivela ku Tixo.
    (All things which are good come from God.)
    *B*aza *b*apendula *b*onke a*b*antu, *b*ati:
    (Then answered all the people and said:)

Boyce quickly made use of his discovery for before the end of 1833 he had completed the first Kaffir Grammar that was ever published. This was printed in 1834 upon the mission press of the Wesleyans in Grahamstown, and was dedicated to the Rev. William Shaw.

Dr. C. M. Doke, the philologist, after tributing the research and recording of the missionaries "to whom Bantu literature owes an unrepayable debt" continues: "The first published grammar of the Bantu language in South Africa goes to the credit of William B. Boyce of the Wesleyan Mission. Boyce's *Grammar of the Kafir Language* was printed in quarto at the Wesleyan Mission Press, Grahamstown in 1834. Boyce was the discoverer of the alliterative concord in Xhosa, 'the key to the etymological structure of the language' as Davis termed it."

This publication produced a new era in Kaffir literature. Previous translations were revised as far as necessary: with greater certainty regarding the structure of the language, a fresh stimulus was given the preparation of translations and other literature. In 1833 Boyce published St. Luke's Gospel, printed on the Wesleyan press in Grahamstown, and the complete New Testament was printed in London by the British and Foreign Bible Society under the superintendence of William Shaw.

Boyce had prepared the way for the long-awaited publication of the whole Bible in Xhosa and that privilege and honour belongs to the Rev. John Whittle Appleyard, to whom now we briefly refer.

Appleyard was a son of the Wesleyan manse in England. Following upon schooling he was apprenticed to a bookseller and printer. After spiritual conversion he became interested in the work of the mission field. He became prayerful and a student of the Scriptures, and was accepted as a candidate for the mission field. He reached Cape Town on 21 January, 1840. He had a knowledge of Hebrew, Greek and Latin, also of Syriac and Chaldee, and in South Africa became an "excellent Dutch scholar", and preached in it. In October he was appointed to the Durban mission (Peddie district) as assistant to the Rev. W. B. Boyce. He knew nothing of the Xhosa language but steadily studied Boyce's Kaffir Grammar, until he was able to preach without an interpreter. Shaw regarded Appleyard as the right man to place in charge of the translating and printing department for, in 1846, he had published the first complete edition of the Kaffir New Testament from the mission press at Peddie and Newtondale. In that year war again broke out on the frontier ("The War of the Axe"). Appleyard became editor and manager of the printing press first at King William's Town and subsequently at Mount Coke. He had for about ten years been working on a Grammar of the Kaffir language, and in 1850, it was printed by him in King William's Town. It was spoken most highly of by philologists, but this is not the place to say more. Mount Coke had newly risen from the ashes produced by war when in 1853 Appleyard was transferred there. In October, 1854, he issued a new and corrected edition of the New Testament issued by him in 1846. Concurrently he had been working upon the preparation of the Old Testament and in fact portions of it were already printed. In his journal, Appleyard records: "Last evening, Sep. 1st, (1859) I corrected

the last proof of the Kaffir Bible, being the closing portions of the Chronicles, revised for the first complete edition of the Old Testament. *To-day the printing of this edition has been finished, so that we have now the entire scriptures in the Kaffir language.*
To God be all the praise."

G. Mears

NOTES

ON

SOUTH AFRICAN AFFAIRS,

FROM 1834 TO 1838;

WITH REFERENCE TO

THE CIVIL, POLITICAL, AND RELIGIOUS CONDITION,

OF THE

COLONISTS AND ABORIGINES.

By WILLIAM B. BOYCE,
Wesleyan Missionary.

Graham's Town:
PRINTED BY ALDUM AND HARVEY, QUEEN-STREET.

1838.

CONTENTS.

INTRODUCTION.

	Page.
Kaffer Irruption into the Colony, December 1834,	i
Colonel Smith's Official Report of the Distress of the Frontier Inhabitants,	ibid.
Public Opinion in England unfavourable to the Colonists,	ii
Influence of the writings of Barrow and others in the formation of Public Opinion at Home,	ibid.
Mistakes of the British Public in reference to the Colonial Character, partly attributable to the growing conviction of the injustice of the European system of Colonization, &c.	ibid.
Popular Charges against the Colonists arranged under *three* heads,	iii
(1) Cases of Individual Misconduct quoted as indicative of the character of the Community,	ibid.
Testimonies of unexceptionable Witnesses in favour of the Colonial Character,	iv
Thomas Pringle (Author of *African Sketches*,)	ibid.
John Fairbairn, (Editor of the *South African Commercial Advertiser*,)	ibid.
Lord Glenelg, (Her Majesty's Secretary of State for	

CONTENTS.

	Page.
the Colonies,) - - -	v
Select Committee on Aborigines, - -	ibid.
(2.) The Commando System, or Militia Force of the Colony,	ibid.
Mistakes of the *Spectator* Newspaper, -	ibid.
Present race of Boers averse to the Commando Service,	vii
British Settlers have never been employed on Commandos against the Kaffers previous to the War of 1835,	viii
(3.) Erroneous Policy of the Colonial Government towards the neighbouring tribes, - -	ibid.
The Colonists not concerned in *this* question, -	ibid.
Animadversions on sundry Mis-statements, - -	ibid.
(1st.) That previous to the War the Kaffers had been driven from their ancient and lawful possessions,	ibid.
(2d.) That previous to the War the Kaffers had been confined within a comparatively narrow space, &c.	x
(3d.) That in the War the Kaffers sustained an enormous loss of lives and cattle, - -	xi
(4th.) That the late War was carried on with unusual and unnecessary severity, - -	xiii
(5th.) Death of the Chief Hintza, - -	xiv
The Cape Colonists suffer from not being connected with any of the leading *interests* of the British Empire,	xv
The Eastern Province especially comparatively unknown,	ibid.
Ludicrous mistakes in England respecting its Localities,	xvi
Unmeasured odium cast upon the moral and christian character of the inhabitants of the Frontier, -	ibid.
Object of the present Work, - - -	xvii

NOTE I.

CAUSES OF THE KAFFER WAR.

Remarks of the Select Committee on Aborigines,	1

CONTENTS.

Page.

Defective and unjust system of Colonization, the source of all the evils resulting from the contact of Europeans and Aborigines, - - - 1
The Kaffers had no regular Settlement west of the Fish River previous to 1776, - - 2
Propriety of the Colonial Government extending the Boundary to that River, 1780, - - *ibid.*
Error committed in not reserving the country west of that River for the use of the Hottentot proprietors, after the final expulsion of the Kaffers, 1811, 1812, - 3
The fatal error of disregarding the Territorial Rights of the Natives, characterized the Frontier Policy of the Colonial Government previous to the administration of Sir B. D'Urban, 1835, - - *ibid.*
Expulsion of Makomo from the Kat River, one of the principal causes of the Kaffer War, 1835, - 5
Rev. W. Shaw's account of that event, - - 6
The Border Policy not the principal cause of the War, - NOTE.
Capt. Stockenstrom and Rev. Mr. Read the principal parties concerned in the depriving Makomo of the Kat River, for the purpose of forming a Hottentot Settlement there, - . - 7
Col. Somerset generally averse to the expulsion of the Kaffers from their lands, - - NOTE.
Dr. Philip an applicant for lands for the use of the Hottentots, out of territory originally belonging to the Kaffers, - - - - 9
False position in which the friends of the Hottentots placed themselves by the acceptance of the Kat River for a Settlement, - - - *ibid.*
Opinions of Messrs. Pringle, Bannister, and Shaw, - 10
Injurious effect of the interference of Dr. Philip and Mr. Fairbairn with the affairs of the Frontier Chiefs of Kafferland in 1830, - - - 11
Vacillating policy of the Colonial Executive calculated to tempt a Kaffer Invasion, - - 14

CONTENTS.

	Page.
Sir B. D'Urban's Anti-colonial prepossessions and benevolent plans,	16
Dr. Philip employed by him as a medium of communication with the Kaffer Chiefs in 1834,	17
Mistake of Lord Glenelg contradicted by Mr. Buxton,	NOTE 18
The conciliatory proposals of Sir B. D'Urban misunderstood by the Kaffers,	ibid.
General desire for war in Kafferland since Makomo's expulsion,	18
Statements of the Rev. S. Young, and Rev. A. Bonatz,	NOTE.
Influence of seditious Hottentots, and the Chief Hinza in urging the War,	19
The War on the part of the Kaffers an unjust and unprovoked aggression, in the *then* state of affairs,	20
Character of Sir B. D'Urban, the Governor of the Colony,	21
Justification of his measures from the charge of cruelty, &c.	23
The Colonists as a body not involved in the remote or proximate causes of the War,	26
Extenuation of the conduct of the Kaffers,	27
Remarks on recent schemes of Colonization,	28

NOTE II.

SIR BENJAMIN D'URBAN'S EXTENSION OF BRITISH JURISDICTION OVER THE BORDER KAFFERS.

The extension of the frontier to the Kei, planned by Sir B. D'Urban in Cape Town, as the most effectual means of preventing future collision, and of securing to the Aborigines the protection of British Law,	30
The expulsion of the bulk of the Kaffer population never contemplated,	ibid.
Explanation of the Proclamation of the 10th May to be found	

CONTENTS.

	Page.
in the measures and declarations connected with it,	31
Interference of the Wesleyan Missionaries in procuring Peace for Makomo, Tyalie, &c., and the retention of their lands,	32
Peace with the Kaffers, Sept. 1835. Their reception as British Subjects,	ibid.
Great Meeting at King William's Town, 7th January 1836,	34
Consideration of the propriety of the extension of British Jurisdiction to the Kei,	48
The Measure did not involve the loss of Territory by the Natives, but simply affected the exercise of an independant Sovereignty by the Chiefs,	49
Kaffer System of Government unfavourable to the continuance of Peace with the Colony,	ibid.
Difficulty of checking the predatory excursions of an independent pastoral community, in the vicinity of civilization,	50
Injurious tendency of the frequent extension of the Colony by the removal of the Kaffers further back,	51
The System of Sir B. D'Urban calculated to prevent the evils experienced by both Kaffers and Colonists,	ibid.
Objections to Treaties with the Kaffers as an independent people,	53
1st. The Chiefs unassisted cannot compel compliance with any Treaty disagreeable to their people,	ibid.
2nd, The serious consequences resulting from any attempt on the part of the Colonial authorities to enforce compliance,	54
These evils can only be avoided by preventive measures, such as those of Sir B. D'Urban,	55
Practical results of the extension of British Jurisdiction over the Kaffers,	56
Testimony of the Writer to the beneficial working of the new System,	57
Opinion of the Legislative Council,	ibid.
Observation of Mr. Cloete,	59

CONTENTS.

	Page.
Col. Smith's Speech at Graham's Town, Sept. 1836,	60
Kaffers not incapable of appreciating the advantages of British Rule,	ibid.
Sketch of the evils of the Kaffer political System,	61
Its oppression and immoral tendencies,	62
Dislike of intelligent and christian Kaffers to their own Government, and their continued migration into the Colony,	63
Injurious consequences resulting from the restoration of Kaffer Independence,	64
Col. Smith's resignation of his authority to Capt. Stockenstrom, Sept. 13, 1836,	65
The Kaffer Chiefs freed from their Allegiance to the British Government by Capt. Stockenstrom, Dec. 5, 1836,	71

NOTE III.

CAPTAIN STOCKENSTROM'S BORDER POLICY.

State of feeling in Kafferland, and the Colony, unfavourable to the System of Capt. Stockenstrom,	72
Unpopularity of the new Lieut.-Governor, and its origin,	ibid.
Extravagant expectations of the Kaffer Chiefs,	74
Sketch of the New System adopted by the Lieut.-Governor in the Treaties of Dec. 1836,	75
These Treaties based in principle, and in many of their details, upon the recommendations of a Letter written by the Author to Sir B. D'Urban, March 1834,	76
Defects of the Treaties,	80
(1) Introduction of Local and Fiscal Regulations, which place no small portion of the property of the Colonists beyond the pale of legal protection,	ibid.

CONTENTS. ix

	Page.
(2) Restrictions on the pursuit of stolen property, which facilitate the escape of the thief, and appear unnecessary obstacles to its recovery by the owner,	83
Enumeration of the facilities afforded for the escape of the thief, - - - -	86
(3) Unjust and heavy responsibility imposed upon the Kaffer Chiefs, - - -	91
This has arisen from a total misconception of the power of the Chief, - - -	ibid.
The Regulations and responsibility imposed upon the Chief, contrary to the principles and practices of Kaffer international Law. - - -	92
These are felt to be a serious grievance, - -	93
The treaties can never be properly enforced, - -	94
Practical working of Captain Stockenstrom's system, -	95
Amount of property stolen from the Colony during 1837, valued at £8,000, - . -	96
Official returns of the balance of losses, during 6 months of the year 1838, amount to about £4,000, -	ibid.
Opinions of the Cape Capitalists of the general insecurity of property on the Eastern frontier, during Capt. Stockenstrom's administration, - - NOTE	97
Expensiveness of the new System, - -	ibid.
Impossibility of enforcing the provisions of Capt. Stockenstrom's treaties without provoking a war, -	98
A proof of this in the attack on the Fingoes at Fort Peddie, August 1837, - - -	99
Injurious effects produced in Kafferland by the vaccilating conduct of the Lieut.-Governor, - -	100
The continuance of Capt. Stockenstrom's inefficient system, attributable to the want of correct information at home, and to the injurious influence of Colonial slanderers, - - -	101

Fallacious statements of the Editor of the Cape *Commercial Advertiser*, in support of Capt. Stocken-

	Page.
strom's measures,	102
Capt. Stockenstrom's departure from the Colony *on leave of absence*, August 1838.	106

NOTE IV.

HINTS FOR THE IMPROVEMENT OF THE PRESENT SYSTEM OF BORDER POLICY.

How can the present system be rendered efficient?	107
Two preliminary measures would facilitate the carrying into effect the amendment desirable,	ibid.
(1st.) The appointing a Military officer as Lieut.-Governor,	108
(2d.) The reception of the Gonokwabie Tribe, under Pato and Kama, as British subjects,	ibid.
This tribe, the faithful allies and peaceful neighbours of the Colony have been systematically neglected by the Colonial Government,	ibid.
Policy of the Colonial Government to conciliate and court its enemies and neglect its friends,	109
Reason of this policy to be found in the peculiar position of the Governor of the Cape,	ibid.
Symptoms of a return to a more manly and honest policy by General Napier,	ibid.
Treaty with the Gonokwabie tribe and the Fingoes by General Napier, June 1838,	ibid.
Good effects of this decisive measure,	110
Advantages which would result from the reception of these tribes as British subjects,	ibid.
Alterations in the Treaties recommended,	111
(1.) Dismissal of the expensive and useless Kaffer Police,	ibid.

CONTENTS.

	Page.
(2.) Some modification of the regulations respecting Thefts,	ibid.
These alterations in the Treaties, if enforced by a vigorous execution may, *for a time* preserve the peace of the Frontier,	113
No solid peace, no stable security, to be expected from any plan which merely contemplates the regulation of our external relationships with the Kaffer tribes,	ibid.
Miscellaneous recommendations,	ibid.
Encouragement should be given to the re-occupation of the Farms on the Frontier,	ibid.
Proposal for rendering the present line of Boundary impassable by cattle,	114
Recommendation of regular official communication with the Tambookie and Amaponda Chiefs,	115
Injurious effects of our neglect of this, experienced by our Tambookie allies,	Note *ibid.*
Large military force requisite for the present on the Frontier,	116
Prospective measures recommended,	ibid.
The Colony to be prepared by degrees for self-government,	ibid.
To be divided into two Governments, with a Legislative Council and Representative Assembly for each,	ibid.
The expenses of the defence of the Frontier to be divided between the two divisions,	117
Natural advantages of South Africa are such, that with felf-government the Colonists would soon be able to pay all requisite expenses,	ibid.
So long as the British Government choose to think and act for the Cape Colony, ignorant of its wants and interests, the British nation must be content to bear the enormous expense,	118

CONTENTS.

NOTE V.

VAGRANCY AND ITS REMEDIES.

	Page.
Supposed number of Vagrants in the Cape Colony,	119
Difficulty of guarding against the depredations of Vagrants arising from the nature of the Colony,	ibid.
Imperfection in the administration of the Criminal Law of the Colony,	120
Inconveniencies arising to the Colonial Farmer from Vagrancy,	ibid.
Injurious effect of Vagrancy upon the industrious portion of the coloured classes,	ibid.
Difficulty of the subject,	121
Its bearing upon the welfare of the coloured classes,	122
A Vagrant Act objectionable, and why?	ibid.
Much may be done towards remedying the evils of Vagrancy, without interfering with the liberties of the coloured classes,	123
Remedies suggested,	ibid.
(1st.) The appointment of an additional number of Magistrates, and the extension of the power and jurisdiction of the Magistracy,	ibid.
(2d.) The establishment of an efficient system of local police or constabulary force,	ibid.
Each Field-cornetcy may be formed into a parish or municipality, and be authorised and required to provide for self-governed and local police,	124
(3d.) Improved prison discipline,	125
The chief remedy the elevation of the social, civil, and moral condition of the black and coloured population of the Colony,	126
Defects of the 50th Ordinance in its imperfection as a measure of justice,	ibid.
Its failure from its being a half-measure, and the	

CONTENTS. xiii

	Page.
injurious consequences experienced by Hottentots and Colonists,	127
Increased mental cultivation, and discontent of the Hottentot population, one of the signs of the times,	128
Duty of the Colonial Government in the present emergency,	ibid.
The locations of the Hottentots on suitable sites at the expense of the Colonial Government,	129
The justice of the claims of the Hottentots upon the Colonial Government,	132
Policy of also locating the (late) Slaves, Kaffers, Bechuannas, &c. domiciled in the Colony,	ibid,
Advantages resulting from the location of the coloured population on suitable sites,	133
Objections considered,	134
Abortive attempt of the Colonial Government to locate parties of Hottentots along the Fish River,	137
Forced and unsuccessful experiment of locating a party of Fingoes on the Zietsikamma,	139
Cautions against the interference of the Colonial authorities in the execution of any plan for the location of Aborigines,	140

NOTE VI.

EMIGRATION OF LARGE PARTIES OF COLONISTS BEYOND THE COLONIAL BOUNDARY.

Occasional temporary migrations previous to 1836,	141
Extent of the migration of the Boers, &c. since 1836,	ibid.
Motives which induced the emigration,	ibid.
Letter of P. Retief to the Governor of the Cape Colony,	142

CONTENTS.

	Page.
Grievances complained of by the Boers,	143
Progress of the Emigrants from the Colony towards Natal,	145
Attacked by Matzilikatzi, and their subsequent punishment of that Chief,	146
Mistake of the Aborigines' Protection Society in reference to the event,	Note *ibid.*
Visit of P. Retief to Dingaan, the Chief of the Zulus,	147
Narrative of subsequent events from Mr. Boshoff's account,	*ibid.*
Account of the murder of P. Retief and his party by Dingaan, February 6, 1838, by the Rev. Mr. Owen, an eye witness,	152
Journey of Mr. Boshoff across the Drakenberg range to Natal, April, 1838	155
Intended occupation of Port Natal by the Colonial Government, (October 1838)	164
Important effects for good or for evil will result from this emigration of the Boers beyond the Colonial boundary,	*ibid.*

NOTE VII.

BRITISH CONTROL OVER EMIGRATION BEYOND THE COLONIAL BOUNDARY, INDISPENSABLE FOR THE SECURITY OF THE ABORIGINES.

Extract from a Letter of Captain Stockenstrom to the Colonial Secretary, containing a fair statement of the case of the Emigrant Boers, and suggesting the only efficient mode of meeting the exigencies of the case,	165

CONTENTS.

	Page.
Facts established by this document,	168
Abundance of unoccupied land in the interior of South Africa,	169
This land might be settled without injuring a single native,	171
The settlement of these tracts *forced* upon the serious consideration of the Colonial Government,	172
The Colonial Government has a choice of two evils,	ibid.
Benefits which might result to the Aborigines from the settlement of Colonies under legal control, and on a well regulated plan in their vicinity,	173
Opinions of the Aborigines Protection Society,	177
Question of most difficult solution stated by Rev. J. Beecham,	178
This question does not interfere with the location of waste and unoccupied lands,	179
Extreme necessity existing for the interference of the British Government,	ibid.

NOTE VIII.

PRINCIPLES OF COLONIZATION ALIKE BENEFICIAL TO THE MOTHER COUNTRY, THE COLONISTS, AMD THE ABORIGINES.

First principle, that the pecuniary obligations of the New Colony should be entirely borne by its own resources,	180
Second principle, that an ample provision for the civilization and christianization of the neighbouring nations, form part of the pecuniary obligations imposed upon the New Colony,	181
Third principle, that the rights of the Natives be conscientiously respected,	183

xvi CONTENTS.

	Page.
Preliminary measures to be adopted previous to the legal settlement of Dutch Emigrants, or the reception of other Colonists, - - -	184
Desirable to commence settlements in three different quarters, - - - - -	188
Advantages of a settlement at Natal, . -	189
Duties of a complex nature,—the result of our position on a vast continent, are incumbent upon us, -	193
Quotation from Dr. Philip in reference to the possible exercise of a beneficial influence on the part of the Cape Government over the whole of South Africa, - - - - -	194
Proclamation of General Napier announcing the intended occupancy of Port Natal, November, 1838. .	195

NOTE IX.

CASE AND CLAIMS OF THE BRITISH COLONISTS OF ALBANY.

Claims of the British Colonists of Albany upon the Home Government undeniable, - - -	196
No attempt made to controvert their statement, -	ibid.
Petitions of the Inhabitants of Albany to House of Commons, 1836. - - - -	ibid.
Statements in reply to the charges of aggression on the Kaffers, - - - - -	205
Denial of the statement of Captain Stockenstrom, -	206
Congratulatory address to the Queen, October, 1837, -	ibid.
Alteration of the constitution of the Legislative Conncil, -	207
Lord Glenelg's reply to the address of January, 1836, -	209
Sir George Grey's speech, July, 1838, - -	211
Napoleon's remarks on Colonial affairs, - -	213
Alison's remarks on the British Colonies, - -	214

CONTENTS. xvii

APPENDIX.

                                                        page.

No. I. Remarks on certain attacks made upon the Wesleyan Missionaries in South Africa, in reference to their conduct and opinions relative to the Kaffer War,   i

(1st.) Address to Sir Benjamin D'Urban, June 1835, Explanation of the Address, May 1837, - *ibid.*

Testimonies of other Missionaries in confirmation of the opinions expressed in the Address, - vi

Rev. Mr. M'Cleland and Mr. Heavyside, Ministers of the Church of England, - - *ibid.*

Rev. Messrs. Laing and Chalmers, of the Glasgow Missionary Society, - - - vii

Rev. Mr. Brownlee, of the London Missionary Society   *ibid.*

Rev. W. Davies, of the Baptist Missionary Society,   viii

Rev. Mr. Bonatz of the Moravian Society, - ix

Remarks of the Editor of the Missionary Register, January 1838, - - - x

(2d.) The Kaffers not described as *wolves* by the Wesleyan Missionaries, - - *ibid.*

(3d.) Morning Chronicle and Mr. Boyce, - xii

(4th.) The late Mr. Pringle and Mr. Boyce, - *ibid.*

No. II. Exertions of the Wesleyan Missionaries in procuring peace for the Kaffers, - - xv

1st Extract, from the evidence of Rev. J. Beecham,   xvi

2d Extract, Copy of a Letter from Mr. Boyce, to Governor Sir Benjamin D'Urban, - - xviii

Journal of Wesleyan Missionaries, while attempting to bring about a general peace, - xx

Course pursued by Rev. Dr. Philip, - - xxiii

No. III. "Wrongs of the Kaffer Nation," by Justus, - xxiv

No. IV. Colonel Somerset and the old Border Policy, - xxvi

No. V. Claims of the Wesleyan Missionary Society upon the British Government for losses sustained by the Kaffer War. - - - xxviii

ADVERTISEMENT TO THE READER.

Circumstances having produced a conviction on the Author's mind, that he cannot efficiently contribute to the spread of what he deems sound views on South African Affairs, without entering upon the discussion of various civil and political questions, which he believes to have a close connexion with the religious interests of the Colonists and Aborigines; he is anxious to apprise the reader, that although he has reason to believe his own opinions accord generally with those entertained by his brethren the Wesleyan Missionaries in South Africa, yet this publication is not to be considered as in any sense compromising *them*;—for the facts, opinions, and reasonings contained herein, the Author takes upon himself the sole responsibility.

INTRODUCTION.

In the last week of December, 1834, the British and Dutch inhabitants of the Eastern frontier of the Cape of Good Hope, were invaded in a time of profound peace, by hordes of Kaffers, against whom, scattered as they were on distant farms, and unprovided with arms and ammunition, they could make no effectual resistance. The result of this invasion was utter ruin to above 7,000 people, who from a state of moderate competency, were in a few days reduced to a miserable dependance upon the charity of the Colonial Government for daily bread. On a very low estimate of losses sustained, it appears that during this irruption of the Kaffers into the Colony, 455 houses, and 58 wagons, were burnt; 5,438 horses, 111,418 head of cattle, 156,878 sheep and goats, were carried off or destroyed; the estimated value of which was £288,625, exclusive of heavy losses sustained in Kafferland, by Traders and Missionaries, amounting to many thousands more.

The state of extreme distress to which this invasion reduced a large proportion of the frontier colonists, is best described by the Hon. Colonel Smith, C. B., in his official report forwarded to Cape Town January, 1835 :—"Already are seven thousand persons dependent upon the Government for the necessaries of life. The land is filled with the lamentations of the widow and the fatherless. The indelible impressions already made upon myself, by the horrors of an irruption of savages upon a scattered population, almost exclusively engaged in the peaceful occupation of husbandry, are such as to make me look on those I have witnessed in a service of thirty years, ten of which in the most eventful period of the war, as trifles to what I have now witnessed; and compel me to bring under consideration, as forcibly as I am able, the heart-rending position, in which a very large portion of the inhabitants of this frontier are at present placed, as well as their intense anxiety respecting their future condition."

This irruption of the Kaffers upon the Colony, naturally and properly directed public attention to a consideration of the causes which had led to an event so distressing and unexpected. With some few exceptions, public opinion was decidedly unfavourable to the Colonists, who by "*the systematic oppression*" of the Aborigines, were supposed to have drawn "*the tremendous re-action of the indignation of an injured people*" upon themselves! Indeed so strong was the prejudice against them, that, "*in the then state of public feeling,*" their friends "*dared not hazard a subscription for their relief.*"* The origin of these impressions, so injurious to the interests of the Colonists, may be easily traced to the influence of the standard work on South Africa, which has given the tone to subsequent writers. Barrow described with no small prejudice, a state of things existing thirty years ago among the Dutch boors of the distant interior. Other writers (with the exception of the learned and indefatigable Lichtenstein), have followed in his wake; and English writers especially, have acted as if it were a point of honour to copy and defend his delineations of the Colonial character. The public, forgetting the changes effected during the last quarter of a century, easily confound the Colonists of the present day, with their predecessors.

In addition to this fruitful source of prejudice, there had been for some time in England, a growing conviction of the injustice of the European System of Colonization, as well as a seasonable jealousy of the Colonial Authorities, both of which had prepared the public mind for the reception of impressions unfavourable to the Colonial character generally. In the course of the discussions arising out of the Kaffer war, the policy of the Colonial Government (in too many

---

* Extract from a private letter received by a Merchant in Graham's Town from his friends in London.

respects indefensible), became the subject of severe and just animadversion; and the censures so freely, and in many instances, so justly bestowed upon the Colonial authorities, and the Border System of the frontier, operated to the injury of the Colonists themselves, who in the opinion of the British public were identified with the support of proceedings, alike impolitic and unjust. In such a state of things, it is extremely difficult for an impartial observer to interpose a few words by way of explanation. A defence of the Colonists is in some minds inseparably connected with the advocacy of territorial usurpation, restrictive enactments, and European aggression. The Sovereign Public is apt to be intolerant, impatient of contradiction, and hasty in its conclusions; hence, as in the present case, we find frequent occasion to dissent from its immature decisions, and wait the more equitable judgment of a calm and dispassionate moment.

The popular charges affecting the Colonists, may be conveniently arranged under three distinct heads. *First.*—Cases of individual misconduct, quoted as indicative of the character of the community. *Secondly.*—The Commando System, or Militia of the Colony. *Thirdly.*—The erroneous policy pursued by the Colonial Government towards the Native tribes on its borders. A few remarks, as brief as possible, on these topics, will form a suitable introduction to a more lengthened discussion of the Foreign and Domestic policy of the Colonial Government.

I.—CASES OF INDIVIDUAL MISCONDUCT, quoted as indicative of the character of the community.

The readers of Barrow and his successors down to Pringle, must have remarked the numerous instances of individual misconduct exposed to public indignation. From the *thorough sifting* to which colonial delinquency has been subjected, it is scarcely possible that many cases of a serious nature have escaped notice, at any rate such as have occurred during the last 30 years. If for the sake of argument, we admit, that *all the cases* recorded are perfectly true, (a point disputed, and apparently on good authority,) is it just, from *isolated cases of delinquency* to draw inferences so injurious to the character of a community as the following? " The treatment of the

"aborigines is one of the darkest and bloodiest stains in the pages of
"history, and scarcely any is equal in atrocity to the conduct of the
"Dutch Boors, ably seconded, according to Mr Pringle, by some of
"the most degraded of the English Settlers." (*Spectator*, 17 May,
1834.) "Civilized christians, have been in South Africa, nothing
"better than a horde of plundering and sanguinary banditti." (*Birmingham Reformer*.) Would it be fair to take the Newgate Calendar, and the police reports of the Metropolis, as a specimen of the British community? To the ignorant prejudices of an excited public, we must oppose the deliberate sentiments of most unexceptionable witnesses.

THOMAS PRINGLE, Esq., the author of *African Sketches*.—In an article written in the *South African Commercial Advertiser*, dated 5 May, 1834, this gentleman speaks with indignation of " the insolent, and flippant tone of the common herd of English travellers;" of " the contemptuous, and revolting account, Barrow has given of the colonists;" and further states, that, " under the circumstances in " which Barrow visited the interior, *it was scarcely possible he could* " *have formed a correct estimate of the character of the inhabitants,* " *or render a fair report of them:*" and again; "We have been led "into these observations, by perusing the manuscript journal of a "gentleman, who takes a very different view of the inhabitants, and "we have little doubt *the more friendly view, is also the more* "*accurate.*"

JOHN FAIRBAIRN, Esq., the talented Editor of the *South African Commercial Advertiser*, whom no one will suspect of undue colonial bias, writes as follows :—

" Mr. Barrow next proceeds to describe the domestic manners, "and habits of the colonists, *confining himself almost entirely to* "*what he found offensive, or thought blameable.*"—(*South African Commercial Advertiser*, March 3, 1834.)

" We are never in danger of giving too ready an ear to the tales " of hasty travellers, or admitting *the six or seven cases of depravity*, " or ignorance, set down in their journals, *as sufficient to characterize* " *a whole people.*"—(*March* 6, 1830.)

INTRODUCTION.   v

"It is not easy to restrain our indignation, when we see a well "educated and travelled man, sitting calmly down to his desk, and "*addressing himself to the vulgar prejudices of his countrymen,* "recomend that they (the colonists) should be ruled with a rod of "iron, because *he* has discovered some instances of depravity among "them; and because *they* do not eat, drink, sleep, and manage their "affairs, as he would have them do. *We might as well expect to* "*find a fair estimate of the genius, and abilities of the English* "*nation, in the Newgate Calendar as a just character of a people* "*in such a Book.*"—(*Ibid.* Nov. 11, 1830.) The book referred to is Barrow's Travels.

The Right Hon. Lord Glenelg, Secretary of State for the Colonies, has expressed the sentiments of His Late Majesty's Government, in his reply to a memorial from the frontier settlers, praying that an inquiry might be instituted into the charges of cruelty &c., advanced against them, from time to time.

"His Majesty's Government disclaims all participation in the "sentiments, which have dictated the reproaches cast on the character "of the Colonists."

The Select Committee on Aborigines, appointed by the House of Commons the 9th February, 1836, delivered its report 26 June, 1337, thus adverts to this subject:—

"We wish it to be understood, that, it is not against individuals, "*much less against the colonists,* or the Military, as bodies, that we "would direct our reprehension. We are convinced that *a large* "*proportion of both, are well, and kindly disposed, towards the* "*Natives.*"

In the Appendix the testimonies of sundry Missionaries, bearing on this subject will be found, to which the reader is referred. And now, *the vindication of the character of the community at large,* may safely be left to the judgment of the candid reader.

II.—The Commando System, or Militia of the Colony, has occupied a prominent place in the charges brought against the Colonists.

In the "*Spectator,*" 17th May, 1834, the following remarks are found:—" For any real or fancied injury (such as the loss of cattle), "it is in the power of the pettiest magistrate to send for a Commando, " surprise and plunder the villages, burn the hovels, massacre the "men, and carry the women and children into captivity, frequently "shooting them on the road, out of wantonness, and impatience at their foot-sore pace." Here it will be necessary to explain to the English reader, that the term Commando is applied to a party of armed Colonists, summoned by the civil authorities of the Field-cornetcy,* or of the District, to aid in the repression of barbarian inroads, recovery of stolen property, pursuit of marauders, &c. It constituted, in fact, the *posse comitatûs*, rendered necessary by the peculiarly exposed condition of a thinly-peopled country, too poor to afford the protection of a regular military force, and too extensive to be defended by any other than a general levy *en masse* of its male adult inhabitants. The institution was certainly liable to great abuse, and from our knowledge of fallen human nature, as well as from well-authenticated facts, we may easily believe that it has been grossly abused in preceding generations. In the present day, the atrocities referred to in the extract are happily unknown; and *during the last* 15 *or* 20 *years, no Commandos on the Kaffer frontier have been called out, except in aid of the military, and under the controul of a proper officer.* A quotation, from " a powerful writer in the colony" (whom I suppose to be J. Fairbairn, Esq.), which is to be found in " *Steedman's Wanderings in South Africa,*" vol. 1, page 109, contains a fair and candid statement of the position in which many of the Dutch Colonists of a former generation were placed, and in which some are now placed, and accounts for their peculiar feelings towards the coloured races. " *It is difficult* "*for people living in security,* under the immediate protection of "magistrates, and a vigorous police, *to maintain uniformly a correct,* "*just, or impartial opinion respecting the feelings, and conduct, of* "*those who inhabit the extensive, and thinly-peopled frontiers of* "*hostile communities.* Armed by necessity, habitually jealous, like " one constantly in the presence of his enemy, the border farmer or " herdsman contracts insensibly the spirit and vigilance of a soldier,

* In the Cape Colony, every District is sub-divided into numerous Field Cornetcies, placed under an officer, termed Field Cornet.

"with a certain contempt for human life, when put in competition
"with property, or the strict observance of the law. Men naturally
"of the most humane dispositions, hold it no sin to kill an enemy in
"war, and repeated injuries, and a sense of danger, whether real or
"imaginary, dispose a man, not over acute at making distinctions, to
"impose that terrible name on an adversary, who has incurred his
"just resentment. It is also notorious, that in his insulated station,
"the borderer has often to act promptly in his own defence, without
"the power of obtaining assistance or advice, and is consequently
"obliged to represent judge, jury, and sheriff in his own person, and
"in his own cause. If he is sometimes induced to assume the rights
"of a legislator also, we need not be surprised at occasional irregu-
"larities in his administration."

It ought, however, to be remarked, in justice to the *present race of Boors*, that they are extremely averse to the Commando Service; and from their known aversion, and repeated refusals to comply with the requisitions of the Field-cornets, &c., Sir Lowry Cole found it necessary, 6th June, 1833, to re-enact the old Commando Law, and enforce its provisions by additional pains and penalties. The correspondence on this subject in the " Parliamentary papers relative to the Cape of Good Hope,"part 2d, pp. 90—96, is extremely interesting, and fully describes the local difficulties attending any other system of defence. Such was the indisposition of the Boors to go out on Commando, a few years before the re-enactment of the old Law, that Captain Stockenstrom, then Commissioner-General, found it necessary to threaten certain Boors with the loss of their farms, should they neglect to join a Commando then collecting for the purpose of entering Kafferland. In a letter addressed by him to Provisional Field-cornet T. Botha, dated 8th June, 1830, directing a levy of men, the following admonitory intimation is appended;—" *Those who are neglectful,* "or have not the fixed number of men on their places, you will im- "mediately report, *in order that those places may be given to others.*" The publication of the Colonial Records (now in progress under the editorship of D. Moodie, Esq.), will probably throw some light on the Commandos of the last century. The apologists of the Boors state, that mutilated extracts from these official documents have been presented to the public, for the purpose of maligning the character of the ancestors of the present Colonists.

The charge respecting Commandos, does not in the least affect the British Settlers in Albany. The only Commando, in which they were engaged, previous to the war of 1835, was sent by the Colonial Government in 1828 to protect the Kaffers, from a marauding tribe the Fikani.—*See Minutes of Evidence before Select Committee on Aborigines. The admissions of the Rev. S. Kay in reference to this subject. Report 26 June, 1837, pp. 90, 91; questions* 602—611.

III.—THE ERRONEOUS POLICY pursued by the Colonial Government, towards the Native tribes on its borders.

As this will form the subject of a separate notice, I would merely observe, that *with this erroneous policy, the colonists had no concern.* They had no control over the conduct of the Civil or Military Government of the Colony, or over the management of its frontier. Against the Border System pursued previously to the war, they have repeatedly remonstrated. Why should *they* be treated, as if identified with the actions of a despotic, and to them, irresponsible executive? This charge affects the Colonial Government, and the Colonial Office at home, and will be fully considered in its proper place.

Various other statements were brought forward in the course of the discussions arising out of South African affairs, *which although properly referring to the colonial executive alone, yet certainly contributed to maintain an unfavourable impression of the colonial character,* and may therefore be briefly animadverted upon in this place. These statements are as follows,—

1st.—Previous to the war the Kaffers had been driven "*from their ancient and lawful possessions.*—(*Lord Glenelg's dispatch* 20 *December,* 1835). This is substantially true, but not in the sense in which it will be understood in England, and the error though trivial, is calculated to give an unfair impression of the conduct of the Colonial authorities. To understand the state of the question respecting Kaffer and Colonial claims on certain disputed territory, it will be necessary to remind the reader, that, originally the Hottentot races inhabited the whole of South Africa from the Cape to the Kei River. The Hottentot and Bushman races are undoubtedly the Aborigines of South Africa, and their migration must have taken place some hundreds of years previous to the Kaffer migration. The Dutch Colonists soon deprived the Hottentots of their country in the neighbourhood of the Cape, and the colonial boundary gradually advanced Eastward. Within the last century the Kaffers advancing *from* the East expelled, and almost exterminated such of the Hottentot tribes as then resided between the Kei and Fish Rivers. It was not until 1776 or or 1785, that the Kaffers crossed the latter river, and were thenceforward engaged in continual wars with the Gonaqua Hottentots, and the advanced posts or cattle farms of the Colonial Government. In 1780 the Dutch Governor declared the Eastern boundary of the Colony to be the Fish River. Of this the Kaffers had no right to complain; since the country west of that river formed no part of their "*ancient and lawful territory*;" the injured party were the Hottentot races, who, when the Colonial Government had, after repeated wars cleared the country of Kaffers, and driven them beyond the Fish River, found their "*ancient and lawful territory*," granted to Dutch Boors, and afterwards to British Settlers. It will be clearly seen, that, *the progress of the Colony as far as the Fish River, has nothing to do with the question of aggression upon the Kaffers.* The Hottentots have a right to complain, that, when the Kaffers were expelled from the country between the Fish and Sunday Rivers, these lands were not restored to them, and the whole race settled there, under the controul and protection of the Colonial Government. Had the Hottentot community in alliance with the Colony been placed as a barrier between the Colony and the Kaffers, and occasionally supported against the attacks of that warlike and predatory people, they would have formed a cheap, and impregnable defence of the Colony; millions would have been saved to the British Treasury, and the Colonists spared all the miseries, inseparably connected with their frequent collision with the warlike tribes of Kaffraria. *With the subsequent*

c

INTRODUCTION.

extension of the Colonial boundary beyond the Fish River, the case of the Kaffers against the Colonial Government properly commences. After that river had been fixed as the line of demarcation, and the right of the Kaffers to the territory East of that line had then been virtually acknowleged, it wss equally unjust and impolitic on the part of the Colonial Government to push its frontier on almost every occasion, in which the predatory habit of the Kaffer tribes provoked punishment.

2d. The second assertion, frequently made, is that the Kafirs,—previous to the war, had been "confined within a comparatively narrow space, where pasturage for their cattle could not be readily found." *(Lord Glenelg's Despatch, dated* 26th *December,* 1835.) And again, "Unless some change of system be enforced by the Government, the nation will gradually perish by murders, by massacres, and by *want*."—*(Spectator,* 17th *May,* 1834.*)*

In order to make out a strong case on the Kaffer side of the question, no necessity exists for describing the loss of land as involving famine, want of pasturage, &c. The injustice of our aggression would be the same, even if it be admitted that there were millions of unoccupied acres in Kafferland, sufficient for a much greater population, which is the true state of the case. The land near the Colony is not valuable to the Kaffers from its extent, or its peculiar suitableness for grazing and agriculture. Indeed, in these respects, it is far inferior to the interior territory; but *they* value it, as a safe position for themselves and their cattle. While the distant tribes of Tambookies, and Amapondos, are continually harrassed, and plundered by barbarous hordes beyond them, in consequence of which, their numbers are rapidly decreasing,* the Kaffers on the Colonial frontier, notwithstanding occasional chastisement from the Colonial Government, have lived in comparative peace and security. No distant tribes have dared to invade them, owing to the terror inspired by the general understanding which

*Having resided four years on the most distant Kaffer Missionary Stations, I can speak from personal knowledge as to this startling fact, so much opposed to the general opinion at home. The domination of the Cape Government has not been productive of unmixed evil: it has saved the Hottentots from extermination by the warlike Kaffers, and more recently the Kaffers have been screened from the barbarous Fitcani and Zulus.

INTRODUCTION. xi

prevails through South Africa, that they are under the protection of the British Government. From data afforded by several Chiefs and ancient Counsellors, I am persuaded, that, within the last 30 years, the Kaffers have nearly trebled their numbers, and their cattle. Mr. Bannister, their partial advocate, admits an increase. " In fact, the population of Kafferland, in spite of many adverse events, has increased continually."—(*Humane Policy*, p. 69.) A most amusing specimen of the ignorance of a respectable and humane gentleman was exhibited before the " *Committee on Aborigines,*" in reference to this very subject.*—(*See Minutes of Evidence, Questions*, 3,899, 3,900.)

In 1816, the Rev. Mr. Read, of the London Missionary Society, then on a visit to Gaika at his residence on the Kat River, observes, " We are astonished to see so *few* cattle in Kaffraria, and were at " a loss to know how a large kraal could subsist; and considering " their customs, and manner of living, we do not much wonder at " their propensity to stealing."—(*Missionary Register*, 1816; *pp.* 478, 479.) The situation of the frontier Kaffers (previous to the war especially), formed a striking contrast to their poverty in 1816; and the improved breed of colonial origin, found in almost every kraal was a proof, that, in spite of occasional losses from reprisals made by the Colonial Government, the Kaffers had been on the whole considerable gainers in cattle by their vicinity to the Colony.

3d.—The loss of life and cattle, sustained by the Kaffers in the late war, is another subject on which considerable errors have arisen. In a despatch of Sir B. D'Urban's, dated 17th February, 1836, an estimate of Kaffer losses, in life, founded on the calculations of the Commissioners for locating, and taking the census of the Gaika and Slambie tribes, makes the number to be about 4,000; and the captured cattle according to the official returns amount to 60,000. Both amounts are gross exaggerations, which can, however, easily be accounted for. The estimate in question was made by myself, but

---

* Among other things this witness states,—" A few days ago, I had a letter from Sir John Herschell, who stated that a Hottentot or a Kaffer was quite a rarity in the neighbourhood of the Cape." I cannot tell what has caused the Hottentot migration, for I saw plenty there four years ago; but as to a Kaffer being *a rarity*, no wonder, since the Kaffers never lived nearer than 600 miles east of Cape Town.

had reference not merely to losses in actual conflict, but also to losses arising from natural causes, old age, disease, &c., for the space of one year, through the whole of the frontier tribes, on the supposition that all had suffered equally with that of Slambie. I am now satisfied, that the data on which the calculation was founded, are inapplicable to above two-thirds of Kafferland; and from all the information I have been able to collect from Kaffers and Colonists, I am convinced that the total loss sustained by the former did not exceed 1,400, a loss of life greatly to be deplored, especially, when we consider how easily the war might have been prevented. The amazing number of 60,000 head of cattle, reported as captured by the Colonial troops, when subjected to a careful examination, shrinks within a very narrow compass. Military men, and others not accustomed to estimate the numbers of cattle grazing promiscuously, are sure to make serious mistakes. For instance, 6,000 head of cattle, reported as captured in the Buffalo Mountains, when counted by an experienced person, were found to amount to 2,400.* The cattle captured in Hinza's country, estimated then at 30,000, were found to amount but to 11,000. From the difficulty of herding, a large number of every lot captured were re-taken by the Kaffers, so that the cattle actually received by the Colonial Commissariat, and disposed of on account of the Colonial Government, amounted only to 18,300. Admitting that many had died, and that all taken were not properly brought to account, even yet, the total loss of the Kaffers in cattle, could not exceed 30,000; whereas they took from the Colony 111,418, besides sheep and horses. I would however observe, that, the Kaffers were not gainers to the amount of the balance apparently in their favour. During the war, they were obliged chiefly to subsist on animal food, and thus immense herds were slaughtered to supply the wants of 60,000 people. The increase of at least one year was lost from the injurious effects of mountain pasturage in the winter season; and the severe rains in the spring following, destroyed thousands of their cattle. The conclusion of the war left them therefore, somewhat poorer in

* Mr. Robert Bowker counted these cattle; on this occasion an officer remarked with great glee,—" Well, we have now taken enough to re-pay the losses of the Settlers."

slaughter cattle, though much richer in that which constitutes *their* riches, a superior breed of milch cows, taken from the Colonists.

4th.—An opinion, that the late war with the Kaffers had been carried on with an unusual, and unnecessary severity, has tended to produce a natural feeling against the Colonial cause, and a more than ordinary sympathy for the Kaffers. Lord Glenelg quotes an official notice of Col. Smith's, which states the number of cattle, goats &c. captured, huts burnt &c. by his troops, while engaged in scouring the country this side of the Kei, during the hottest period of the war. Lord Glenelg infers, that, because the Kaffers offered *" no organized opposition,"* therefore, all this was unnecessary.—*(Despatch,* 17*th February,* 1836.*)*

These remarks arise from a total ignorance of the nature of Kaffer warfare; they proceed on the supposition, that, because the Kaffers dared not meet our troops in fair open fight;—therefore they offered *" no organized resistance."* In time of war, the Kaffers retire to their fastnesses, from which they harass their enemy by plundering expeditions, and by cutting off small parties; a mode of warfare, tedious, and almost insupportable to regular troops, who are not permitted to enjoy any respite from action, and yet seldom come fairly in contact with the enemy. Such a guerilla warfare can only be met, by cutting off the supplies of the enemy, and thus starving him into submission. This plan was adopted by Sir B. D'Urban, in preference to the sort of war, which would have been carried on under the old Commando System. Sir Benjamin having imbibed a strong aversion for the previous policy of the Colonial Government, and being in some degree prepossessed in favor of the Kaffers, entered on the war with the greatest reluctance. Two plans of operation were before him, either to array the disposable militia of the Colony, usually termed a Commando, and to fall upon the Kaffers, by detached parties of Colonists acquainted with the localities of the country, and able to follow the enemy into their hiding places; or to carry on the war with regular troops chiefly, and keeping the Militia of the Colony in strict Military order. The former method, which is in fact the only effectual mode of opposing a guerilla warfare, and is by far the least expensive, might possibly have finished the war in a few weeks; but in the excited state of feeling in which the Colonists *then* were, owing to recent losses of life and property, it was deemed unadvisable on the ground of humanity, to send 3 or 4,000 of them armed, and unrestrained by Military discipline, as the avengers of their own wrongs. The other plan, necessarily involved delay, and expense; but was likely to be attended with a much less degree of suffering, and was therefore adopted. The troops marched through Kafferland along the main roads, occupied prominent positions, made few attempts to follow the enemy into his fastnesses, but endeavoured by cutting off his supplies, to oblige him to submit. Meanwhile, the Colony was plundered almost daily by small parties of the enemy, who generally escaped with their plunder to the mountains, a mode of warfare much more natural and advantageous for the Kaffers, and more destructive to the Colony, than any "*organized opposition*" could have been. In the conduct of the war, no blame can possibly attach to Sir B. D'Urban. The humanity displayed by himself and the troops under his command was highly commendable; the lives of thousands were spared, who certainly would have fallen, had he adopted the cheaper, and more efficient system of warfare. The charge of inhumanity has been abandoned in the *High* quarters, in which it originated, and the Secretary of State himself has made the *amende honorable*, to the parties accused. Nevertheless, be it remembered, the effect of the hasty accusation remains, in the continuance of the first prejudiced impressions on the public mind, the retraction of the Noble Secretary, not being generally known.

5th.—The death of the Chief Hinza, and the circumstances attending it, produced a strong sensation in England, extremely unfavourable to the character of the Colonists. It became the subject of a Court of Inquiry, held at Fort Willshire 29th August, 1836, the proceedings of which have been published. The conclusion to which it came, appears to have been perfectly satisfactory to the Colonial Secretary, Lord Glenelg, as appears from the language of a late despatch:—

"With regard to the case of the Chief Hinza, I am happy to "state, that, the information now transmitted, clears up the doubts,

"and difficulties, which in my despatch of the 26th December, 1835,
"I described as connected with that subject. It is, I think, now
"established, that, if not the fomentor of that invasion, that Chief
"was at least engaged in a secret conspiracy with the authors, and
"was availing himself of such advantages as it offered him. On
"himself, therefore, rests the responsibility for the calamity in which
"he and his people were involved by the contest."

Much of the misrepresentation of South African affairs, arises from the fact, that the Colonists labour under the peculiar disadvantage of being entirely unconnected with the powerful interests, which in England press the claims of the Colonists of other British dependencies upon the attention of Parliament and the Public. The interests of the Indo-Britons of the East and West, are identified with the welfare of most of the influential families of Britain. Our North American Colonies, have their popular assemblies and salaried agents, appointed by themselves. New South Wales, as a penal settlement, and more recently, as the adopted country of a large number of respectable emigrants, has been more or less before the public eye, since the very foundation of the Colony. The Eastern Province of the Cape Colony is comparatively unknown, and while its superior natural advantages, and its peculiar position, in reference to warlike tribes on its borders, give it a distinct character of its own, it is continually confounded with the Western, and more frequented division, the inhabitants of which are placed in a very different position, and generally speaking, are as much unacquainted with the state of the Eastern frontier, as the people of England themselves.

The Eastern Province has been gradually rising into importance since the location of the British Settlers in the district of Albany, about 18 years ago. As the standard works on the Cape, with which alone the Public are familiar, were written previous to that period; and as recent travels &c. have obtained but a limited circulation, little is known in England, even of the site of the new Colony, and still less of the peculiar circumstances in which it has been placed. The misfortunes of the first settlers, served to check further emigration, and the settlement itself, after exciting for a brief period the sympathy of the British Public, was soon forgotten; or if casually noticed in the journals of the day, was described as a scene of disappointment, and distress, and adduced as a proof of the impracticability of successfully colonizing South Africa. Hence, when the recent irruption of the Kaffers again called public attention to this part of the world, not one in a thousand of the well-informed, reading population of Britain was acquainted with the situation of the settlement, much less with its origin, or local peculiarities. In consequence of this general ignorance, a few amusing blunders have found their way even into some of the most respectable prints. In 1832, when the Colony enjoyed an unusual degree of prosperity, the well known weekly paper " the Atlas," inserted a paragraph, stating, that, " in consequence of disturbances in the " interior, there would be no settlement in Graham's Town that " year!!" About the same time, Sir Richard Phillips, an extensive publisher, informed the reader of one of his multifarious epitomes of knowledge, that, " Algoa Bay is a trap for needy emigrants, and " that, the few surviving British settlers are living in great distress !!" During the Kaffer war, another periodical displayed its ignorance both of facts, and localities, when it informed the public, that, " Port Elizabeth on the Fish river, had been captured by the Kaffers !!"

But mistakes of this nature are unworthy of note, when compared with the unmeasured odium cast upon the moral, and christian character of the inhabitants of the frontier, especially in reference to their intercourse with their Kaffer neighbours. Specimens of the usual language employed have already been quoted, and the causes which gave currency to such unfounded calumnies, have also been pointed out. From the carelessness of the periodical press, and the thoughtlessness of the British Public, the Colonists have suffered much injury. It is impossible to estimate too highly the influence, and general excellence of the periodical literature of our native country. Among its many merits, we cannot however name, what Erasmus terms, " *a superstitious adherence to truth.*" While it is readily admitted, that there exists no disposition, intentionally to malign the character of distant communities, there is yet a lamentable want of the *care requisite to avoid that evil.* Men who make literature a profession, and who are engaged to furnish a certain quantity of matter within a stated period, and matter which *must* be calculated to interest, have not always time either to think or to examine. In most cases the picturesque or striking; rather than the true and common-place; is likely to be the most attractive; and by an easy mistake, exceptions, noticed by cursory observers, are mistaken as average specimens of colonial feeling, and even quoted as exemplifications of colonial conduct.

In consequence of recent events, as well as from the attention which the appointment of the Parliamentary Committee excited, it is highly probable, a thorough revision of our Colonial System will be the result. In the furtherance of so desirable an end, the writer desires to contribute his share of information, and trusts that a residence of nine years on the colonial frontier, and in various parts of Kafferland, enables him to throw some light on the affairs of both. As a Wesleyan Missionary, independent alike of the Colonists and the Colonial Government; naturally identified by his very position with the interests of the Aborigines; he may surely claim to be heard when his testimony, notwithstanding this, is favorable to the Colonist; at the same time, when he pleads *the just claims of the Aborigines*, he hopes his statements will be viewed, not merely as the special pleading of a partial advocate, but as the unbiassed opinions of an impartial observer. A partizan on either side of the question might find abundant materials for a strong case; but the pacification, and prosperity of South Africa, depend, not upon one-sided favouritism to either class of the community, but upon equal-handed justice to each, whether Colonists or Aborigines; whose real interests are in fact one and the same. What he has written will equally offend those in England, who consider the unqualified condemnation of the colonial character as an indisputable duty, and *the few* in the Colony, whose strong antipathies, and narrow prejudices form the sole ingredients of their factious patriotism.

NOTE I.

CAUSES OF THE KAFFER WAR.

In reference to the late war, the Select Committee on Aborigines make the following judicious observations:—
"It is sufficient to express our opinion, that the system which has long been pursued in our intercourse with the natives of South Africa, has been productive of most injurious effects, *both to the Colonists and the Kaffers; exposing the former to constant insecurity and frequent severe sufferings and loss*, and subjecting the latter to great injustice, and to treatment which could not fail to occasion feelings of irritation and hostility. We look upon the late war as one among many illustrations of these evils. While we purposely abstain from dwelling upon the circumstances which immediately produced it, we, without hesitation, name its real, though perhaps remote cause;—it was *the systematic forgetfulness of the principles of justice in our treatment of the native possessors of the soil.*"—(*Report*, p. 43.)

The defective and unjust system of Colonization adopted by all European nations, is undoubtedly the fertile source of all the evils resulting from the contact of civilized and uncivilized man. This is well described in the following extracts from Rev. J. Beecham's pamphlet, entitled,—

"*Colonization; being remarks on Colonization in general,*" &c., 2d edition, London, 1838:—

"The natives have had to surrender their lands without receiving for them any adequate remuneration. No painful collision has taken place, perhaps, in the first instance. The Colonists have needed only a portion of their territory on which to commence operations, and for this they have treated with the natives. The forms of a bargain have been gone through, and a price has been paid; but the moral wrong which was committed by us in legislating respecting the disposal of their lands—when they were not only not consenting parties, but, at the distance from us of perhaps half the circumference of the globe; were utterly ignorant of our proceedings and our plans, and perhaps nearly so of our very existence as a nation—has been aggravated by the fraud practised upon their ignorance in the price which has been given for the lands first ceded by them. A few beads, or other trinkets, or something equally worthless, have been the consideration paid down for lands and possessions of incalculable value.

"But, however peacefully our Colonies may have been commenced, while the natives remained in ignorance of our designs and the extent of our plans, circumstances have ere long taken place which have awakened unfriendly feelings, and led to painful collision. The natives have soon discovered, that their means of subsistence have been diminished; and, goaded by hunger and stimulated by revenge, they have begun to trespass upon the lands of the Colonists, and commit depredations upon their property. Then the struggle has fairly commenced; and the Colonists have found themselves under the necessity of passively yielding up their property to the natives, or defending it by force."

Previous to 1776, the Kaffers had no regular settlements west of the Fish River; the extension of the boundary of the Colony to that point in 1780, was a measure perfectly just on the part of the Colonial Government, *provided it had shewn itself in this case the guardian of the rights of its Hottentot subjects and dependants.* Colonel Collins' account of the first emigration of the Kaffers west of the Fish River is perfectly satisfactory, as to the non-existence of any just claims of theirs to the country from which they were finally expelled in 1811, 1812.* The great error of the Colonial Government in appropriating this rescued territory to European settlers, instead of establishing there a respectable Hottentot community, has already been noticed in the Introduction prefixed to these pages. For this fatal mistake, whether originating in a simple error of judgment, or in mere cupidity; the frontier settlers have suffered severely in their persons and property, and the British Treasury has had to pay to the extent of fifty times the marketable value of the lands thus unjustly and unwisely appropriated. "The systematic forgetfulness of the principles of justice," manifested in occupying lands which rightly belonged to the sole free remnant of the injured Hottentot races, thus placed the British Colonial Government in 1811, 1812, in immediate contact, and as an almost certain consequence, in collision with the warlike tribes of Kaffraria.

From this period, to the administration of Sir Benjamin D'Urban, which commenced in 1834, the same fatal error of disregarding the territorial rights of the Aborigines characterised the frontier policy of the Colonial Government.†

---

* "Soon after Zaka (Chaka) had been promoted to the rank of Chief, he proceeded to the neighbourhood of the Bæka River. Zuurveld (Albany) was then inhabited by Ghonaqua and other Hottentots, under the command of a Hottentot named Ruiter. His country being well stocked with game, Zaka applied for leave to hunt in it, and at first paid for his permission; but wishing to remove from the vicinity of his powerful neighbours, Zlambie and Langa, he was induced to try to establish himself on the right bank of the Great Fish River; as a justification of his conduct, he gave out that he had purchased the Zuurveld. Incapable of affording an effectual resistance, Ruiter, after some skirmishes and remonstrances, retired by degrees to the Bushman's River."—(*See Papers relative to the Cape of Good Hope, p.* 41. *See also Stockenstrom's Evidence, Committee on Aborigines, pp.* 46, 47. 218.

† No reflection is here meant to be cast on the individuals who administered the Colonial Government. My theological creed teaches me to judge men according to their several dispensations of light and knowledge. That of a

It is freely admitted, that, the Kaffers were from their predatory habits, most troublesome neighbours to the Colonial farmers; and that in *most cases*, they deserved the frequent chastisements they received from the Colonial authorities.† It is also admitted, that, decisive measures were requisite for the defence of life and property from the continued attacks to which both were subjected; but the measures of the Colonial Government were neither *just* in their nature, nor *wise* in their application to the circumstances of the parties concerned. It was unjust to punish by expulsion from their lands a whole Kaffer tribe or a considerable portion of it, on account of the cupidity or weakness of the Chiefs which prevented their putting a stop to the systematic plunder of the colony. It was equally impolitic and unwise to attempt to remedy an evil partly originating in the too great extent of the Colony compared with its limited population, by a process involving territorial enlargement, and thus tempting that scattered population to a still further dispersion.

Allowing that the proper duty of a Government is the protection of its subjects from aggression, this duty must nevertheless be discharged in strict accordance with the immutable principles of justice. The practicability of an equitable system of international intercourse, providing for the mutual punishment of offenders against the laws of

Colonial Governor is *precedent*, and his path of duty, in the absence of special instructions to the contrary, is supposed to be a strict adherence to the general principles of Government adopted by his predecessors. We have no right to expect Colonial Governors, any more than other men, to rise above their dispensation; and it is very questionable whether an original genius, administering the affairs of the Colony according to his own notions of propriety, would be cordially supported by the Home Government.

† Certain advocates for the Kaffers have taken false ground in attempting to extenuate their robberies, &c., and have represented them as a plundered people, driven by their own losses to retaliate on the Colonists; this is a totally mistaken view of the case. Individual cases of injustice to Kaffers have no doubt occurred, *but as a nation they are verily guilty in the plunder of the Colony, and have on the whole been considerable gainers, so far as the cattle account is concerned.* The injuries of which the Kaffers have a right to complain, are the occupation of their territory east of the Fish River, and the neglect of an enlightened and christian Government, in not establishing long ago a system of international intercourse, which would have prevented most of the evils we now unavailingly lament.

either party, should have been tried ;—or if at any time stern necessity demanded the extension of the British jurisdiction, and the military occupation of any portion of the Kaffer territory, as the only efficient method of preserving the peace of the Colony ;—even then the right of the population to the full and free occupancy of their lands, undisturbed by grants to European settlers, was a measure required no less by justice than by sound policy. The right of the Chiefs of Kafferland to the government of their respective tribes; and the right of the Kaffer population to the possession of the Kaffer territory, are two distinct things. Circumstances may arise which may render the modification of the loose and inefficient system of Kaffer Government absolutely necessary to the peace and safety both of the Cape Colonists, and of the Kaffers themselves;— but *no case can be imagined in which a nation can lawfully forfeit its claims to its undoubted territory ;*—and hence the expulsion of a whole people, though occasionally resulting from the political schemes, or unsated vengeance of conquerors, has ever been reprobated as an act of the grossest injustice. This plan was, however, pursued by the Colonial Government. The aggressions of the Kaffers were punished by piece-meal expulsion from their lands, between the Fish and Keiskamma Rivers. Sometimes they were allowed to return and occupy as a favour their former possessions, but as frequently were compelled to re-cross the Keiskamma and thus a constant irritation was kept up, which in the end produced results equally injurious to the interests both of the Colonists and Kaffers.

It is unnecessary to enter into the details of all these unfortunate measures, which have been already before the public in various popular publications, as well as in the evidence before the Committee on Aborigines. One transaction however requires a particular notice. This is the expulsion of the Chief Makomo from the Kat River in the year 1829, *an event which more than any other continued confirm the suspicion of the Kaffer tribes, that the gradu usurpation of their territory formed part of the policy of t*

Colonial Government. To the jealous feeling created by this expulsion, we may trace the real origin of the Kaffer war of 1834-5,* and the whole affair on many accouuts demands the serious attention of the reader.

The brief account of a Missionary then in Kafferland in-includes the main facts of the case.—*(See Rev. W. Shaw's letter to the Earl of Aberdeen,* 1835*)*:—" A kind of agreement was made with Gaika in 1819, by which our Government understood, that he ceded the lands now called the Neutral Teritory. Some time afterwards, (1832) Makomo the son of the late Gaika, re-established his clan on a certain tract of the neutral teritory by the connivance of the Colonial Government. At length, however, this land, a very fine and beautiful tract, was wanted for the purpose of forming a Hottentot Settlement, and Makomo, whose people were charged with committing various depredations on the Colony, was warned to remove from the land in question; but he refused; alleging that they had never been ceded by his father, and entering into a dispute as to the boundaries fixed in 1819, which he maintained preserved a portion of the Kat River mountains as Kaffer territory. The Colonial Government,

* I am aware that the *Border Policy,* as it is termed, is generally considered the principal cause of the war. By the Border Policy is meant the system of allowing patrols of soldiers, attended by Boors, &c., who had lost cattle, to follow the " spoor" (traces of the cattle) to the kraal, when it can be traced, and take the value of the cattle stolen. Although sometimes productive of injustice, this system was in accordance with Kaffer usages, and was not so much objected to by the nation generally. They knew that in the cattle account they were every year considerable gainers. It was, however, a very objectionable mode of preventing theft, unless regulated by a strict authority, which would prevent justice from degenerating into vengeance. The Kaffers had of late years been uncommonly sensitive as to *land,* and especially land near the Colony; and nothing was more calculated to excite jealous and revengeful feelings, than the occupation of their favourite grazing ground by the Colonial Government. In reference to the system of reprisals, it must be observed, that the right of entering Kafferland to follow the " spoor" of cattle, &c., was freely granted by Gaika, Slambie, and other Chiefs as the best means of checking depredations. To this system the Chiefs are attached in preference to being made individually responsible, for in cases of seizures made by the Colonial Government, they incur no trouble, and cannot be blamed by their people; whereas in the latter case they incur personal risk and responsibility, and lose popularity among their people; but this subject will be discussed in another place. See Abo. Com. Colonel Wade's Evidence, pp. 278, 279.

however, notwithstanding the mediation of some of the Missionaries, persisted in its claim, and the Kaffers were forcibly expelled by our troops, the huts being burned to prevent them from returning to occupy the lands."—*(See also Pringle's Narrative p. 465.)* This expulsion took place May, 1829; and thus after seven years undisturbed possession, a powerful and talented Chief was deprived of his territory, for reasons which, however cogent in their influence on the minds of the advisers of the Governor, could not be fully comprehended by Makomo himself. The main reason assigned for his expulsion was, that he had made war on a certain Tambookie clan, and had pursued them across the Colonial boundary into the Tarka district. This, though an offence, was certainly not of a sufficiently serious nature to demand a punishment so severe, and one calculated to make a brave and spirited Chief an enemy for life. And there is fortunately sufficient proof before us, to enable us to infer, *that the expulsion of Makomo would never have taken place, had not certain parties, at that time been influenced by ulterior motives of a partially benevolent character.*

It appears that in 1822, Capt. Stockenstrom, (then Landdrost of Graaff-Reinet) was opposed to the re-occupancy of the Kat River by the Chief Makomo, deeming the possession of such a strong hold by Kaffers most injurious to the Colony. His objections were overruled through the influence of Colonel Somerset,* the Commandant of the Frontier.—*(Evidence Aborigines' Committee, p. 84.)* On the arrival of Sir Lowry Cole, as Governor of the Colony,

* No officer of Government has been more abused by certain reputed friends of the Kaffers than Col. Somerset; and yet, it is singular, that in the statements made before the Aborigines Committee, he appears to have been generally opposed to the expulsion of the Kaffers from their territory. In one respect, as a public functionary, *his* hands are clean;—*he* has no grant of a splendid estate out of lands wrongfully taken from the Kaffers. When Captain Stockenstrom (then Landrost of Graaff-Reinet) himself asked for, and obtained from Sir Rufane Donkin, the acting Governor of the Cape 1821, the grant of the Kaga farm, (now worth about £2000) he furnished his opponents with strong reasons for doubting the sincerity of his professed regard for the just rights of the Aborigines, and more especially for that right which of all others is the *most important in its bearing upon their continuance as a people, namely;—the undisturbed possession of their lands.*

Sept. 1828, Captain Stockenstrom (then Commissioner General of the Eastern Division) proposed that *the whole of the Neutral Territory should be occupied by Europeans and respectable Hottentots* (*see page* 288); this scheme was also negatived. In the month of January, 1829, the expulsion of Makomo was decided upon at Cape Town, and in April, the Commissioner-General left the Cape for the purpose of superintending that measure. It is admitted by Col. Wade, *(page* 287-8*)* that the desire of locating the Hottentots emancipated by a recent Ordinance, had previously been felt at head-quarters, and yet, when the measure of Makomo's expulsion for a mere trifle, *from a locality exactly suited to the pressing claims of the Hottentot races* was decreed, we are expected to believe, that the plan of placing *them there had never been thought of!!* We may easily believe, that Major Dundas and Col. Wade were not in the secret, and that Sir Lowry Cole had not fully decided, and we may further believe, that the Commissioner General had made no *official* proposal for the formation of a Hottentot settlement there; but no one can read the evidence of Captain Stockenstrom *(page* 84-5*)* without being conscious of an impression, that in *his* mind the idea of that settlement had long been entertained as a desirable measure. He states that the thought occurred to him in the month of April, 1829, during his passage by sea from the Cape to Algoa Bay. The Rev. J. Read, of the London Missionary Society, then residing at Bethelsdorp, with whom Captain Stockenstrom consulted, fully approved of the plan; observing, "*It is just what Mr. Bannister and I lately discussed.*" From Uitenhage, Captain Stockenstrom wrote his proposals to Colonel Bell, the Colonial Secretary, in a letter dated 17th April; Sir Lowry Cole's answer was dated 8th May. The preparedness of the Rev. Mr. Read's mind, *to accept for the Hottentots, lands then actually in the possession of the Chief Makomo,* (whose expulsion would naturally involve the destruction of the Mission Station of Balfour, established by a kindred Society;) and the equal readiness on the part of Sir Lowry Cole, to consent to a measure involving so many serious political considerations; are circumstances entirely unaccountable on the supposition that no previous discussion respecting this scheme had taken place. Without attempting to impeach Captain Stockenstrom's veracity, we may be allowed to suppose, that in narrating the thoughts and actions which occurred six years previously, his memory was not in all cases minutely faithful in reference to time, place, or circumstance. The speed with which this plan was carried into effect is most extraordinary, on the supposition of its being until that time unpremeditated; but is easily accounted for, if we may suppose it to have been the result of a previously understood arrangement, between Captain Stockenstrom and Mr. Read, to which the consent of the Governor was subsequently obtained. *In April the scheme is thought of; by the middle of May the Governor's consent is obtained; by the end of May Makomo is expelled; and in June the settlement of the Hottentots commences!!* It is impossible to view the whole affair in any other light, than as resulting from a determination on the part of the Commissioner-General to embrace the first fair pretext of stripping Makomo of a most desirable and extensive portion of his territory, for the purpose of forming a Hottentot settlement there. To this injustice Mr. Read must be considered as accessary probably before the fact, but certainly after, by the acceptance of the territory in question for the use of the Hottentots, and it must be admitted that he has well as other friends* of the Hottentot race "placed them-

---

* Rev. Dr. Philip, Superintendent of the London Society's Missions, subsequently applied for an additional grant of land for a body of Hottentots, the site to be "the spot which was occupied by the late Mr. Williams," and "a few places in its immediate neighbourhood on the Kat River."—(*See Letter to Sir B. D'Urban,* 14*th March,* 1834, *in Evidence before Abo. Com.,* p. 493.) This land was part of the original Kaffer territory which Dr. Philip believes to have been wrongfully taken from the Kaffers; and yet in June, 1836, Dr. P. is so obtuse as to their rightful claims to this territory, that in answer to the question,—" Did you not, in 1834, apply to Sir B. D'Urban for lands within the precincts of the territory of the Kaffers, or some of the other natives of South Africa, on which land you proposed to locate a large body of Hottentots?" He replied, "I never did;" and refers to the document above quoted in proof. Either Dr. P. has very incorrect notions of the territorial rights of the Aborigines, or else he has some method peculiar to

selves in a false position when they concurred in the acceptance by the Hottentots of lands, the title of which, to say the least was, of a very equivocal nature."—*(Shaw's Letter, p. 11.)*

The readiness with which men of undoubted rectitude could connive at actions of the most unjust nature, when favourable to the prosecution of their own schemes, is one of the melancholy features of this case. The colonial functionary appears to have calculated correctly, that in certain influential quarters, "the end would sanctify the means," and that the purpose to which the land thus unrighteously wrested was to be applied, would atone for the injustice by which it was acquired. The event answered his most sanguine anticipations. The agent of the London Missionary Society is entrapped into the approval of a measure, which Mr. Pringle terms, " in itself alike iniquitous and impolitic," and even he who pronounces this decisive judgment, is himself induced to believe, that, the evil and injustice is " amply atoned for by the Hottentot settlement!" Bannister more consistently (in his *Humane Policy*, page 94), admits that the settlement of certain Hottentots upon the spot in debate, is a remarkable proof of the little consideration in which the Cape Government estimate the feelings or the just claims of the natives ;"and adds, " To obtain land for any portion of that oppressed race, is so good an act, that it would be ungracious to look harshly at the mode of doing it, if our character for justice to others were not involved in the particular way chosen." It is but just to observe, that in this transaction no *selfish* motives can be ascribed either to Mr. Read or Captain Stockenstrom ; it was simply an error of judgment, arising from loose notions of the respect due to native rights. In its effects, however, it was a most serious error, for, *from that day, the irruption of the Kaffers into the Cape Colony was, with them a mere question of time and*

himself of reconciling a positive denial of facts, previously admitted, with that scrupulous regard to truth, naturally expected from his station as a Minister of the Gospel.

opportunity. A sense of the general insecurity of the whole of their territory pervaded the tribes of Kaffraria, and nothing but the prompt measures of Sir Lowry Cole prevented an immediate outbreak, and the anticipation of the scenes of 1835 in the year 1829. On this subject we have the testimony of the Rev. W. Shaw, who then resided at Wesleyville :—" I am persuaded that the '*sore place in the heart*,' as they themselves would phrase it, was occasioned by the forcible seizure of their lands. Residing in Kaffraria at the time, I had opportunities of observing how greatly the Kaffers were exasperated ; and if Makomo could have persuaded the other Chiefs to unite with him, I have no doubt that disasters, similar to those we now deplore, would have happened some time ago."—(*Letter to Earl of Aberdeen*, 1835.) In confirmation of Mr. Shaw's direct evidence on this point, the reader may refer to Bannister's *Humane Policy*, pp. 96—100, in which will be found a series of extracts from the public papers, and private letters, of the Colony, at that period, indicating the general impression of alarm on account of an anticipated war, arising out of the natural resentment of Makomo at his expulsion.—*See Report Abor. Com., pp.* 35, 36.

Hitherto Missionary influence had, however, been sufficiently powerful to prevent open collision, and the Missionaries of the various tribes had been uniformly considered as the medium of intercourse between the Chiefs and the Colonial Government. The advantages resulting to the Colony and to the Missions, from the position of the Missionaries as mediators are obvious. It afforded the Missionaries an opportunity of obtaining a hearing from the Colonial Government for the Chiefs, and of being fully made acquainted with the plans of the Chiefs, and thus they were enabled to interpose, and effectually prevent many a rash scheme, which if hurried to an immediate execution, without their knowledge, might have produced serious consequences. The value of this influence exercised by the Missionaries is evident, from the fact ; that *in the only case where it has been fully preserved*, *the great evil of collision with the colony has been averted, and the tribes have been saved from the horrors of war.* Witness the case of the Gonokwabie tribe and a portion of Slambie's, where the influence of the Wesleyan Missionaries was sufficient in 1835 to prevent their joining in the war against the colony. By the well meant, but injudicious interference of two individuals, the one connected with the editorship of a respectable Cape paper, and the other the superintendent of the London Society's Missions, this influence was destroyed, *at least in that part of Kafferland, where from recent events, its existence and active exercise were most necessary.*

In the beginning of 1830, Mr. Fairbairn and Doctor Philip visited the frontier Mission Stations, and held formal conversations with the Chiefs, respecting their claims upon the neutral territory, and other complaints against the Colonial Government. By the Wesleyan Missionaries at Wesleyville, and Mount Coke, this interference on the part of entire strangers was remonstrated against, as calculated to produce useless irritation. In this way, they incurred a measure of resentment, which has since found so many opportunities of manifesting itself; but they also saved their respective Chiefs from the delusions which involved the other Chieftains of Kafferland in the war of 1834-5. The Chiefs connected with the Missions of the Glasgow Society, namely Makomo, Tyali, Eno, and Botman, were in consequence of this visit led to regard strangers at Cape Town as entitled to their confidence, in preference to the Missionaries residing among them. Mr. Read, of the Kat River settlement, from that time became a medium of communication between the parties. The Missionaries stationed in the country, became comparatively of less importance in the estimation of their respective Chiefs, and thus being deprived in a great degree of their confidence; the zealous and praiseworthy interference of the Glasgow Society's Missionaries failed to prevent the irruption of December 1834. Nothing could be more unfortunate for the mutual interests of Kafferland and the colony, than the transfer of any degree of the confidence of the Chiefs from Missionaries resident on the spot, to individuals removed from them by a distance of 600 miles.

It would be ridiculous to imagine, that the individuals in question wished to inflict an injury, either on the colony or on the Missionaries, or even that they anticipated such a result from their proceedings;—but the consequences of their imprudence were not the less injurious. It is easy to be imagined, (and it can be proved) that the Kaffers formed very erroneous notions respecting the advice given by these gentlemen, and entertained very extravagant expectations as to the good to be anticipated from their advocacy. In the middle of the year 1834, Doctor Philip repeated this visit, and the impression made on the mind of the Chief Tyali, (probably from the representation of others) is best stated in his own words, " Philip said, *this is your land*, I shall speak in the Governor's ear. Philip made great inquiries and said, *the land is yours on this side the Fish River;* I shall write to the King of England and speak to the Governor;—*this and the Hottentots talking to us, set us on fire.*"—*(See proceedings of Court of Inquiry, respecting the death of Hinza, page* 59.) The facts, *that the war originated with the Chiefs, thus partially alienated from their proper Missionaries and natural advisers; and that the Chiefs whom the Wesleyan Missionaries saved from this injudicious tampering took no part in the war,* are a sufficient proof of the evils resulting from the uncalled for interference of strangers in affairs, which properly belong to Missionaries resident on the spot; and who being themselves perfectly acquainted with the probable consequences of their own counsels, as well as with all the circumstances of any subject of local dispute, are more likely to give judicious advice, than persons not possessed of similar local knowledge.

The interference of the agent of one Missionary Society with the Chiefs and people of another, is a breach of those understood rules of courtesy, which have hitherto been acted upon by the responsible directors of all Missionary Societies, and it rests with the directors of the London Missionary Society, to express their disapprobation of all future officious intermeddling on the part of *their* agent, in the proper and peculiar concerns of other Missionaries. In the present case, the evils of a foreign interference were soon exemplified. The Chiefs of the Gaika family ceased to consider their Missionaries as possessing much influence either with the Colonial Government or the Colonists; hence in a time of difficulty, when they most needed peaceful counsels, those who gave that counsel were not listened to; the influence which if retained by the Missionaries unimpaired, might have prevented the war, had been diverted into other and distant channels; and thus the calamities of December 1834, and the following month, are in part traceable to the injudicious and thoughtless interference of Dr. Philip and Mr. Fairbairn, in 1830.*—(*See further Colonel Wade's Evidence, Abor. Com. Questions* 2,778, 3,490, 3,533.)

The policy of the Colonial Government seems to have been guided by a maxim the very reverse of that excellent

* This interference of Dr. Philip in the affairs of Kafferland, was not warranted by any extensive Missionary connexion with that country. The London Society had, at that time, one Missionary station connected with a very small tribe near the frontier. With Makomo, Tyali, &c., they then had no Missionaries. From the language employed by this gentleman, and his colleague, Mr. Read, while in England, the public must have been led to suppose that all Kafferland was under their pastoral care; whereas the London Society has hitherto found sufficient employment for its Missionaries within the Colony, and amongst the Griquas and Bechuanas to the northward. Even now, (Oct., 1838), the London Missionary Society has only two stations in Kaffraria, while the Glasgow Missionaries occupy five stations with the tribes of Gaika, Makomo, Tyali, &c, near the frontier. The Wesleyan Mission stations are nine in number, and extend from the Fish River to the Zimvoobo, a distance of 300 miles from the Colony; *and the opportunities afforded to the Wesleyan Missionaries for acquiring information respecting Kafferland, are of course much greater than those enjoyed by others who occupy a comparatively confined locality.* When Mr. Read boasted at Sheffield,—" *We* have 300,000 Kaffers," he might with equal truth have said,—" We have 300,000 Esquimaux." He should have stated what *he* and his colleagues in Kafferland had done for the benefit of so numerous a flock. *He* had helped to deprive them of the Kat River lands, and had thus been indirectly concerned in involving them and the Colony in the late ruinous contest. The forming of christian villages and churches; (with the single exception as stated above,) the composition of grammars, &c., and the work of translating the Scriptures; had been almost entirely left to the abused and maligned Wesleyan Missionaries, and those of the Glasgow Missionary Society.

one of Mr. Pringle's, "a determination neither to do, nor to suffer wrong." After first irritating the Kaffers by an unjust invasion of their territorial rights, it appeared as if it tempted them to make aggressions on the lives and property of its own subjects, by neglecting to enforce their just claims to protection, whether in the colony or beyond its boundaries. In 1828 the Attorney General of the colony declared his opinion to be, that, "when any theft or other serious crime has been committed by these savages, or when they are seen in arms in any considerable numbers they may be pursued with hue and cry."—"In no case should fire arms, or other deadly weapons be used, until all other means have proved abortive."—"Should the life of a Kaffer be lost in the affray, it will be the duty of the Clerk of the Peace to institute a preparatory examination; and the duty of the Resident Magistrate to commit or discharge, according as upon evidence adduced, it shall appear to him that unnecessary or premature violence, was used, or the contrary." When it is stated that Kaffer robbers usually choose the night for their attacks, and that the farm houses in many places are from 5 to 10 miles from each other, and sometimes still more distant, and that the population is comparatively scattered; the absurdity of pursuing them by hue and cry, or of defending property and life, without the use of fire arms will be sufficiently obvious. In the same year, a banditti had taken up a position on the Mancazana, and systematically plundered the neighbourhood; a farmer who in self-defence had shot one of them, was apprehended and tried. In consequence of this, the Field-Cornets positively refused to afford any assistance to the plundered farmers, lest they should involve themselves in trouble, and this state of things continued until the evil was cured by the more rational decisions of the Judges of the Circuit Courts. In the beginning of 1833, the Chief Eno, then residing on the neutral ground, (during good behaviour) caused a Hottentot man and his family, consisting of a wife and two children, to be murdered for the sake of his cattle and goats. This man was furnished with a colonial pass, and was on his way to the Mission Station Wesleyville. Evidence of this murder was furnished to the Colonial Government, the parties were pointed out, who were the actual perpetrators of the murder; on searching the place, the skeletons, and part of the clothes of the murdered persons were found near Eno's kraal, but although the witnesses were ready, yet no further notice was taken by the colonial authorities. In 1834 an English trader was murdered in Hinza's country, for which no redress was demanded. This submission to murder, as well as to their combined depredations, led the Kaffers to imagine, that the Colonial Government was unable to punish their aggressions, and they were thus by degrees tempted at length to hazard an open inroad into the colony.*

At this period, Sir Benjamin D'Urban arrived in the colony, and from his humane feelings, as well as from the instructions received from the Home Government, he was extremely desirous of coming to an amicable settlement of all the disputed affairs of the frontier. Two distinct communications appear to have been made by him to the Kaffer Chiefs; the one in the middle of 1834, the other in or about October of that year, as appears from his despatch, dated 5th January, 1835. "I had in the middle of last year, caused communication to be made to the Chiefs of the Kaffer tribes on the eastern frontier, expressive of my disposition and intention, to enter into a new order of relations with them, upon a footing which could not but be advantageous and agreeable to them; but that the carrying these friendly intentions towards them into effect must mainly depend upon themselves, since they were founded on a belief that they desired relations of amity and reciprocal good offices with the colony and would be disposed to act

* The whole of Colonel Wade's evidence deserves an attentive perusal by all who desire to understand the affairs of the Cape and Kafferland, previous to the war of 1835. His, is unquestionably the ablest defence of the Colonial Government, and his manly straight-forwardness commands respect, even where we differ from his opinions.

accordingly; and that of consequence, if they wished or expected to be dealt with as friends, they must cease to act as enemies, and to discontinue the acts of robbery and depredation constantly committed by their people. Upon their manifesting this disposition, it was added, I should be prepared upon my visit to the borders, to enter into such treaties and agreements with them as had been described. This communication was made to all the border Chiefs accordingly; and I afterwards availed myself of a tour which Doctor Philip, the head of the London Mission, made through these tribes late in the year, (he having several* Missionaries residing among them) to explain to them more fully and in detail, the nature of the agreements, into which I should be prepared to enter with them, provided that, in the mean time, they abided by the line of conduct which I had suggested. The greater part of these Chiefs (with the exception of Tyalie) expressed themselves well pleased with all this, and for a short period the depredations were in a great degree suspended."—*(See papers relative to the Cape, part* 2, *pp.* 117, 118*).*†

* The London Society had two Missionaries stationed in Kafferland with a Chief (Tzatzoe), of extremely limited influence; but was this a fair reason for stating that Dr. Philip had "*several* Missionaries resident" among the Kaffers? Such, however, seems to have been the impression left on the Governor's mind, by the statements made to him. It may appear trivial to notice such slips, but as exaggerations and distortions of the truth, however trivial in themselves, are in this controversy connected with important conclusions, it is necessary sometimes to point them out, not so much from their own importance, but as indicative of the *animus*, and as discovering the *tactics* of the party employing them.

† For some reason or other, the employment of Dr. Philip, by Sir B. D'Urban was denied in England, and the Governor of the Cape was considered as having stated this merely to aggravate the guilt of the Kaffers in making war; hence Lord Glenelg in his despatch, 26th December, 1835, observes,—" I have before me evidence the most conclusive to shew that *Dr. Philip did not either in his own person, or through the agency of any other of the Missionaries of his Society,* make those communications to the Kaffer Chiefs, with which you state him to have been charged by you. Whether he misunderstood your instructions, or whatever circumstance may have occasioned it; of the fact itself there can be no doubt. He neither negotiated as the agent of the local Government with the Kaffers, *nor ever delivered any message from you to the Chiefs.* We are, therefore, not entitled to impute to the Kaffers the fault of having burst into the Colony regardless of the obligations to forbearance imposed upon them by the pendency of such negotiations as you have mentioned " *(Par. Papers, Kaffer war, and death of Hinza,p.* 63.*)* This point blank contradiction was made public 30th May, 1836, and undoubtedly tended to destroy all faith in Sir B. D'Urban's assertions. No doubt Lord

These pacific overtures very probably served to convince the Kaffers, that the Colonial Government had from sheer weakness, and from the absence of sufficient military force, made such liberal offers of a conciliatory nature. Whatever might be the sober opinions or wishes of the Chiefs and old councillors, the great bulk of the Kaffer adults capable of bearing arms had long desired war; for some years previous, in fact ever since the expulsion of Makomo from the Kat River; the probability of a war, and the best and most efficient manner of annoying the colony, had been frequent subjects of common conversation.* The Kaffers were well

Glenelg was misled in this instance, and some pains must have been taken to impose upon His Lordship; but the result as to Sir B. D'Urban was that he remained for some time under the imputation of having made a false statement in a public despatch; whereas about three months after Lord Glenelg's despatch was written, viz. on the 14th March, 1836, while Captain Beresford was being examined before the Aborigines' Committee, the Chairman, T. F. Buxton, Esq., *actually made public a letter from Dr. Philip, admitting all that Sir B. D'Urban had stated—See Evidence Abor. Com.*, p. 268. The following is an extract:—" It is probable that the Colonial Secretary will, in justification of the severity which may be exercised upon the Kaffers, lay much stress on the facts, that the Governor had through my medium, made promises to the Kaffer Chiefs, that when he should arrive on the frontier, he would take into consideration their affairs, redress their grievances, and that a secure and an equitable system of relations between them and the colony would then be introduced. *That the Governor made such promises, and that I communicated them to a few of the leading Chiefs, is correct.*" The denial is, however, after all explained as meaning that Dr. Philip did not consider himself *officially* charged with messages from the Governor. p. 679. "I never appeared in Kafferland as the accredited agent of the Governor. I never said to the Kaffers that I had any instructions from Sir B. D'Urban. I never on any occasion dropped any hint as if I had come from the Governor, or that I had had any personal intercourse with the Governor." This is surprising! The *solemn denial as to making any communication at all,* turns out to be nothing more than this, that Dr. P. *did not consider himself as " an acredited agent."* It requires a most jesuitical system of morals to reconcile such miserable equivocations with the christian sincerity of *yea* and *nay.* It is also very singular that *the Kaffers,* (as not only I but others can testify) considered Dr. P. as sent by the Governor; nay, his own colleagues understood the matter in this way. When I landed at Algoa Bay from a short visit to England, January 1835, I was informed by a friend of Dr. P.'s, as a secret not generally known, though surmised, that Dr. P. had been sent by the Governor to the Kaffers with a message, and on his return, such was his haste to deliver their answer to the Governor, that he could not devote any time to other affairs which were likely to detain him on the road.

* Of this all the Wesleyan Missionaries are aware; I frequently heard the subject discussed, and also occasional threats, while at Mount Coke, 1833; but in common with others, I regarded their talk as merely the idle bravado of vain young men. A letter from the Rev. S. Young, dated 10th August, 1830, Wesleyville, contains the following passage:—" The Kaffers now say that if they have another war with the Colony, they shall not all come in a body as before; but they will divide themselves into separate parties, and

aware of the small number of troops on the frontier, which were divided among many military posts, few of them being capable of defence in the event of war, from the difficulty of sparing men sufficient to keep up a communication between them. The valuable and numerous herds of colonial cattle grazing on the frontier, were tempting objects to a predatory people, aware that there was no military force at hand capable of defending them, or of recovering them when taken.* Add to this, the injurious effects produced by the misrepresentations of various seditious Hottentots, some of them residing with the Chiefs in Kafferland, others on the Military posts, and a few in the Kat River settlement. These pretended to understand the sentiments of the Kat River Hottentots as being averse to any further subjection to the English Government.† Meanwhile Hinza, influenced by emissaries from the frontier Chiefs, and by the advice (as is with apparent reason supposed) of one Treckard,‡ a renegade boor who had for some time resided near the Ameva, in the northern part of Hinza's territory;

each party must have their route appointed them; and in this way, they say, they can avoid our troops, and come upon the settlers and boors before they can have time to collect themselves together."—(*Wesleyan Magazine for* 1831, *p.* 55.) In this fashion they actually made war in December, 1834. The Rev. Mr. Bonatz, the *Moravian Missionary* stationed at Shiloh, in the Tambookie country, thus gives his opinion:—"The last war was by no means a party outbreak, for I had heard of the design three years before; and the only cause which I can assign for it, is the irreconcileable enmity which the Kaffers cherish against our Government for repressing their depredations." (*See Missionary Register for* 1837.) This was one reason certainly, but not the *only* reason.

* In December, 1834, when the war broke out, the whole of the troops, European and Native, on the frontier, amounted to but 741 men, of whom 189 were mounted; 430 men, including 12 mounted, were kept at Graham's Town and Port Elizabeth; and thus on the immediate frontier 311 men, of whom only 177 were mounted, had to guard the whole extent of the boundary line between the Colony and Kafferland. These 311 men were divided among seven military posts.

† See "Minutes of the Court of Inquiry as to Hinza's death," p. 57, Tyali states: "The Hottentots and us, in the Kat River and Fort Willshire, were one; we expected every help from them, arms and ammunition."—"When my cattle were taken, the Hottentots sent to say, in five days they would set a house on fire at Fort Willshire, on which Makomo desired all his people to assemble there to witness what was going on."—"The Hottentots induced us to go to war, they assured us we could beat the English." See also the depositions of Enno, Botman, Ganya, Yo Yo; pp. 59—66.

‡ See Tyali's deposition, Court of Inquiry, p. 56.

at once removed with his people from the Mission station at Butterworth, took up his residence on the Ameva, from which situation he and his people could more easily support the inroad of the other Kaffers upon the colony. This removal took place about 3 months before the actual outbreak in December, 1834. In this state of affairs, Lieutenant Sutton and Ensign Sparks' patrols did not *cause*, but merely precipitate the war by a few months. The shooting of Xo-xo, which has been so plausibly assigned as one of the causes of the war, was a mere excuse, as is proved by a witness on the spot.* The unlooked for success which attended the first experimental predatory incursion, precipitated almost the whole of the tribes of Gaika and Slambie, together with a portion of Hinza's upon the colony; and thus commenced the late Kaffer war, which continued from December, 1834, to September, 1835, to the mutual injury of the Kaffers and Colonists, but especially of the latter.

In reviewing the circumstances which at length issued in this untoward event, we cannot but acknowledge that, had the Kaffers made war previous to the notification of Sir Benjamin D'Urban's conciliatory proposals for restitution; the justice of the cause would have appeared to be on their side, and on the Colonial Government must have devolved much of the guilt of the war.† But their knowledge and implied consent to Sir Benjamin D'Urban's proposals, completely alter the case. *In the then state of things*, the war

* Rev. Mr. Chalmers, of the Glasgow Missionary Society, who thus writes: "We were never more astonished when we entered Xo-xo's hut and found him looking as healthy as usual, having no bandage on his head, nor any appearance of any wound, although his head was shaved. We asked to see the wound, and were surprised to find it a mere scratch." See also the Chief Congo's statement to the Rev. S. Young. (*Evidence Abor. Com., p.* 659.)

† The relative position of the two parties was thus :—The Kaffers had a clear case against the Colonial Goverment for *territorial* aggression. The Colonial Government had an equally clear case against the Kaffers for a series of depredations on the *property* of its subjects. From the returns in the colonial office Cape Town, it can be clearly proved, that from the year 1810, to the end of November 1834, the Kaffers had plundered the colony of—

	Cattle,	Horses,	Sheep,
	54,204	1,864	2,682
Of which there were recovered,	15,787 ,,	594 ,,	
Balance due to the colony.	38,417 ,,	1,270 ,,	2,682 ,,

was on their part an *unjust and unprovoked aggression*. Such it was considered by all the *christian* Kaffers, *not one of whom joined in the war*, and to the present time, I have never met with any Kaffer who would attempt to defend their attack on the colony, even on the principles of their own law.

The injustice of throwing the odium of the war and its consequences upon the Governor, or upon the colonists, will appear evident from the preceding considerations; and it may not be amiss here to remark on the character and conduct of the individual, upon whom at that time devolved the duties and responsibilities of the Government, and military command of the colony.

Sir Benjamin D'Urban, is a Lieutenant General in the British army, his military career is well known to have been alike honourable to himself and useful to his country. The duties of his civil appointment in the West Indies, first in Antigua, and then in Demerara, were discharged to the perfect satisfaction of His Majesty's Government, as well as of the parties more immediately interested;—the white, free coloured, and slave population of these colonies. For his conscientious enforcement of the protective enactments in favour of the slave, he received the formal thanks of the Anti-Slavery Society. His well known attachment to the best interests of the coloured and slave population, and the personal (not merely official) zeal displayed by him in the support of every benevolent and religious institution,— rendered his appointment to the Government of the Cape, a subject of congratulation among the tried friends and supporters of Missions in England. We have the testimony of one who in Cape Town possessed many opportunities of personal acquaintance with him, that, "his head and heart were unrivalled, and that his talents were alike suited to the cabinet and the field, and that although a Governor he could afford to have a conscience."[*] Upon the minds of those

---

[*] Speech of Doctor Philip at the Anniversary Meeting of the Infant School, Cape Town, March 1835.

whose avocations placed them in frequent contact with him, an impression was generally left, favourable to the foresight and comprehensiveness of his understanding and the overflowing benevolence of his heart. It was his great misfortune to arrive in the colony at a crisis of peculiar difficulty, arising from the change in the laws affecting slavery, and the outbreak of long smothered discontent in Kafferland. From these and other causes a pressure of business fell upon him, which his utmost industry, though exerted to the injury of his health, failed to compass. The great defect in his character,—and in his situation, a serious one,—arose from the excess of a rare virtue, the " charity which hopeth all things, and thinketh no evil." Hence his confidence was in some cases misplaced upon men who misled him, if not by their advice, by their countenance, into the commission of some of the most serious mistakes of his administration. The apparent carelessness, observable in the wording of many of His Excellency's public despatches, and proclamations, and their consequent ambiguity of meaning, must be ascribed to the circumstances by which he was constantly harassed in body and mind, and which left little time for a careful revision, so desirable in documents of such an important character. Here His Excellency committed serious mistakes, of which his enemies took advantage. He was condemned for a few hasty expressions, tortured from their fair meaning as explained by the context, *and the true meaning of which should have been sought in his actions.* His statesmanlike plans of comprehensive benevolence were never fairly brought before the prejudiced public, and men who had not the local knowledge requisite to comprehend his schemes, or who perhaps felt dubious as to their ability to carry them into execution, were permitted to supersede the system of christian and humane policy, commenced by him at the close of the war, and which if persevered in but for one generation, would have rendered the semi-barbarians of Kafferland a nation of free and civilized subjects of the British crown.

In the Introduction, some remarks have already been made on the unfounded charges, of cruelty &c. so lavishly bestowed upon Sir Benjamin D'Urban. It would be preposterous to attempt to reply to the rabid virulence of certain party writers in England, some of them the editors of religious periodicals.* A paragraph, however, in Lord Glenelg's despatch 26th December, 1835, claims attention, as it reflects upon the conduct of Sir Benjamin D'Urban, and from its vagueness, and the implied sin of omission which is therein hinted at; no doubt produced on the public mind a most unfavourable impression. "So far are they (the London and Glasgow Society's Missionaries) from thinking the sword the only remedy, that on the contrary, they insist even with importunity, on the certain efficacy of other methods, of which kindness, conciliation, and justice, should form the basis." *(See Parliamentory Papers Kaffer War, p. 65)*.

It is difficult to understand the bearing of this passage. If the object be to *contrast* the opinions of the Missionaries of the London and Glasgow Society, with those of the Wesleyan Society, which is the natural inference drawn from the context, the affair is more properly between the Missionaries themselves, and Sir Benjamin is but very remotely concerned in the discrepencies of their opinions. The *supposed* difference of opinion, *here so erroneously assumed as existing, and the unfair interpretation* (and wilful perseverance in that interpretation) of the sentiments of the Wesleyan Missionaries by the noble Lord, will be more fully referred to in the APPENDIX. The natural inference which the public at large will draw, and have drawn from the frequent quotation of this isolated passage in the public prints is; that in the opinion of the Missionaries the war was unnecessary, even when the Kaffers had invaded the colony, and

---

* Among these may be mentioned the "Congregational Magazine." The virulent abuse indulged by its present editor, is only matched by his thorough ignorance of every fact connected with the Kaffer question. He certainly labours hard, and to do him justice, *with some success*, to degrade a periodical hitherto deemed respectable.

that *even then,* " *the certain efficacy,*" of conciliatory plans ought first to have been tried ; or in other words, that the Chief Magistrate of the colony, ought at that distressing period to have borne "the sword in vain," instead of becoming "a terror to evil doers." In justice to the Missionaries above referred to, it should be stated that they never uttered any such ridiculous opinions. They simply insisted on " the certain efficacy of other methods" in reference to a period when the war having ceased, it would be necessary to arrange a system of policy to meet the new circumstances of the colony and Kafferland ; and in this view of the case, no man possessed of common sense, to say nothing of christian feeling, could differ from them. The war having broken out, there was but one opinion in the colony as to the necessity of defending its inhabitants, and punishing the aggressors. Mr. Fairbairn, the editor of the South African Commercial Advertizer, wisely observed 7th January 1835, "This is not the time to deal in accusations. The Kaffers who have dared to invade the colony must be chastised, and taught the difference (to use their own phrase) between a deer and an elephant." Dr. Philip himself, could feel no scruples as to the justice of the war, when he used his influence to cause the Hottentots residing on Missionary Institutions to volunteer their services against the Kaffers.—*(See Evidence Abor. Com. p.* 709 *).* But it is needless to refer to authorities. Any disinterested person must be convinced, that the question being once agitated, by an appeal to arms, whether a horde of barbarians should possess supreme power, or a civilized Government, the interests of humanity and civilization, apart from any other considerations of duty or policy ; required a prompt and efficient chastisement of the invaders, and the establishment of British supremacy over them, as the only sound basis of a future peace.

Lord Glenelg's opinion as stated in a previous paragraph, is confirmatory of the above statement, and amply justifies Sir B. D'Urban, who during the whole of the war did no more than is there stated to have been his "*clear and indispensable duty.*" Adopting the language of Lord Aberdeen, " I concur entirely with him in declaring it to have been your clear and indispensable duty, to arrest the progress of the invaders and to compel them to retire within their own territory. Nor was this the whole extent of your duty in that critical state of public affairs; you were not less distinctly bound to take effective measures for putting down within Kafferland itself, all assemblages of men, who had either formed, or were in the act of forming themselves into bands hostile to the colony, you were also entitled to take effectual securities against the recurrence of similar invasions."—*(See Parliamentary Papers Kaffer War, p.* 61.) Sir Benjamin D'Urban in his conduct during the Kaffer war, *did not exceed the strict letter of these instructions.* He compelled the Kaffers " to retire within their own territory,"—he took " effective measures for putting down within Kafferland, all assemblages of men &c.," *as far as he could consistently with humanity;* it is admitted that he *might* have used more *effective measures*, by letting loose the frontier militia, hurrying to avenge recent losses, but this he refrained from doing, lest possibly and probably indeed, an indiscriminate vengeance should go beyond the limits of justice. He took " effectual securities against the recurrence of similar invasions," and *the only effectual securities*, namely, *those arising from plans distinguished by a wise foresight and a comprehensive humanity; having for their object the civilization and christianization of the Kaffers themselves.* It is therefore frequently and naturally asked by those who are acquainted with the true version of these affairs; why was Sir Benjamin D'Urban removed from the government of the Cape colony? Why was *he* made responsible for evils, the result of previous mismanagement? It is by no means improbable, that the error into which his humanity led him was the main cause of his removal. The enormous expense occasioned by the local difficulties in the transport of stores, and the *materiel* of war, &c. for so many regular troops, for so long a period, rendered necessary by the humane system of warfare substituted by him, instead of the less expensive, but more destructive war which might have been carried on by the armed militia of the colony; was peculiarly annoying to the treasury; and this is stated by some who profess to be in the secret, to have been the *real*, though not the ostensible cause of the recal.

It is equally unjust to consider the *colonists as a body*, as involved either in the remote or proximate causes of the war. While we admit that the real cause of the Kaffer, as well as of other wars, between colonists and aborigines, may be traced to the unjust system of European colonization, we must in justice remember that, "An important distinction is ever to be made between the founders of the colony and the colonists themselves. The main body of the settlers have nothing to do with originating the plan of any colony, or obtaining the Act of Parliament for its formation. They are generally persons who have not profoundly gone into the question of colonization, with reference to the principles upon which it is based; but captivated by the flattering offers and the glowing statements made by the authors of the scheme, they have been induced to go out as emigrants, and seek a new home in the distant land, which the pen of the eloquent writer and the pencil of the artist have been employed to deck with all the charms of "the land of promise." "In some cases it would be a difficult question to settle, whether the natives, who have been induced by the founders of the colony to surrender their lands, or the emigrants to whom those lands have been allotted, were the subjects of the greater deception and delusion. In such circumstances what else could have been reasonably expected, but that which has really happened, when the rights of the natives and the claims of the colonists have begun seriously to clash?"[*]

The above extract, while it so justly characterizes the

[*] "Colonization," being Remarks on Colonization in general, &c., by Rev. J. Beecham; 2d edition, London, 1838.

nature of European colonization in general, *exactly describes the position of the British colonists on the eastern frontier of the Cape colony.* Their emigration in 1819, was the result of a scheme patronized warmly by the British Government. They were lured to Africa as to a land of promise. They afterwards found they were placed as a barrier against Kaffer inroads, and as a protection to the older districts of the colony. They had no voice in the arrangements of the border policy, and are not justly accountable for its real or supposed delinquencies. *In the question as to whether the Kaffers were justified in invading the colony or not, the British settlers are no parties concerned.* Were it clearly proved that the Kaffers had been driven to make war by the oppression of the Colonial Government, (which is supposing an extreme case, such as only the veriest partisan would dare to state), even then, the colonists would not be justly chargeable with the painful results of the misconduct of their rulers, over whose actions they could have no control.

While, however, a sober and dispassionate observer will fully acquit the Settlers of any share of guilt in provoking the late war,—he will with equal impartiality refrain from a sweeping condemnation of *Kaffer* character and conduct.

The Colonists, smarting under recent losses, may, perhaps, be excused if *they* speak strongly; but impartial men will find certain extenuating circumstances which considerably soften the otherwise unfavorable estimate of Kaffer character. A series of unfortunate collisions between the Kaffers and Boers of long standing, an unsettled and disputed line of boundary, together with the vacillating policy of the Colonial Government sometimes unaccountably careless of the property and lives of its subjects, and at other times unnecessarily severe; in a word, the total want of plan and system which characterized our border policy previous to the war, are reasons sufficient in themselves to account for the existence of considerable excitement and irritation in Kafferland. The temptation afforded by the wealth of the colony, almost unprotected, was too powerful to be easily resisted by a warlike, predatory, and heathen people. We must not pass judgment upon such a people according to the strict rules of christian morality. The moral, political, and social condition of the Kaffer tribes, act as a stimulus to their predatory habits, and until these are changed, the frontier of the colony can only be kept secure by a strong and preponderating military force. And even this of itself will not be sufficient to keep the colony in peace and security, unless the power of the Colonial Government be guided by wisdom and justice. When *concurrently* with increased means of *religious instruction* for the Kaffers, we have a Government which will " *neither do wrong, nor suffer wrong,*" THEN, AND NOT TILL THEN, WILL THERE BE PEACE AND SECURITY.

It has been shown in the foregoing pages, that to a system of territorial aggression, pursued from the earliest periods, and carried on by the Dutch and English Colonial Governments, (sanctioned of course by their superiors in Europe), we owe the Kaffer war. Had the true principles of colonization, and the just claims of free communities of natives been understood by the Home Government, and by the people of England, the evils adverted to, would long ago have been checked. Shall we profit by past experience? or is it true, that while individuals *sometimes* learn wisdom from experience, yet nations *never?* Recent schemes of colonization which have found some favour in the eyes of the British public, and have even been advocated in some of the religious journals, afford reason to fear, that " the thing that hath been, is that which shall be." Let this question be fairly met. Considering the mixed character of the population of a new colony, the weakness of a colonial administration, the peculiar difficulties naturally arising from the juxta-position of European and Native, mutually ignorant of each other's modes of thought and action ; is it possible for colonies to be formed in the vicinity of *powerful* tribes of aborigines, without the almost absolute certainty of an eventual collision, which *must* end in the subjugation of the weaker party? In such a case, it is impossible but that offences will come; and should the proposed colony be established in New Zealand, we may fully anticipate, that before the next generation, the "New Zealand war," like "the Kaffer war," will occupy the attention of the legislature and the public.*

* Since these observations were penned, the news has reached South Africa, that the scheme for the Colonization of New Zealand has been rejected by the British Parliament. Thanks to the enlightened zeal and philanthropy of many real friends of the Aborigines of that distant country. It is, however, remarkable, that some who were most forward to vituperate the unfortunate British Settlers of South Africa, for alleged aggressions made by them upon the Kaffers; seem to have been perfectly regardless of the probable consequences to the New Zealanders of this new scheme of colonization. It does not appear that they have taken the least share in defeating the proposed measure. How is this to be accounted for? Have not the New Zealanders as great a claim on the justice and benevolence of Britain as the Kaffers? Or is there some difference in the two questions, with reference to *party* views and proceedings? Sir W. Molesworth on one occasion declaimed at length, in his place in Parliament, against the territorial aggressions of the colonists at the Cape; and yet during the same session he was the warmest advocate of a plan for alienating the choicest lands of the New Zealand tribes!

NOTE II.

SIR BENJAMIN D'URBAN'S EXTENSION OF BRITISH JURISDICTION OVER THE BORDER KAFFERS.

From the beginning of the war, the grand measure to which Sir Benjamin appears to have looked for ensuring permanent peace and security on the frontier, was the extension of British jurisdiction on the Kei. That this was no sudden thought, is evident from His Excellency's statement, and from the fact that his intentions in this respect were generally known in the colony, even so early as the end of January, 1835; and previous to his arrival on the eastern frontier. The measure itself was no after thought, suggested by "*interested Colonists*," but was planned by His Excellency, when under the influence of any other than favourable impressions towards the frontier authorities and inhabitants, as the most effectual means of preventing future collision, and of securing to the Aborigines the protection of British Law; as well as for providing a secure frontier to the colony against the predatory tribes beyond. This measure was never intended to imply the expulsion of such of the native inhabitants *as were willing to abide in their old territory in peaceable submission to British Laws*, though the ambiguous wording of several public documents gave too much countenance to the statements of those, whose purpose it suited to describe the annexation of the new province to the colony, as necessarily involving the expulsion of the old inhabitants, and the granting of their lands to Colonial Settlers. The proclamation of the 10th May, 1835, in which the taking possession of the new territory was first formally announced, certainly states, that, "the Chiefs Tyali, &c. with their tribes, are for ever expelled, and will be treated as enemies if found therein." But the sweeping sentence of expulsion implied in this incautious expression, was immediately corrected; for *two days after*, on the 12th May, 1835, His Excellency states, that, provided the belligerent Chiefs will cease hostilites, and surrender themselves, or voluntarily pass beyond the Kei, "I will only require the expulsion from the aforesaid territory of the Chiefs aforesaid, and those Kaffers who were engaged in inroads into the Colony, or in the murder of British Subjects:" and then immediately follows a statement, that, "ample lands" shall be provided for Sutu, and her son Sandili,* &c. the representatives of the Gaika family, for Nonibe and her son Siwane* the representatives of the Slambie family, and for such of their respective tribes as they recommend, or permit to reside with them. Sir Benjamin D'Urban appears to have thought, that, the Chiefs thus condemned to banishment, would have been forsaken by all, save a few of their immediate dependants; that the bulk of the tribes would have submitted to the legitimate heads of their Chief's families ruling under British protection, and that the banishment of the Chiefs, and those concerned in the war, and in the robbery and murder connected with it, would have secured the peace of the new province, and would have prevented the agitation of many difficult questions on the part of the injured Colonists, as to the restoration of stolen property, and the punishment of the known deliberate murderers of their

* It may be here requisite to remark that Sandili is the acknowledged head of the family of Gaika; and Siwane is the legitimate successor of the late Chief Dushani, who was the great son of Slambie. These youths are both minors; but when they come of age, Makomo, Tyali, &c. who are, at present, better known, will be inferior to them both in rank and power.

friends and relatives. In this he was misled, and a perseverance in his declared intention of expelling the belligerent Chiefs beyond the Kei, would have prolonged the war many months, and would have caused a lamentable destruction of human life, as well as an enormous additional expenditure on the part of the British Government.

Previous to the commencement of the second campaign, 27th July, 1835, the Wesleyan Missionaries deemed it their duty to state their views as to the impolicy of renewing the war for the purpose of effecting a measure, which, if possible to effect, was of a very questionable nature, and would, at all events, be accompanied with a vast addition of human suffering. His Excellency having already committed himself to insist upon the expulsion of the Chiefs, and the evident impossibility of his receding from his original terms, while the enemy yet remained unsubdued; were serious obstacles in the way of a pacific termination of this ruinous contest. These were, however, obviated by an offer on the part of the Wesleyan Missionaries to open an intercourse with the belligerent Chiefs, and to give them such advice as would lead them to supplicate for peace, and for a residence this side of the Kei within the bounds of the new province, and to be received as British Subjects, under certain modifications, suited to their peculiar circumstances. The consent of His Excellency to this arrangement having been obtained, the Missionaries, at considerable risk, succeeded in opening a communication with the Chiefs in the Amatoli mountains; and within three weeks after the subject had by them been brought under His Excellency's notice, the Kaffer Chiefs sent to desire peace, and to be received as the Governor's children. Negotiations ensued, which ended in the pacification of the 19th September, 1835. *(See Evidence Abor. Com., pp. 495, 496.)*

By the treaties then entered into, the Chiefs of Kafferland, on this side of the Kei were, " *at their earnest request,*" received as British subjects, and accepted from the Governor grants of territory of greater or less extent, in proportion to the number of their people. Certain reserves of land between the locations of each tribe, were preserved for the purpose of planting trading stations, military posts, &c. The principal Chiefs were appointed Magistrates, to exercise a delegated and legal jurisdiction over their people, subject to the controul of an English Agent; the usages and customs of the Kaffer councils were not to be interfered with, and the old laws remained in force; *care, however, being taken to provide for their equitable administration, by reserving to Kaffers of every rank, a right of appeal from the court of the native Magistrate, to that of the English Agent;* and thus a foundation was laid for the gradual, but certain, introduction of an improved state of society, which the natural capabilities of the Kaffer mind, aided by the religious training of the Missionaries, and placed under circumstances thus favouring intellectual and moral development; would speedily have produced.

To carry these treaties into effect, to explain the principles of the new system about to be introduced, as well as to complete a census of the population of each tribe, &c.; a number of Commissioners were appointed. At the *special request of the Chiefs*, the Missionaries with whom they had been previously connected, were placed on this Commission, the details of which it would have been difficult to carry into effect without their assistance.* The general opinion of the Commissioners being unfavourable to the retention of the reserved lands, the whole of the Kaffer territory was in a few months restored to the respective tribes. Colonel Smith, C. B.,

---

* This part of the conduct of the Missionaries has been censured, and they have been represented as "entering Kafferland triumphantly as Commissioners under the Conqueror." Thus, under the influence of party malignity, their willingness to expose themselves to all the unpleasantness arising out of their position as mediators in settling difficult arrangements, has been converted into the appearance of a triumph, indulged in at the expense of the natives!! No further refutation of this calumny is necessary than the above statement of facts, but it may be right to add that the services of the Missionaries, as Commissioners, were gratuitous.

was placed at King William's Town as Commander-in-Chief of the New Province of Queen Adelaide, and English Agents were appointed to reside with the principal Chiefs, agreeably to the provisions of the treaty. These preliminary arrangements being completed, the new regime was formally introduced, and the Magistrates were installed, at a public meeting held at King William's Town, 7th January, 1836; of which the following account, written by Mr. Greig, one of the spirited projectors of the *South African Commercial Advertiser*, will be read with interest; as it affords a fair specimen of the ability and tact with which the enlightened Commander of the New Province discharged the duties of his important office:—

"On Thursday, the 7th of January, a gathering of all the Kaffer Chiefs, now under British jurisdiction, took place at King William's Town, in the Province of Queen Adelaide, for the purpose of administering the Oath of Allegiance, to the Magistrates and people who are become voluntary subjects of the King of England; for initiating the Chiefs, and other heads of kraals, into the offices severally of Magistrates, Field-commandants, and Field-cornets; and also for explaining to these functionaries the leading points connected with the duties which they are expected to perform.

"The greater part of the Kaffers arrived on Wednesday afternoon, and were bivouacked for the night on the slopes of the hills which surrounded the camp. The tribes of Makomo and Tyali presented a very imposing appearance, mounting about 600 men on horseback, besides about 1,000 on foot. The other Kaffers came up with order and regularity, some of the tribes singing their war songs, and whistling in a peculiarly deep and thrilling tone. Early on Thursday morning the troops, consisting of detachments of the 75th and 72d Regiments, a body of cavalry from the Cape Mounted Rifles, and the provisional company of the 75th, with Artillery, and Sappers and Miners, in all nearly

600, began to assemble on the ground. From that time until twelve o'clock was consumed with the collecting and arranging of the respective Kaffer tribes, who appear to move but slowly. At length the signal gun was fired, and Colonel Smith walked to the marquee, accompanied by Mrs. Smith and Mrs. Major Burney, and the officers of the staff, &c. On the ground also were the Commissioners for locating the several tribes, some Missionaries, several gentlemen from India, Cape Town, &c. The *coup d'œil* was exceedingly interesting. To those accustomed to see large masses of civilized men, the exhibition of this day furnished no analogy. It had a character altogether novel, and was rendered highly picturesque by its wildness. In the centre was the tent of the Commander-in-chief of the province. On his right hand sat Makomo, and on the left Tyali, each dressed in a suit of blue clothes. The countenance of the former indicates candour, and his eye and mouth firmness and decision. His brother Tyali, looks selfish and sensual, is indisposed to talk much; and it seems, he imitates John Bull so far already, as to be slow in forming intimacies with strangers. Next to him sat Sutu, Gaika's queen wife; then Nonube, the Regent of Dushanie's tribe during the nonage of her son Siwane. Then came Cobus Congo, Pato, and William Kama, the latter of whom is a very respectable looking man, adheres to one wife only, sends his son to school, and shows many other pleasing marks of civilization. Jan Tzatzoe sat next. This Chief is said to be more advanced than any of the others. He has, in fact, stepped up to the agricultural state; he too has but one wife, and has long been conspicuous for encouraging improvement among his people, by means of Missionaries, &c. Botman, Stock, (Eno's eldest son and representative), and Gazelle, (from Slambie's tribe), followed; then Matwa and Tinta, younger sons of Gaika, and Sonto, who was distinguished during the war by riding on a *white horse;* several Chiefs of minor note sat around, but apart from the body of their people, and these completed this curious group. The Fingoes with their war shields were intermingled with the Kaffers on friendly terms.

"The business of the day was opened with an impressive prayer in the Kaffer language, by the Rev. Mr. Chalmers.

"While surveying the athletic forms of these uncouth men, (who evince a most pastoral contempt for nether garments,) the mind was irresistibly led to reflect upon the late conflict in which we were engaged with them. Utterly reckless of human life themselves, bold and cunning, inured to hardships, with few wants, despising labour, and caring less for their wives than their cattle, to obtain possession of which no sacrifice appears to be too great; one could not view them but as a most dangerous enemy, and, in their present state, uncertain friends; and, as the best efforts of civilization proceed with very slow steps, there appears no alternative but that of keeping up the present military force, or of abandoning the frontier districts altogether. Doubtless an intercourse of stern and rigid justice, tempered with kindness, as at present pursued, will be productive of beneficial effects. But while the Kaffers continue to consider it degrading for a man to till the soil, or sow, or reap, or bear a burthen,—while they indulge in the practice of polygamy, and have to obtain wives by means of cattle only,—while the baneful custom of witchcraft is upheld among them, by which men of wealth in oxen are robbed by their Chiefs, and thus driven to steal for subsistence, and while they exercise worse than servile tyranny over their wives, whose lives are in their hands, for certain crimes,— so long will it be, in the opinion of the writer, unsafe to entrust the security of the frontier to any scheme less formidable than that of military posts throughout the country. It is admitted by men of intelligence, well acquainted with the Kaffer character, that the Chief has but little, if any, influence over them for *good purposes*. To make war, to head a foray or predatory expedition, to steal cattle, are they ever his ready and willing instruments.

But were he to attempt to induce them to relinquish any habit or prejudice affecting their own interests, they would refuse, or leave him and join another Chief, or, mayhap, depose him. To disengage his interest from their's, and to make him depend upon, and look up to, another power, therefore, seems to be a desideratum of no mean importance, as the first step to the breaking up of that clan-ship, which appears to be strong only in evil; and, entertaining these opinions, the writer thinks the object aimed at by Colonel Smith, as explained in his speech of this day, to be very judicious and highly important, namely, that of rendering the Chiefs *stipendiary Magistrates*, and making them responsible to colonial authority for any infraction of, or relaxation in, their duties. It is highly desirable that this line of wise policy should be confirmed and followed up hereafter.

"Before reading the address, Colonel Smith took off his cocked hat, and waiving it, called out in his wonted martial manly tone of voice, "Long live our good King William the Fourth," which was responded to by a shout from the Kaffers, loud, long, and deafening. They raised their hands high in the air, snapping their fingers as they yelled, with singular effect. They then sat down on their hams, and it appeared incredible that 2,000 men could be stowed away, as it were, in so small a compass. Colonel Smith then read, in a clear and audible voice, the important document subjoined. The whole of this address was interpreted, passage by passage, by Mr. Shepstone, jun., with striking ease and fluency, which made it obvious that he is perfectly acquainted with the construction and *spirit* of the language. Thus, where allusion is made to the 'immortality of the soul,' the writer was curious to learn how an adequate interpretation of this expression could be conveyed to men ignorant of a future state. The words were rendered by 'a life that has no end.' Such an interpreter is invaluable to the cause of fair dealing and humanity.

"The reading of the paper occupied upwards of an hour;

yet the Chiefs, and a great majority of the Kaffers, paid untiring attention to it, and at several parts Makomo showed much emotion, which may have arisen in part from Colonel Smith's emphatic manner. When it was finished the Colonel said, 'Makomo and Tyali, and the other Magistrates, I now wait to hear anything you have to say.' After a short pause, Makomo turned round and said,— 'Although my people are stupid, and ignorant, and naked, I and they are perfectly sensible when good words are said to us. I will always tell you if anything happens among my people, as you are the representative of the King and the Governor, and I will obey your instructions.' To which the Colonel replied,—' Makomo, you have shown yourself to-day the same man I have ever found you; and I again urge you to remember these words,—You are now British subjects, and no man can injure you with impunity. I am glad to hear you are ready to live and act as an honest man. In the bush you were *brave*. Now show yourself *true*. Last year was an arduous one for me. I speak not of my own labours; but as I then punished you, and saw your distress, so I am happy that I can now address you as friends. I thank you and Tyali for the rectitude of your own conduct, and the orderly behaviour of your people. You may rely upon my protecting you in all that is good.'

"Tyali then spoke briefly. He thanked Colonel Smith for all he had done for him and his people. 'They do not see the King, nor the Governor, but only Colonel Smith, who is here for the King. But Tyali and his people appreciate the Colonel's goodness, and will try to be good subjects; and he promises to keep nothing from the great Chief.'

"Thus ended this memorable meeting. The parties quietly dispersed, each tribe of Anglo-Kaffers marching off to their place of occupation. And it should not be omitted to be stated, that on this occasion the Kaffers evinced the most undisguised and unquestionable confidence in the British character. Although our troops were armed on the ground and there were two pieces of artillery loaded, they left their assagais on the ground where they halted, and came lightly and boldly to the place with a walking-stick only. Considering how recent is the peace, and the proverbially cautious character of savage men, this fact may be regarded with pleasure and satisfaction. And it was no less remarkable to observe the entire confidence and attachment shown by all the Chiefs to Colonel Smith. Let the writer be joined by the reader in the expression of a fervent hope, that the present good understanding may never again be disturbed by mischievous policy on the one side, or by reckless treachery on the other.

ADDRESS OF COLONEL SMITH.

"Having closely applied myself to become thoroughly acquainted with your wants, I have now lived long enough amongst you, my children, to be able to observe them.

"Field-commandants, Field-cornets, and heads of kraals—The laws of a country are rules established by the authority of its King or Governor and his councillors, to direct the conduct and secure the rights of its inhabitants. You have all lately been received at your own request and humble desire, and in the mercy of His Excellency the Governor, as British subjects, consequently are now governed by the British law, which, widely differing from your own, will require on my part some little explanation, in order to point out to you the necessary procedure in cases where the interposition of the law and its coercive power is required. Having been placed over you by His Excellency the Governor as your ruler since the day peace was concluded, and as he holds me strictly responsible to him to see justice duly administered to all,—that the laws are neither outraged nor individuals oppressed or ill used,—so have I since that period, as you all well know, watched over your rights and interests for your benefit, so to govern you, that gradually you might become so accustomed to our manner of proceeding as to enable you to observe the impartiality with which the law is enforced, falling equally heavy upon those who are its transgressors, rich or poor, black or white, and equally protecting all. I have, therefore, called together this large assembly, personally to explain to you to the best of my ability, the mode you are to adopt as Magistrates, when crime is brought under your observation, in conjunction with the British Resident.

"Whoever it was amongst you who first suggested the idea of your becoming British subjects, deserves to be marked by you as a man who has rendered you the most eminent service. Did not your great father Gaika on his death-bed assemble his sons around him, and with his dying breath tell them to hold fast the word of peace with the English? this you did not do; what ensued? you were almost utterly destroyed; soon would have been annihilated, and driven from your native country; your women and children were starving, almost the prey of wild beasts, and the widows of four thousand of your warriors lament the loss of their husbands slain during the war; the greater part of your cattle and flocks starved or taken; your plunder so treacherously seized from the colony, lost to you by the robberies of others; you were in a lamentable, nay, deplorable plight; you sought and asked for mercy, it was granted you. You also begged to be received as British subjects, this has been granted you, and you *are now the subjects* of the most powerful nation, whose laws, manners, customs, and institutions, are the admiration of the world. This was your state when I took you 'out of the bush,' since which three moons have barely passed over your heads; land has been given you,—your gardens are flourishing—your clergymen have returned to you, hoping to forget your sins in the observance of your penitence,—a trade is established for you,—your persons and property are protected by the equity of the British law,—no man can now be 'eat up' unless found guilty of crime, and condemned by your judges; and in place of being the beaten, degraded, humbled and mortified people you were in the bush, you are taken by the hand and called brother by the inhabitants of the greatest nation under the protection of Almighty God. You tell me that you are naked and ignorant, that I must teach you to clothe yourselves, to know good from evil, that you are willing to learn, and that you wish to be real Englishmen. Mark me then;—Years ago the English were as naked as you, as ignorant as you, as cruel as you were in the late war; but the bright day which has opened to you dawned upon them; they first learned to believe in the omnipotent power of God Almighty, who judges every man according to his actions; worshipped, honoured, and obeyed him; they loved their neighbours as themselves; and respecting their property ceased to be thieves; they believed all that the ministers of God told them; they sent their children to be taught to read and write; they learned the use of money, and carried on an honest trade with each other, selling their skins, &c. and buying clothes, as you see us all now dressed; some were labourers in the field, some tended the herds and flocks, some made implements of husbandry, built houses, made guns, and every thing you see your brother Englishmen possess, while others made laws to govern the whole, under the King, whom we all love. Thus civilization gradually advanced, while we became acquainted with works of art, knowledge increased, we threw off the yoke of despotism and barbarism, cast away our vicious habits, and put to death and banished by the law every one who by sin, crime, and wickedness, was a pest and an enemy to society at large. Do you suppose we have all these things by lying sleeping all day long under a bush? no; but by habits of daily industry, working as you see me do and all my people around me, each day becoming wiser than the other; and, by avoiding the evils of yesterday striving to improve ourselves to-day. Such now may be your case provided you cease to do the following things:—

" 1. 'To eat one another up,' this is theft.

"2. To murder or kill any one.

"3. To believe in witchcraft. This is all folly and ignorance of the worst description. Did not Eno's 'rainmaker' desire you to go to war, and encourage you by telling you that you would beat the English, the greatest nation in the world, whose power exceeds yours as much as the waters of the Keiskamma do the pools of the Peula rivulet? How dared the villain tell you such lies? Was he not the first man shot when the troops moved on Eno's kraal, after I came amongst you, and was then as much your bitter enemy as I am now your true friend?

"4. Perjury, or giving false witness against any one.
"5. Setting houses on fire, and destroying property.
"6. Rape. And above all (having this day taken the oath of allegiance)
"7. Treason, or lifting up your assegais against the King, the Governor, his officers, magistrates, soldiers, and subjects. The English law punishes these crimes with DEATH, and by avoiding them we have become the great, powerful, enlightened, and happy nation you see, going about the world teaching others to imitate us, and we are *now instructing you*. Do you wish then to be real Englishmen, or to be naked and almost wild men? Speak, I say, that I may know your hearts.

"You have spoken well, your brothers will assist you; this day has His Excellency the Governor clothed your chief Magistrates and Field-cornets according to their rank, to show you how England expects her subjects to appear. From this time henceforth no more presents of clothes will be given you; by trade (as we do) must you clothe yourselves, and look no more to me for presents but for some important and good service rendered to the state. Such I will reward, because His Excellency the Governor loves to reward merit.

"Since you have been under my protection, the oldest men tell me that there has been less crime than they ever knew;

but this, though it pleases me, does not satisfy me; there shall be no stealing one from the other, above all from the King, or, as you would term it, the great kraal, the Governor, or his people. Beware, I say, of theft; and as I protect you, so will I punish you, until the law, by the rigour with which I will wield it, shall root out this evil from amongst you. Our clergymen will teach you what God expects of you, what you must do in this world to expect God's mercy and love in the next; thus you will all learn to love God. You must send your children to school, or you are wicked and base parents; and by your good example, and by speaking the truth, teach them what they may become with the advantages of an education, which you have not nor could receive. Above all do not despair or despond, or say we are poor people, we know nothing; rouse yourselves, remember what I have told you that the English were once as you now are, and that you may become what they are at present.

" In the great change of laws by which you are now governed, one of the most important is that of not tolerating your being ' eaten up.' Now this protects the weak; the strong, from time immemorial, possessed amongst you this power, which custom made a right of the Chief, though it was a curse to you; do not, therefore, suppose that the English law while it protects one party injures the other; no, such is not the case; your Chiefs, who from custom possessed this power, by which their kraals were filled with cattle, and by which they were enabled to reward those who performed good services, must, your merciful and provident Governor says, receive an equivalent; besides, being now your Magistrates, much of their time and attention will be taken up in labouring for your advantage. You must, therefore, contribute to their support and dignity.

" A regulation is now framing that each kraal pay so many cattle or calves in the 100 annually to each Chief, on the day the ox is paid to the King of England for the land which you possess, and which he had conquered from you; no time will be lost in carrying this arrangement into effect. Thus *you* see, Makomo, Tyali, Umhala, and the others of your kindred, who from birth possess rights and privileges, *you* will be hereafter amply provided for.

"To you, Makomo, most particularly, do I return my thanks for your conduct since I have taken you out of the bush. Some errors you have committed; no man is faultless. Confide in the laws you now live under, assist in carrying them into execution, and of this be assured, hereafter no man can injure you, or any one of our new British subjects, who obeys the law. In the high Magisterial situation in which you are placed, in conjunction with the British Resident, much labour, exertion, and example, is expected from you. It rejoices me to hear the readiness with which you established, close to your own kraal, the Missionary Kayser, and I hope to hear of your constant attendance on Sundays, that your son receives the advantages of education, and that your people follow your footsteps.

"You, Tyali, are yet young, but remember that the charge left you by your father, Gaika, is a great one; you are now responsible to the King of England and the Governor, and I hope to observe that steadiness in your conduct, which can alone ensure the good, the happiness, the welfare of your people. The good example you set the other Sunday, in attending Divine Service at the Chumie, with your wives and family, I highly applaud; and I trust your innate feelings were inspired by those religious principles, which, while they teach us to be good, honest, and upright, ensure our happiness. Being now satisfied with your conduct, I invest you with the seal of your office as a Field-commandant under Makomo. Wear it, and preserve it, by being just and equitable, and implicitly obeying orders at your peril.

"You, Gazelle, you must tell Umhala he has much to

do as Field-Commandant; your people are much scattered, and somewhat divided among themselves; the greater energy and exertion, therefore, is required of you. Set a good example to all around you, by activity and industry; learn to trust to your own resources to improve your own situation. I hope speedily to establish a Mission Station near you to assist you. I was highly pleased with one of your people the other day whom I sent for, by name "Dadazi;" he came to me neatly dressed in clothes, which he had purchased from the sutler; why do you not all do so? This England expects of her subjects. Leave off this trash of brass, beads, wire, clay, &c.; replace them by soap, linen, and clothes, if you will be real Englishmen.

Suta, you have a Missionary Station close to you; you must attend to the education of your son, or you will lose the good character you justly hold amongst the missionaries; induce your people to attend Divine Service, and to send their children to be taught.

"Nonibe, you have behaved well upon all occasions, and have been a faithful friend to the English; attend to the education of your son Siwani, or you will not be a good mother.

"The Commissioners have recommended to His Excellency to appoint Field-cornets under the Field-commandants:—

For the Slambie Family,—Gazela, T'syolo, Quasana.

FIELD-CORNETS FOR THE GAIKA FAMILY.

Sutu and Sandili	Hlahla, Vena, Anta, Madaam, Isiplai,	Tyali.	Vonko, Mabomba, Clew, or Xo-xo, Kapai, Katse,
Makomo.	Bungalo, Sonto, Lalwana, Messanie, Panyakwa,	Matwa,	Tenti, Soga, Maduma,
Eno,	Stock, Casa, Isaba, Faka,	Botman.	Vandana, Flata, Bongola,

"You are responsible to the Field-commandants—they to the English Resident Agents,—the whole to me,—I to His Excellency the Governor, whose instructions I obey, and it is he whom you must thank for all the good things conferred upon you, and projected for your welfare now and hereafter.

"Pato, Kama, and Congo, are already appointed Field-commandants. Umkye is recommended for his people and those of Nonibe, and Jan Tzatzoe for his own. These men are willing to learn, and are rapidly progressing towards civilization; they are clothed by their own industry; some have ploughs drawn by bullocks; all know the use of money, and attend to the Clergymen.

"From you, Pagati, much do I expect; many of you were the councillors of your Chiefs; aid them now to do good by the English law—strive to prevent crime,—attend Divine worship—send your children to school, and show that example which the confidence placed in you demands.

"To the heads of kraals or villages do I now address myself:—

"You are now responsible for the good conduct of the people of your village, if you exert yourselves and do your duty, crime will be checked, and ultimately stopped altogether. No man ought to be absent without your knowledge, no man can return with cattle or horses without your knowing it, and whenever a crime has been committed by a kraal, I will make the whole responsible to me, if they do not produce the offenders and stolen property. You shall leave off this wicked practice of stealing from one another in the way you do—the English law will make honest men of you—you shall not steal.

"You must see that your people are active and industrious, that they work in the gardens; it is the duty of the men to work in the fields—not of women, they ought to make and mend your clothes and their own, to keep their chidren clean, wash your clothes, cook your food, and take care of the milk. You well know from observation, what work the Englishmen do, and what their women, this you must imitate, and not sleep half your time, and pass the rest in drowsy inactivity; these things you must do, and you will soon reap the fruits of your labour.

'Magistrates, and all assembled, as you wish to be real Englishmen, you must observe their habits and customs in every thing, and as you are rapidly ceasing to believe in witchcraft, and at the death of any of your friends and relatives, (an affection to which we are all liable) beginning to omit the witch-dance, and the burning your huts and clothes, so do I now call upon you to bury your dead, as you see us do, and not drag out the corpse ere the vital spark is extinct, and cast it forth as food for wild beasts and birds of prey; the thought even makes a christian and civilized man shudder. To the first man who has the misfortune to lose one of his relatives, if he decently inter him will I give an ox, How can you bear to see those whom in life you loved and cherished, your aged father who taught you your manly exercises, and provided you with food; your mother who nursed you as a child, who attended you in sickness,—who for years watched over you, contributing to your wants or wishes; your brother, sister, nearest relatives, or dearest friends, dragged from amongst you ere dead, and thrown out as a dog. We English not only make coffins to bury our dead, but raise upon the spot, where our dearest friend's earthly remains are deposited, monuments to perpetuate their virtues, and when wicked men, whose lives have been forfeited to the offended laws of our country, for any of the crimes which I have enumerated to you, are buried (for we even bury them also,) such spot is marked with the merited ignominy it deserves, and our youth, as they pass the tomb of the good man, have an example of the respect due to virtue set before them, or are taught to abhor the crime which merited an ignominious death, by the wretched mound which

K

marks the sinner's grave. Thus, as you loved your relatives in life, so are you bound to cherish their memory, and decently deposit their mortal remains in their parent earth. Englishmen not only do this, but the clergyman prays over the grave; and these matters of moment, connected with the immortality of your souls, Missionaries will teach you, when you attend Divine Worship; but your dead you must bury, as I point out, if you wish to be real christians and Englishmen.

'At this great meeting, let me impress upon you, that all previous animosities amongst yourselves be forgotten, and while the great English nation now regards you as British subjects and brothers, love your neighbour as yourself,—Fear God, and honour your King, and the Governor his representative. Now let any man speak who wishes it.'

"Umhala, from the Slambie tribe, not having arrived until the evening, the ceremony of installing him and the other captains in their offices was postponed till Friday the 9th, when the whole of the above document was read to him, and interpreted by Mr. Shepstone, jun. On this occasion there were present five delegates from Creili, who also requested Col. Smith, in the name of their Chief, to administer the Oath of Allegiance to them; to this Colonel Smith assented, asking them if they distinctly understood that Creili and they took this step at their own suggestion, and had become voluntarily, and without solicitation on his part, British subjects."

The propriety of extending the colonial boundary to the Kei River, and of placing so large a portion of Kafferland under British jurisdiction, remains to be considered. It will be necessary to guard against the common misrepresentation of the measure, which supposes it to involve the expulsion of the inhabitants, and the occupancy of their territory by Europeans; *the whole of the Kaffer territory* **added by Sir Benjamin D'Urban to the colony, was within a short period after the pacification of September 1835,** restored by him to the native tribes; and *not one acre was granted, or any right of occupation by settlers, reserved by the Colonial Government.* The expulsion of a whole people from their lands, would have been an abuse of the rights of war and conquest, but the subversion of the Kaffer political system, by the transfer of the supreme power to the British Government, is a question quite distinct from the right of the Kaffer people to the proprietorship of their native soil. If the continuance of the independent exercise of sovereignty by the Kaffer Chiefs was inimical to the continuance of peace between the Kaffers and the Colonists, and was then calculated to prove in its consequences equally detrimental to both parties, it will be evident, that, the Colonial Government was bound in justice to its own subjects, as well as by a regard to the interests of humanity, to embrace the opportunity afforded by the result of the war, to make such arrangements for the future, as were necessary to ensure the peace of both communities. To this desirable end, nothing was more likely to contribute, than the dissolution of a loose and inefficient system of government in Kafirland, which experience had proved to be at once a nuisance to its neighbours, and a curse to its own subjects.

The residence of a pastoral and predatory people, under its own independent Government, in the immediate neighbourhood of a civilized community, has ever proved incompatible with the existence and spread of civilization. Witness the history of Southern and Central Asia, which is but a record of civilization occasionally advancing to a certain limit, and then crushed under the invasion and domination of barbarous hordes of warlike shepherds. The Barbary States, Syria, Kurdistan, Persia, Abyssinia, &c., exhibit in their past history and present condition, proofs of the impossibility of the steady progression of improvement, whether in agriculture, or in the more complex arts of civilized life, while the settled and industrious portion of the population is exposed to periodical predatory inroads, or to a series of petty exactions, equally destructive of all sense of security of person and property. On the eastern frontier of the Cape colony, the constant exposure to Kaffer depredations, and occasional inroads, has produced similar effects.* Industry and enterprise have been paralyzed, and the scattered farmers have considerably retrograded in civilization, feeling no desire for the improvement of property, or the accumulation of conveniences and comforts, of the peaceful enjoyment of which, they were not for one moment secure. The Cape Colonial Government was placed in a most difficult position. It was its undoubted duty to protect its own subjects; but hitherto, all the means tried had failed, as to any result beyond a mere temporary and deceptious quiet, so long as the influence of some terrible chastisement, operated upon the fears of the Kaffer people. *A war with the Kaffers was always ruinous to the exposed farmers of the frontier*, and the expence to the Government far beyond the value of cattle captured in its successful prosecution. In time of peace,

---

* The deliberate opinion of that well known and tried friend of the Kaffers, the Rev. W. Shaw, may be quoted as a dispassionate view of the evils necessarily connected with the present social and political condition of Kafferland.—"From the days of Vaillant, it has been the practice of various writers to give such glowing descriptions of the noble and generous-minded Kaffers, that many persons, after reading their publications, find it difficult to believe that a Kaffer Chief would degrade himself by sanctioning robbery and murder. Nothing can be more misleading than statements which produce this impression. That there exists in the minds of many of the Chiefs a proud self-respect, which sometimes produces a noble bearing, and magnanimous conduct, I can testify; and it is a quality which might be turned to advantage by a skilful agent of Government: *But they have very indistinct notions of the rights of property, and they are fearfully reckless of the destruction of human life*. They are not wholly ignorant of the science, or destitute of a form, of government; but that which has been established amongst them from time immemorial is something like the antient feudal system of Europe,—*a kind of government which unhappily is very favourable to the doctrine, that ' might gives right.' All nomadic tribes are robbers*, unless the propensity be checked by religion, or by circumstances which they cannot controul. Within these limitations the Kaffers may be regarded as coming under the general rule; for, while the Chiefs protect in a considerable degree the rights of property among their own vassals, *the tribes have ever been addicted to engage in war with each other for the purpose of carrying off the cattle of their neighbours*. The frequent robberies committed by them, within the colony, ought not therefore to be wholly attributed to any aggressions of the Colonists; but may fairly be ascribed, in a great degree, to their own imperfect moral perceptions, deeply-rooted habits, and defective mode of government."—*Letter to the Earl of Aberdeen*, 1835.

the Chiefs of Kafferland were generally either unable or unwilling to check the predatory habits of their people, and the farmers were continually plundered. The plan of expulsion from one river to another, had been repeatedly tried by preceding Governors of the colony; this was a relief to that part of the colony which then became far removed from the frontier; but the new line of country occupied, remained as much exposed as the former frontier line. The colony was injured by the additional stimulus thus given to the spread of its scanty, and already too scattered population; while on the contrary, the Kaffers were concentrated, so as to render them more capable of co-operating in any attack upon the colony.

Sir Benjamin D'Urban was the first Governor who avoided the error of all preceding Colonial administrations, and discovered the only safe frontier defence of the Cape colony, in the step which he took of rendering the Chiefs and people of the nomadic and predatory tribes on its borders, subject to the supremacy of British Law.* The defect of the Kaffer political system, rendered the existence of the Kaffers as an independent people, in the vicinity of a civilized and powerful nation, humanly speaking, impossible,

* The opinion of Dr. Philip on this subject accords with that of every man of sense, who is in the least acquainted with the circumstances of the colony and Kafferland:—" Ever since I have formed fixed opinions on this subject, I have always considered it of the last importance to have belts of civilized natives between the Colonists and their less civilized neighbours. The people in our immediate neighbourhood, who have worked themselves up to a knowledge of our character and power, and who have acquired any portion of the civilization of Europeans without losing their sympathy with their uncivilized brethren, would unite the Colonists and the uncivilized tribes by internal bonds, and operate in preventing collisions from taking place between them. On this principle I think it will be a matter to be regretted if the new province shall be again dissevered from the colony."— (*Evidence Abor. Com.*, p. 635.)

"I should have no objection to see the whole country from the Keiskamma to the Kei, or even from the Keiskamma to Delagoa Bay, included within the limits of the colony, *on the plan adopted by the ancient Romans, which led them to spread themselves* and their institutions over the countries which submitted to their government. The British Government might in this way prove a great blessing to Africa, as it has been to India; and *nearly* all the Chiefs in Kaffraria, and *all* the people, would be rejoiced at the adoption of such a measure by the British Government."—(*Dr. Philip's Letter to Sir B. D'Urban, dated* 17*th March,* 1834: *Evidence Abor. Com.*, p. 693.) I should be sorry to see " the plan of the ancient Romans" adopted in *all* its

from the laxity of feeling among the Kaffers on the subject of plundering their neighbours, and the incapacity of the Chiefs *under ordinary circumstances* to repress such practices, frequent collisions naturally arise, which must end, as hitherto, in the removal or extermination of the weaker party. These collisions, so painful to humanity, and so ruinous to both Colonists and Kaffers, and this impolitic extension of the colonial territory, were at once prevented by the plan adopted by Sir Benjamin D'Urban. The strict and impartial execution of *the Law* by independent Magistrates would soon have completely destroyed the predatory habits of the people. Their territorial rights sanctioned by *Law*, would have been as secure as those of the Colonists, and the military occupation of the country, insured the safety of the Colony, by preventing the possibility of any extensive combination of the Kaffer Chiefs against its peace. In creating a British interest in Kafferland among the Chiefs and leading men,—in gradually withdrawing the people from their blind subserviency to the will of their Chiefs, and attaching them by a sense of interest to the regular legal authorities, (the impartial dispensers of justice to all, whether Chief or vassal) a sure foundation was laid for the permanent peace and security of the colony,—for the conservation of Kaffer territorial rights, and for the civilization and christianization of the Kaffer people.* That an end so praiseworthy in itself, and pursued by means so perfectly just,—and that a system in full and efficient operation, securing at once the colony from plunder, and the

particulars, especially their summary mode of planting military colonies, regardless of the rights of the Aborigines, and thus "*spreading themselves*" over the countries they had conquered; but no doubt the spread of their *institutions* was beneficial; though I suspect the injury inflicted on the native inhabitants of Gaul, Spain, and Britain by the severe methods deemed necessary to tame their notions of independence, was much greater than we are willing to believe.

* By this means a process similar to that which was introduced into the Highlands of Scotland after the Rebellion of 1716 and 1745, would have produced eqnally beneficial effects. The ever turbulent Highlanders are now among the most orderly and peaceable of the inhabitants of the British islands; and *black mail* is no longer paid by the formerly plundered Lowlander. Would not Sir B. D'Urban's system have rendered the eastern frontier of the Cape colony equally safe?

Kaffers from oppression; should have been sacrificed to the influence of party views, is one of the many events which the philanthrophist must ever lament as an almost irreparable injury to the interests of humanity and religion.

It is, however, imagined by some, that just treaties, stipulating for the recovery of stolen property, &c., and supported by a strong military power,—ready to enforce their fulfilment, would have met the evils complained of; and have proved far more simple and preferable to a plan which burdened the colony with the difficult and delicate task of the Government of 70,000 new subjects, and the military occupation of 7,000 square miles of additional territory.

Difficulties would, however, have arisen in an arrangement of this kind, from two causes; FIRST, the inability of the Chiefs *unassisted*, to compel their people to comply with the treaty; SECONDLY, The serious consequences which would result from any attempt to *enforce* compliance.

FIRST.—That the Chiefs are *generally* unable to enforce provisions of a treaty disagreeable to their people, is a fact, well known to all acquainted with the state of Kafferland; and is the natural result of the position of the Chief in reference to his people.* His power depends upon the

* The case of the Gonokwabie tribe, under Pato, Kama, and Kobus Kongo, is an exception which cannot be pleaded as a general rule. To the Divine blessing upon the efforts of the Rev. W. Shaw, the first Missionary who went among them (1823) their uniform good conduct is mainly owing. Circumstances of a peculiarly favourable nature, and the possession by Mr. Shaw of talents singularly adapted to create and preserve commanding influence over a barbarous people, contributed to secure the peaceful behaviour of these (until then) thievish clans. Much no doubt might be effected by Missionaries possessing influence similar to that of Mr. Shaw, but few men acquire that degree of influence, which is the result in his case of peculiar talents, aided by a combination of favourable circumstances, and opportunities; the possession of the one, and the occurrence of the other, are not to be calculated upon. At present (1838) the three Chiefs of this tribe, assisted by the three Wesleyan Missionaries, have enough to do to repress the desire for plunder, which naturally arises in the minds of a pastoral people, who cannot help observing the facility and safety with which their neighbours rob the colony, and yet escape with impunity. The continuance of the present weak and timorous frontier policy, (a terror only to its own subjects) will in a few years, probably induce the Gonokwabie clans, to return to their old predatory habits.

number of his fighting men, and as from the sub-division of power among the junior and collateral branches of the great families, the number of the Chiefs is continually on the increase, every Chief is compelled by a sense of his entire dependance upon the willing services of his people, to avoid doing any thing which will offend them, lest they should desert to other Chiefs, and thus add to the power of their rivals. The evils resulting from this state of things are increased in proportion to the small number of people attached to a Chief; for if his men be but few, he is the more anxious to avoid offending even one of them, and must, on all occasions advocate with a blind and wilful partizanship their cause, be their guilt ever so clearly proved. Of his own accord, the Chief will never detect or punish offences against other nations or tribes, as this would be most unpopular; thus, in his political relationship with the colony, he is comparatively powerless for any good. If he be occasionally able to enforce restitution, and punish them, it is only when the fear of serious consequences compels his leading men to assist and carry into effect his wishes, and thus give a temporary display of vigour and efficacy to his authority. The making a Chief responsible for thefts, &c. which he cannot prevent, and expecting him to enforce restitution without lending him the assistance of a patrol, powerful enough to prevent any attempt at resistance,* is calculated to sour the minds of the Chiefs against the Colonial Government, and will eventually render them its determined enemies.

SECONDLY.—The serious consequences which must ensue from any attempt to compel the observance of the treaties by Colonial force, independently by the Chief, *are such as will ever prevent their being enforced at all*; except when the

* In March 1834, when adverting to this subject, in a paper written for Sir Benjamin D'Urban, I stated the necessity of assisting the Chief with a patrol, to enable him to recover stolen property. "The Chief should be allowed the assistance of a patrol, when circumstances rendered it necessary, as thieves are sometimes supported by influential men, with whom the Chief would be too weak to contend, in which case a patrol would prevent bloodshed."—*(Cape of Good Hope Papers, p. 46.)*

evil has continued for so long a time, and to such an extent, that it is no longer supportable. This is the very evil complained of in the old border system. Considering the awful responsibility resting upon the Executive of the eastern frontier in the event of a war with the Kaffers, arising from the wide-spreading ruin of extensive districts, and the enormous cost to the Government, no man will dare to *enforce* restitution so long as the Kaffers content themselves with plundering the colony *in detail.* The public mind at home forgets that the aggregate amount of these *details* is enormous, and would deem a collision arising from the conscientious enforcement of the *principle* of the treaty unwarrantable. The Executive of the colony will, therefore, accept every excuse from the plunderers, and then becoming annoyed at the reproaches and complaints of its own subjects, will be insensibly led to adopt a sort of partial advocacy and extenuation of the conduct of their enemies. And thus, while the public complaints are loud and frequent, public documents will be framed to prove that these complaints are not warranted by the facts of the case. The Home Government naturally inclined to view favourably the acts of its officers, suffers the evil to continue, until the truckling passiveness of the Colonial Executive having tempted the Kaffers to serious aggressions, war and extermination become the order of the day, and the British treasury pays for all. This is in part history (1838) as well as prophecy.

These evils can only be avoided by the application of preventive measures to the very root and source from whence they spring, and this constituted the distinguished excellence of Sir B. D'Urban's system; which not merely aiming at palliating symptoms, was adapted to effect a radical and thorough cure of the disease, which had hitherto proved so destructive to the mutual welfare of the Colonists and Kaffers.

The practical *results* of the occupation of the new province of Queen Adelaide, during the administration of its affairs by Colonel Smith, were such as gave abundant promise of the great advantages which would accrue to both the colony and Kafferland so soon as the irritation caused by the war should subside; and men not otherwise sanguine, were led to anticipate that after so many years of frontier distraction, peace and prosperity were about to be secured. The rule of Colonel Smith, was on the whole satisfactory to all parties; which, in his difficult and trying situation, was no small proof of its wisdom and justice. The Colonists were inspired with a sense of safety, to which they had long been strangers, knowing that in the then state of Kafferland a general inroad on the colony was impossible; and further aware that every theft traced fairly into the new province would be at once redressed, and that no attempt would be made by the authorities to screen the delinquency, for the sake of giving a deceptive impression of the existence of an unprecedented state of security. In consequence of the impartial administration of justice, irrespective of rank and station, the Kaffer serfs were emboldened to throw themselves and their property under the protection of *Law*; and the unjust exactions of the Chiefs were almost universally resisted. This was one gratifying proof, that, however attached the Kaffers might be to their hereditary Chiefs, they were still more attached to their property, and were ready to support cheerfully any system of government which secured them in the free enjoyment of their own. It was sufficiently manifest from the confidence which British rule inspired, and the alacrity with which the decisions of the Magistrates were obeyed, that the general feeling of Kafferland was decidedly in favour of the equitable system, which had introduced the great mass of the people to the enjoyment of the rights of free men. The power of the Chiefs was completely neutralized by the *new feeling* so generally experienced by all classes. The Chief Makomo made many attempts to induce his people to resist the new order of things, or withdraw beyond its jurisdiction, but met with repeated refusals; and his most influential men, tired of his importunity, at length informed Colonel Smith of his conduct. Others of the principal Chiefs were sensible enough to perceive the decline of their influence, but they felt their inability to resist; the current of public opinion being decidedly against the *old regime*, from which the Chief and his immediate favourites had alone benefitted. In order, however, to recompence the Chiefs for their losses, arising from fines formerly levied, and from other means of raising a revenue, which had ceased to be available, it was in contemplation to allow them a small monied salary as an equivalent, a measure in itself just and politic. Had this comprehensive system of benevolence been carried on for a few years, *with the introduction of such improvements as experience would have suggested*, there can be no doubt but the predatory habits of the Kaffer tribes would have been destroyed; new trains of thought and feeling would have been established; the influence of the Chiefs, apart from the degree of respect naturally paid to birth and rank, would have ceased to exist; their former power being exercised by the constituted European and Native authorities, employed in the actual administration of the affairs of the new province. I can speak from my own knowledge to the good effects resulting from Colonel Smith's rule, and to the general consternation excited among the bulk of the people, by the first announcement of the probability of their being abandoned to the oppression of their own Chiefs.

Other testimonies may be adduced, in reference to the practical working of this new experiment, so interesting to humanity. And first, the following " Opinion to be entered upon the minutes of the proceedings of the Legislative Council," Cape Town, August 24th, 1836, deserves to be considered of no small importance, from the character of the individuals whose signatures are appended to it :—

"1.—We the undersigned members of the Legislative Council, deem it due to His Excellency the Governor, to record our unqualified approval of all those measures which were adopted and carried into effect in repelling the late Kaffer invasion.

"2.—That the treaties entered into between His Excellency the Governor and the Kaffer Chiefs, on the 6th and 17th of September, 1835, (based on the desire, as expressed by the latter, to be received under British protection), appear to be best calculated to ensure the tranquillity of the eastern frontier of the colony, to raise the Kaffer tribes in the scale of civilization, and to fit them for the blessings and advantages of christianity.

"3.—That the measures subsequently adopted by His Excellency, in carrying the humane principles of those treaties into effect, have eminently conduced to the unprecedented tranquility which at present exists throughout the eastern districts of the colony; and that those measures have only to be followed up consistently, to ensure both to the eastern Colonists and the Kaffer tribes, a degree of prosperity and happiness which otherwise would be unattainable by either."

H. CLOETE, Ls.,	P. G. BRINK,
J. B. EBDEN,	JOHN BELL,*
C. S. PILLANS,	J. G. BRINK,
H. ROSS,	A. OLIPHANT.†

Captain Fawcett (of the Bombay army), a gentleman by no means disposed to think favourably of the administration of frontier affairs, thus writes to the editor of the *Commercial Advertiser*, in reference to the new province. "Our present excellent border policy, a policy which if persevered in, will rank the present Governor and Colonel Smith amongst the high list of worthies which England has produced."—(*Graham's Town Journal, February*, 1836). This opinion is not quoted for any value placed upon it, as if Captain F. were to be regarded as an authority; but simply to show the impression which the candid and liberal

---

* Secretary to the Government. † Attorney-General of the colony.

conduct of Colonel Smith produced upon the most prejudiced observers.

An eye-witness of the results of the new system, in writing from King William's Town in the new province, thus expresses himself:—

"Thus stands the government of the Kaffers; the protection afforded by the present system to the colony is admitted by all to be extraordinary when compared with former years; and then, be it remembered. that this order of things has been commenced only nine months. In respect to the Kaffers, the mass of barbarism has been thoroughly changed without spilling one drop of blood; freedom is enjoyed, while the ordinary laws are enforced by a police of their own people. Let the most prejudiced enthusiast compare such a state of society with the maddening frenzy, the hatred and animosity which existed in the latter end of the year 1834, and he must be constrained to admit—even if a doubt has been indulged as to the equity and spirit of the war—that the Kaffers have gained all the advantages which have resulted from it."—*Graham's Town Journal*, 28*th July*, 1836.

In the Legislative Council, 24th August, 1836, Mr. Cloete made the following observations :—

"He was bound to admit that, though he had looked for favourable results from this measure, the effects produced had far surpassed his most sanguine expectations. It was matter of absolute wonder to find that in the short space of eleven months, these people had been not only redeemed from the tyranny of witchcraft, but had been brought into a state of tranquillity and peace, equal to what is enjoyed in the nearer districts of the colony. There can be no doubt that the Kaffers look to the continuation of the present policy as the Magna Charta of their liberties—as the bulwark of their happiness and prosperity; while the Colonists also regard it as the only means of preserving the peace and security of the country. He hoped, therefore, he should not be taxed with presumption in saying, that the name of Sir BENJAMIN D'URBAN will be handed down to future generations, not only as the friend of the colony, but the true friend of the Kaffers themselves."

The opinion of Colonel Smith himself (who from his connection with the practical working of Sir Benjamin's system, was able to speak as to its tendency and practicability), was unreservedly stated at the public dinner given to him in Graham's Town, 22d September, 1836 :—

Speaking of the Kaffer, he says,—" He was generously and humanely received by His Excellency as a British subject; the whole of his lands have been restored to him, as established in 1819; for twelve months I administered the government of 100,000 souls; and, while I introduced just and salutary laws, I banished tyranny, oppression, and witchcraft; and I am vain enough to hope, that while my utmost energy and enthusiasm were employed to ameliorate the condition of the degraded barbarian, the vigour and decision, tempered by kindness and generosity, with which I governed him, afforded that security of property to the frontier Colonists, which previously they had not known. And if the system established by His Excellency, and worked by me, be steadfastly pursued,—while just and equitable laws protect life and property, the schoolmaster teaches the youth, and the missionaries disseminate the blessings of Divine truth and revelation,—if the statesman and the churchman thus proceed hand in hand, the barbarian may become an honest neighbour and a christian. But without this union every partial effort will fail, to the misery of the Kaffer and to the injury of the Colonist."

It has been imagined, that the Kaffers were incapable of appreciating the advantages derived to them from their new position as British subjects. Europeans are apt to underrate the capacity of a semi-barbarous people, fancying them incapable of valuing the benefits arising from the impartial administration of justice. It is true that it is difficult to make them comprehend our free but complex constitution, but they can, and *do*, contrast the enjoyment of personal freedom, and the security of property formerly enjoyed under British rule, with that which they now experience since the abandonment of the new province by the British Government. Equitable as the Kaffer laws generally are, and well adapted to the circumstances of the Kaffer social state, they are rarely administered with impartiality. The man whose family connections are numerous, and willing to support him, generally escapes with impunity, or with a mere acknowledgement of guilt; because the Chief dare not offend so powerful a clan. Men feeling no protection in innocence, are compelled in all the various gradations of rank, from the Chief to the Fingo, to attach themselves to powerful individuals able to defend them, and are of course ready to aid and abet their protectors in return. This connection of patron and client, together with the strong feeling of clanship which pervades all Kafferland, sadly interferes with the due execution of law. Justice is only granted to weak and powerless individuals, when some foreign or extraneous influence is exexerted (as for instance the interposition of a Missionary) or when the chief council (Amapakati) deem it politic to humble some unpopular, though powerful man; or in the few cases in which plaintiff and defendant are of equal importance. It is a mere party affair, the abstract question of right or wrong being generally least thought of. None but those living in Kafferland, acquainted with the people, and in a situation to hear their complaints, can form any idea of the oppression and wrong which is daily perpetrated, and submitted to as a matter of course.

The main cause of this defective administration of justice arises from the weakness of the executive, the Chief being unable to controul his influential men; and the law which regulates the succession, unfortunately tends to perpetuate and extend this evil. The "*great son*" of a Chief, not his eldest son, succeeds to the authority and rank of the father;

this successor is the son of the "*great wife*," and in selecting her, not only is regard paid to noble extraction, but to the will of the *Amapakati*. Most commonly she is the wife of the Chief's old age, and her son, the heir, is a mere child at the death of his father. Perhaps in this there is some management on the part of the leading men, as during a minority, each retains his influence unchecked by a superior, and the most influential of them, in connection with the collateral branches of the royal family, contrive to alienate the national stock of cattle, most of which, when the Chief comes of age, are in the possession of these dishonest guardians and their adherents, who have thus firmly established *their* power at *his* expense, and with the cattle which by law and right belong to *him*. All this he knows well; he has seen the system of robbery going on for years; perhaps his mother and a few old men are his real friends, as are also the young men who were circumcised with him, and their friends; his party is gradually increased by the accession of many whom the ruling powers have injured during his minority. At a proper period he assumes the government and receives the remnant of his father's cattle, and presents from all his leading men; these he judiciously distributes among his followers, regretting at the same time his poverty, compared with the wealth of his father. After a while, on the death of some of the wealthy old men, the young Chief contrives to seize the lion's share of their cattle, and increases his own party by the addition of most of their retainers, who begin to feel confidence in his ability to act as a Chief, and to claim his own. By this time, he feels himself on safe ground, the minor branches of his family look up to him, and are ready to support him; he gradually claims his cattle, and mulcts or plunders his spoilers. Those who are too powerful to be dealt with openly according to law, are brought under the charge of witchcraft, which at once cuts them off from all sympathy, and deprives them of all support. By cunning, and by judicial murders, the power of a Kaffer Chief is obtained and consolidated. Owing to his unfortunate position, the Chief is almost necessarily compelled to be guilty of treachery and murder. His whole life is a lie, as his safety and success depend upon simulating, and dissimulating; and hence the imperturbable temper of the Chiefs, even under most provoking circumstances, which is not the result of principle, but arises from a cool calculation of the certainty of a glorious revenge at a convenient season; and if that convenient season be long in coming, he can wait. Relationship, friendship, important services, are of no account when they stand between the Chief and his victim. Hence we see every year instances in which brothers, nephews, and cousins of Chiefs have suffered, the pretence being witchcraft, the real reason being the desire of the plunder of their property, or jealousy of their power. The influence of such conduct in high places, in destroying the moral sense of the people, and its reflex operation through all classes of society, render every Chief a curse in his day and generation; a sort of moral upas tree, within the reach of whose influence no noble or generous feeling can exist; and to this influence of the Chief's conduct, operating upon the natural obliquity of our fallen nature, we may in a great measure trace the moral desolation of Kafferland.

Now it requires no profundity of research on the part of the Kaffer, to discover that the freedom and security of life and property enjoyed under British rule, was far superior to this state of things; and accordingly we find that the most valuable and intelligent of the Kaffers, as soon as they acquire property, hasten to remove into the colony, to live *" onder de wet,"* (under the law.) As Missionaries, we feel disappointed at finding the men upon whom we have calculated as agents for the facilitating the improvement of their countrymen, so anxious to leave their own land, and reside in the colony, but it is impossible to blame their motives, or combat their reasons. Of this class there is a large number in the colony, who will never return to Kafferland to reside, so long as they would there be subject to the irresponsible controul of the native Chief. Had Kafferland continued "*onder de wet*," these would have remained, and their principles and general intelligence would have helped to leaven the inert and unintelligent mass. As it is, every obstacle to christianity and civilization remain in full force, having been carefully built up and fostered in the mistaken zeal of the benevolent people and Government of Britain for the restoration of what has been termed "Kaffer independence." To preserve to a few Chieftains (most of them of depraved character, and degraded habits), the exercise of their hereditary tyranny, a whole nation has been deprived of the freedom and equal justice it had enjoyed under the temporary supremacy of *Law*. They have thus been thrown back at least 20 years in the march of improvement; and what makes it the more distressing is, that this blow at the incipient christianity and civilization of Kafferland, comes from those who warmly desire its moral and intellectual advancement. We cannot say, "An enemy hath done this;" these are the wounds she hath received in the house of her friends. The undiscriminating and unreasonable prejudice of a class of philanthropists in Britain, has thrown back the Kaffer to his former degraded condition, as the vassal of a tyrannical feudal lord; it has again legalized murder on account of the absurd charge of witchcraft; it has restored the "*Punhlo*," and has thus sent the maidens of Kafferland to the customary annual pollution of a Chief's kraal; it has deprived the bulk of the Kaffer people of all protection either of property or life, and by a natural consequence, it has transferred the numerous victims of oppression, into banditti engaged in the plunder of the colony; it has stimulated the predatory habits of the Kaffer people, which are decidedly on the increase (the Gonokwabie tribe excepted); in a word it has laid the foundation of a series of evils, which if unchecked within a short period, will lead not only to the desolation of the colonial frontier, but will endanger the very existence of the Kaffer tribes. Those who influenced the Colonial Secretary to determine upon the abandonment of the new province, are not to be envied the feelings with which, as humane men, they must contemplate the results of their well-meant, but injudicious, interference in a matter, of the true bearings of which they were totally ignorant.*

We have now to detail the circumstances connected with the withdrawal of legal controul, and the restoration of the old Kaffer system.

On the arrival of the Lieutenant-Governor, Captain Stockenstrom, the retirement of Colonel Smith was of course to be anticipated. A formal meeting of the Chiefs was held at King William's Town, 13th September, 1836, in which Colonel Smith formally resigned his authority into the hands of the Lieutenant-Governor. Of this meeting the following interesting account was furnished by an eye-witness:—

"King William's Town, September 13, 1836.

"This morning the meeting took place. The troops were drawn up in line, and the Kaffer Chiefs and people assembled on the grand parade to the number of from 3 to 4,000. The ceremony began by giving three hearty cheers for *King William*, after which a prayer was offered up by the Rev Mr. Brownlee, of the London Missionary Society. Colonel Smith, the commander of the province, then came forward, and with great emphasis and feeling delivered the following address:—

"The King, our great Chief, has sent a Governor to rule over you, who will watch over your interests with zeal for your welfare, happiness, and prosperity. You must obey him as you did me, or I shall cease to regard you as worthy of the exertions made for your improvement.

---

* The expense attending the civil and military charge of the new province has been stated in justification of its abandonment. But what are the facts of the case? the civil expenditure of the eastern frontier connected with Kafferland is greater now (1838) than it was during the occupation of the new province; and *the military force on the frontier is much larger than was considered, by Colonel Smith, necessary for the support of British supremacy in Kafferland, and the security of the colony, provided the new system had continued.* More troops are even now required, and have been asked for by General Napier.

"I now, therefore, transfer the power I held over you, to His Honor the Lieutenant-Governor. Be faithful to your oaths of allegiance, and obedient to your rulers. Circumstances over which I have no controul oblige me to leave you, my children. I have now watched over you with, I may say, parental care, since I took you out of the bush (made peace). I have introduced those just and equitable English laws among you, by which life and property are so respected, that every one lives in security; and as I have brought good among you, so have I endeavoured to expel evil; such as tyranny, oppression, robbery, witchcraft, murder, ' eat up,' or general confiscation of property upon imaginary grievances or representations. I have endeavoured to excite you to industrious habits, to acquaint you with the use of money, and to be kind to each other; in all of which I have succeeded, in many instances, far beyond my expectations. Some of you have led out the waters of the rivers,—have ploughs,—all bury your dead as I desired,—most of you have shaken off witchcraft, the sin of all others to be most dreaded,—many of you have reformed from your predatory habits,—all your native Magistrates have assisted me in carrying forward every measure which I conceived would contribute to your welfare; the industrious and persevering Ministers of the Gospel have been much better attended. There was a set among you opposed to the Missionaries,—these are now their staunchest advocates. I have taught you that you ought to be clothed,—that by education you can alone prosper. I have been endeavouring to introduce schools of every description among you, which, I hope, are in contemplation and progress. Above all, I have taught you that when you abstain from evil, the white man is your friend and brother.

"I will not revert to the horrors of the late war, which you brought upon yourselves, but I must warn you against such enormities in future. You have seen the power of England; you have felt, you have experienced the kindness and generosity of Englishmen, and the liberality with which you have been treated. Contrast the latter with the former; judge for yourselves between good and evil, happiness or misery. I trust I have been the humble instrument of Providence to place your future prospects on a foundation, upon which the fabric of my future hope has been reared; and I equally trust no one will seek to undermine or beat down this column which can alone support the feebleness of humanity, rescue you from barbarism, and render the colony safe and secure from future inroads and aggressions.

"That civilization has made much progress, I will assert, that if the plans I have proposed were adopted for your religious instruction—for your education, to teach you mechanical arts, and every habit of industry, its advance would be most rapid. The want of occupation of both mind and body—in other words, indolence is the author of mischief, discontent, and every bad feeling human nature is prone to. Arouse yourselves, therefore; profit by the lessons I have for some hours daily instilled into your minds, and the frequent messages I have sent among you, expressive of my desires, to all of which you have attended. Persevere, therefore, as you are now doing; you possess the same attributes and understanding with the white man, and may and will become equally civilized, if equal advantages could be introduced among you.

"You must learn to check this unbridled humour you possess to have cattle, and by honest industry endeavour to obtain them,—not by predatory inroads on your neighbours. You may then become a brave and intelligent people, rapidly advancing towards civilization, and speedily understanding all that your brothers, the English, know. My object has been insensibly to check your faults by introducing a wholesome power, sufficient to curb the propensities of your nature, as experience familiarized me with your wants; so as gradually to wean you from the vices to which you are most prone, and by an active and masculine energy to enforce obedience to whatever I might desire; for well was I aware that immediately succeeding a war, there would be among you many loose, dissolute, and desperate characters, who are urged on by the indolence of repose to the danger of enterprise; but few are the instances in which these characters have dared to commit crime, and few in which the culprit has not been detected.

"It might have been expected that the freedom and liberty which I have been instrumental to produce among you—which, however plain to those accustomed to it, would, as is generally the case in new forms of government, have caused bloodshed, disorder, and confusion; for the greater the new power created, the greater must inevitably be the horror and contempt with which the old, and the instruments of its tyranny, would be regarded; but few acts of insubordination have been brought under my observation, and I again tell you to persevere in this system of moderation, and you will become respectable among the civilized nations of the world.

"I know it has been asserted that the policy to adopt towards you was to break your spirit, and to awe those whom it was a vain hope to conciliate. This advice have I avoided as ungenerous, impolitic, and unstable; but to awaken curiosity—to excite interest—to point out the good from the evil way—has tended, I hope, to confirm habits of attention and good will; to teach you to speak and act rather from your reason than your feelings; and to curb your ardent desires by a just restraint.

"Your intercourse formerly with the colony was of that doubtful nature which inspires mutual disgust and contempt; by your being British subjects you have learned the honor and integrity by which they are guided—and you have ascertained that the only friends you have are the English, who have received you as brothers, pardoning your former crimes and enormities. Your future welfare, therefore, depends upon yourselves; none can befriend you if you persist in being your own enemies.

"He who undertakes to conduct the affairs of a nation in the rapid transition from an oppressive, tyrannical, and arbitrary government, to the liberal, just, and salutary law of freedom, which, as British subjects, you have enjoyed, without bringing into collision either of the parties which this change most affects, has undertaken no ordinary task; one which in the commencement, I candidly admit, I dared not hope to effect without some cause for deep and dire regret; but the omnipotent God has been bountifully pleased to lead you, ignorant people, from the paths of tyranny and oppression to those of liberty, security of person, right of property, freedom, and from the evils of, and the fascinations of witchcraft, without one solitary instance of violence, and few of reluctance or ill-will. Persevere then, I pray you Chiefs, in judging as you would be judged; let the mild, though energetic, manner in which I have administered the just laws you have lately experienced, guide you: you will then see your people happy and prosperous, loving, and ready to protect you.

"And you, who have all so long called me your father, be obedient to the King's representative and to your Chiefs : yet be faithful to your own liberties—to the country which has adoped you—and cherish the patriotism which I have endeavoured to make so evident to you; that what at first appeared as a vision, I trust has sprung into life and continual vigour. Remember your brothers, the English, were once ignorant and naked as you are; remember the many things I have instructed you; spurn the idolatry of witchcraft, the folly, cruelty, and oppression of which I have so often explained to you; it is, I again tell you, a hellish instrument, by which the strong oppress the week, by an old wretch pretending to possess a supernatural power, which no mortal is endowed with. God alone knows the thoughts and actions of others, and this witchcraft is the offspring of an evil spirit; avoid it if ye wish to be happy, and possess your herds and flocks; avoid it if ye wish to attain to civilization, and to become christians.

" My children, this may be the last time I may thus collectively address you. Remember twelve moons have only passed since I brought you out of the bush into which you precipitated yourselves headlong to your utter ruin and destruction, had not the clemency of the Governor saved you by thus generously and humanely receiving you as British subjects.

"I leave you, my children, with deep regret, but which is softened by a certainty that you will be well taken care of by the Lieutenant-Governor. We must all obey our superiors : yet, go where I may, your interest and welfare shall be nearest my heart. It is the poor and ignorant who require friends; be humble, and strive to do good; abhor sin; and when you think of me, ever exclaim,—He loved to see us good—he punished us when we did evil. And may the Omnipotent GOD lead you from the paths of sin and darkness into those of honesty and light,"

"His Honor the Lieutenant-Governor next addressed the meeting in a short but firm manner, to the following purport;—

"Many of you no doubt are personally acquainted with me; many of you have heard me advise you often as a friend; and you must feel that if you had followed my advice, many of the misfortunes whice have befallen you on account of your own conduct would have been prevented. I stand now before you as the Representative of the King of England, and as such I assure you I have no other earthly wish respecting you than your future welfare. Colonel Smith, who has just addressed you, came amongst you while you were at war with the English, and fought against you as a soldier. Since the peace he has been your best friend and real father, and it only depends on yourselves, whether I follow his steps or not. You have seen a *little* of the power of the English, but very little, and it will be to your advantage, if I am not obliged to shew you more of it; only presevere to the utmost of your power to prevent evil, and it will be well with you."

"His Honor concluded by desiring them to speak, if they had anything to say. Makomo then stepped forward, and after thanking him for the " news," &c., spoke for some time in a very animated manner, expressing his desire for more land, especially for that which had been given to Pato. Also that he might be permitted to punish for *witchcraft* as formerly. Colonel Smith replied to this, that although *he* (Makomo) might wish it,'*his people* did not; and on this being interpreted by Mr. Shepstone, an approving smile was perceptible on the countenances of many of the crowd around. The Lieutenant-Governor observed to Makomo, that he had willingly signed treaties with the Governor, which treaties he held in his hand, and that he would insist on their being fulfilled; that whilst he supported their just rights, he was determined to make them respect the laws, and that he would punish them severely if they did not do what was right. He had not come there to break treaties, or to make new ones; but to witness the power of and authority hitherto held by Colonel Smith, made over to him by that officer, and that they might take leave of their *best* friend. The Rev. Mr. Kayser then offered up a prayer, and the ceremony was concluded.

"Afterwards the Chiefs and all the great wives and women of distinction assembled to take leave of Mrs. Smith, on which occasion a scene was displayed truly interesting. This most excellent woman had endeared herself to all around her by her affability and undeviating kindness, and the crowd on being admitted to her presence, wept aloud. Mrs. Smith appeared quite overcome by the intensity of her feelings. The assembly, without any exception, tore their bracelets from their arms and presented them to her, praying her to take them, and keep them in remembrance of *her children* whom she was leaving behind. The devotion which was also shewn to the gallant Colonel admits of no description."

On the departure of Colonel Smith, no attempts were made on the part of the Colonial Government to uphold the system of which *he* had been the life and soul. It being generally understood that, the giving up of the new province was already a fixed point with the Home Government; the troops simply retained the military occupation of certain posts, and the ruling powers ceased to interfere with the civil affairs of Kafferland. On the 5th December, 1836, Captain Stockenstrom finally freed the Kaffer Chiefs from their allegiance to the British Government, and entered upon a totally different line of policy, the consideration of which will be the subject of the following note.

NOTE III.

CAPTAIN STOCKENSTROM'S BORDER POLICY.

In discussing the merits and practical working of a system which has been the subject of so much controversy, it will be requisite to take into consideration the state of feeling in Kafferland and the colony at the period of its introduction. In justice to Captain Stockenstrom it must be confessed that the most efficient system, if brought into operation under circumstances similarly unfavourable, would have fallen short of producing the desired results. These "untoward circumstances" were, 1st. Captain Stockenstrom's personal unpopularity, and 2dly. The extravagant expectations of the Kaffer Chiefs,—the natural consequence of so sudden, and to them unaccountable, change in the policy of the Colonial Government.

1st.—The unpopularity of the new Lieut.-Governor arose from his having made certain statements before the Aborigines' Committee seriously affecting the colonial character; from his refusal to receive an address from the British Colonists of Albany, in which he was requested to explain these derogatory statements;[*] and from his subsequent

---

[*] The evidence of Captain Stockenstrom has long been before the public in the report of the "Aborigines' Committee;" the nature of that evidence may be gathered from an extract from the address of the British Colonists, which Captain Stockenstrom refused to receive at Graham's Town, Sept. 3, 1838.

"They would also be wanting in candour—and might, in some respect, be considered as having forfeited their claims to consideration as indepen-

imprudence in identifying himself with a party in Cape Town, which the bulk of the Colonists consider as directly opposed to their welfare. Into the merits of this party controversy, it is needless to enter.

dent men and subjects of a free country—did they affect to conceal from your Honor their conviction that the evidence lately given by yourself before a Committee of the Representatives of the British people, has made an impression on the public mind exceedingly derogatory to their character for humanity and justice; injurious to their future prospects as a young and rising community; and fatal to their claims to that Compensation for their losses by the late barbarian inroad, to which in equity they conceive they are entitled from a paternal government.

"Under such circumstances, and with these views and feelings, they address Your Honor, on assuming the duties of Lieutenant-Governor of this Province; and they now, at the earliest moment after your arrival among them, request respectfully, but firmly, and as an act of unquestionable justice, that your Honor will be pleased to state—

"1. Whether, in your opinion, the conduct of the British Settlers of Albany has ever been, in any one instance, such as to justify the Native Tribes adjacent in making incursions upon them, and in laying waste the country in which they have been placed by the British Government?

"2. Whether Your Honor has any knowledge of their ever having, as a community, acted inconsistent with the British name and character?

"3. Whether it is your opinion that the Frontier Farmers in general derive any advantage by hostile collision with the Natives? or whether, on the contrary, it is not within the knowledge of Your Honor that the inhabitants along the whole of the inland Frontier of this Colony have been continually suffering from the daring and unprovoked inroads of the Native Tribes upon them; and which have often resulted in the murder of their families, the destruction of their dwellings, and generally in the loss of property, which constitutes, to a colonial farmer, the means of subsistence?

"4. Whether, in short, the evidence given by Your Honor before a Committee of the House of Commons was intended to make on the public mind such impressions as are calculated to lead to a conclusion that the inhabitants of this Colony, or this Frontier, deserve, as a people, by their ill-treatment of the Native Tribes, or any other course of misconduct, to be reproached by their country with having brought disgrace upon the British name, or acted inconsistent with the requirements of humanity and justice.

"It now only remains for them distinctly to state, that whilst they claim for themselves the indefeasible right of questioning the merits of public men who may be called to exercise authority over them, or the expediency of measures which affect their most vital interests; and whilst they present themselves to your Honor on this occasion in the exercise of this sacred birthright; they, at the same time, deprecate any imputation of being actuated by factious views, or by partial or local feelings and prejudices. On the contrary, they take credit for an anxious desire to uphold the institutions of the country,—for a firm determination to respect and support lawful authority,—and for unshaken and ardent attachment and loyalty to their King and country."

It is to be deeply regretted that Captain Stockenstrom did not feel himself at liberty either to reply to these queries, or to return a courteous and conciliatory answer to the Address. The unquestionable ability, and great local knowledge, possessed by that gentleman, had inspired many of the British Settlers, and others interested in the welfare of all classes, both within and beyond the colony, with a hope that notwithstanding the great excitement occasioned by the character of his evidence before the Aborigines' Committee: he would nevertheless prove to be an able Governor; and that in due time,

2dly.—The extravagant expectations of the Kaffer Chiefs were the natural result of so sudden a change in the policy of the Colonial Government. After the departure of Colonel Smith, the absence of *the master spirit* was soon felt in the new province. The intermission in the exercise of the wonted authority of the executive, and the preparations making for the evacuation of the Kaffer territory, were naturally viewed by the Kaffers as proofs of weakness. The unexpected addition of the country between the Kat, Fish, and Keiskamma Rivers to their former territory, at a time when so far from appearing to merit the favour by their peaceable conduct, they were on the contrary engaged with redoubled ardour in predatory raids on the border farmers; served yet more to convince them that they might rely not merely on indemnity for the past, but also on *impunity for the future*. It was most unfortunate that *such a time* should have been chosen for the cession of new territory to the Kaffers. Had the Chiefs engaged in the war of 1835, been carefully excluded from it, until by a perseverance in peaceable conduct for a given time, they had given proof of their ability and willingness to perform the conditions on which it was granted, the evil effects resulting from the unguarded precipitancy of this mistimed concession would have been avoided.*

the various and conflicting border interests would, under his management, have been harmonized; ensuring thereby the peace and security of the country. That these anticipations, indulged by a moderate and respectable class of the community, have not been realized, has always been, to the writer, a subject of great regret; but in his opinion, this result should not be attributed so much to Captain Stockenstrom's plans and intentions, before leaving England for the scene of his Government, as to the exertion of a baneful influence over his mind by a small party at the Cape, who (having certain ends to attain), unfortunately succeeded in involving him in a series of difficulties, personal and political, out of which it was impossible even for his sagacity to find a way of escape, either with credit to himself, or with advantage to his country.

* This cession of the neutral territory to the Kaffers was opposed to Captain Stockenstrom's known and avowed opinions. Perhaps Captain Stockenstrom viewed the country as originally belonging to the Hottentots. It is true that in 1752, the Kaffer was unknown on the west of the Keiskamma; for on the 31st July of that year, Ensign Butler addresses the Dutch Government from that river, and states, "I have only now returned out of Kafferland, and am encamped on the further side of the Thyskamma, *which*

The new system of border policy adopted by Captain Stockenstrom, commenced 6th December, 1836, and is fully developed in the five treaties entered into with the following Chiefs; one with Makomo and Tyali, for the Gaika family; one with Pato, Kama, and Congo, for the Gonokwabie tribe; one with Umhala, Umkye, &c. for the Slambie family; one with the Fingo Chiefs, settled near Fort Peddie; and one with the Tambookie Chief Mapassa. These treaties provide for the settlement of the boundary line,—

forms a boundary between the Hottentots and the Kaffers." Nevertheless, the Dutch Government, and subsequently the English Government acknowledged the Kaffers as *de facto* possessors of the country to the Fish River, and the question of their right to that territory founded on conquest, is one which *we* have no right to agitate. The Cape Government committed itself on this question in 1788, as appears from the following minute of council, taken from the records of the Dutch Government.

Extract.
[TRANSLATION.]
Tuesday, Nov. 14, 1780, in the forenoon.
All present.

The Governor further stated, that on his extensive tour in the interior, in 1778, he had agreed with the Kaffer Chiefs, that, in order to prevent all disputes with our inhabitants living in that neighbourhood, the Fish River should serve as a boundary between them, and that accordingly the said Kaffers should not cross the said River, with their cattle, into the fields occupied by our inhabitants; and that on our side our people should also remain on this side of the said River; but that *the said Kaffers, however, contrary to their solemn promises to him, had crossed the said River, and had encamped, with their cattle, on the very farms of our inhabitants, which was the chief cause of the disputes which had arisen with the said Kaffers:* whereupon it was resolved, now again, to fix upon the said Fish River as a boundary between our inhabitants and the Kaffers, and to make this known in the instructions for the Field-Commandant of this remote District; with further instructions to the same, in case the above-mentioned Kaffers should not quietly fulfil their promises to the said Governor, and return to the other side of the Fish River, then compel them by force so to do.

This done and decreed in the Castle of Good Hope, day and year as above.
(Signed) J. van PLETTENBERG, &c.

With Captain Stockenstrom's views of the impolicy of this cession of territory, his consenting to carry it into effect, naturally excited surprise; especially as in his zeal to distinguish his administration by cession of land, he actually presented the Tambookies with a tract of country between the Stormberg Spruits and Kraai River, (already settled by a number of boers) which never belonged to them or any other tribe, or had, in fact, been inhabited within the memory of man, except by a few Bushmen. In a country quite unsuited to natives, as it has no bush. The boors had constructed dams, built good houses, and planted gardens and vineyards; all their improvements were then lost to them; they were ordered out of the country, which remains to this day unoccupied, except as a rendezvous for murderers and robbers. The Tambookies had no claim to the country as a compensation for lands taken from them by the colony, as they had never lost any by colonial aggressions, and if there were any proprietors, these were the scattered bushmen, *very few* in number.

the cession of the neutral territory to the Kaffer Chiefs on certain conditions, and for the appointment of European Agents or Consuls by the Colonial Government, to reside in Kafferland in a "diplomatic capacity," to act as a medium of intercourse, and as checks upon or protectors of British subjects in Kafferland, as the occasion may require. A variety of regulations respecting the recovery of property stolen from the colony were embodied in them, which are hereafter to be considered. In order to facilitate the discovery of the thieves, the Chiefs engaged to appoint Amapakati (influential counsellors) at the principal fords on the Fish River, whose duty it would be to receive reports of loss of cattle from the colony, and use any effort to trace them. Native policemen appointed by the Agent, and paid by the Colonial Government, were to be stationed at the military post, who were to assist the Colonists and follow the *spoor* or traces of cattle into Kafferland. The entrance of Kaffers into the colony, and of Europeans into Kafferland, was subjected to certain wholesome restraints, (the only drawback to which, is the impracticability of enforcing them), and finally, the Chiefs bind themselves "to abstain from any way molesting or interfering with the Fingoes who are or will be located in the said ceded territory, but to consider them as under British protection."

These treaties, containing many stipulations just and reasonable, neutralized however by others of an injurious and impracticable nature, are based *in principle* and in some cases *in detail*, upon the recommendations contained in my letter of March 1834, addressed to Sir Benjamin D'Urban, at his request. That the leading provisions of the treaties are manifestly taken from this document, will appear from the following comparison of the recommendations of the letter, with the particulars of the treaties themselves.

1st Extract.—" Unsettled state of the Colonial boundary. This is a source of jealousy to the border Kaffers; if they were informed officially, that beyond a certain line it was not the intention of the Colonial Government to permit the advance of the Colonists, and that they might rest assured that their lands were not an object of desire, then their suspicions of the ulterior motives of the Colonial Government would be removed."—*See Letter to Sir Benjamin D'Urban, Parliamentary Papers on Kaffer War, p.* 45, *for this and subsequent extracts.*)—The *second* article of the treaties strictly defines the boundary line between Kafferland and the colony.

2nd Extract.—" I do not think it desirable that this country (the ceded or neutral territory) should be given to the Kaffers as their own absolute possession, but that they should continue to hold possession during good behaviour." The *fourth* article of the treaties, states that the Chiefs accept as *a special mark of grace and favour*, any part of the territory between the Keiskamma and Kat River, *as a loan:* and the *fifth* article specifies that this *loan* is to be held *in perpetuity, never to be reclaimed except in case of hostility committed, or a war provoked* by the said Chiefs or tribes, or *in case of a breach of this treaty or any part thereof*, and for which breach satisfaction or redress shall not be otherwise given or obtained.

3rd Extract.—" It would be desirable for the military Governor to enter into written agreements with the Chiefs separately." This has been done: there are five treaties, one for each principal family of Chiefs. The reason of this treating with the Chiefs separately is the obvious inexpediency of at present accustoming the Kaffer Chiefs and people to consider themselves as one nation.

4th Extract.—" If the Chiefs were assured that *in accordance with Kaffer customs*, they and their people would be held responsible in cases where the spoor of cattle was traced to their neighbourhood, they would soon find out the thieves." The *twenty-fifth* article of the treaties, provides that after the end of one month, from the time that any case of theft, clearly traced over the boundary, is laid before the Chiefs and council, if they cannot discover the plunderers, they shall at once indemnify the person robbed to the full value of the property lost. The unfortunate provisions which prevent the Colonist from tracing his property *according to Kaffer custom*, and which in consequence impose upon the Chiefs of Kafferland a responsibility, *not in accordance with Kaffer custom*, and by which the good which might have resulted from this enactment is neutralized, form no part of *my* recommendation.

5th Extract.—" In all cases the legal fine varying from four to ten for *one*, should be taken from the kraal where the thief resides, and this fine should be divided between the Chief and those who have assisted in detecting the theft. It would be impolitic to allow any part of the fine to go to the Colonist, as it might encourage unprincipled men to be careless of their property, if assured of its restoration and a recompence besides." The *twenty fourth* article of the treaties provides that the amapakati and police in the employ of the Colonial Government shall receive *compensation for their exertions, according to Kaffer usage*. The *twenty-fifth* and *twenty-sixth* articles stipulate that the person robbed shall be indemnified to the *full value* of the property lost and *no more*.

6th Extract.—" The Chiefs should be allowed the assistance of a patrol when circumstances rendered it necessary, as thieves are sometimes supported by influential men, with whom the Chief would be too weak to contend, in which case a patrol would prevent bloodshed." *Substantially* this recommendation has also been adopted, although the *twenty-third* article of the treaties is so worded as apparently to forbid anything of the kind. " No patrol or armed party of any description," shall be allowed on any occasion to cross the line of boundary for the recovery of cattle, &c. stolen. This is however evaded by allowing the policemen (armed Kaffers) to follow the spoor and recover the cattle stolen. It is difficult for a dispassionate person to see the difference in principle between *an armed body of soldiers* and *an armed body of policemen.* What difference there may be, is certainly in favour of the employment of armed soldiers, for *these* would be under the controul of a responsible officer; but the *armed* police, are under no controul, and if it suited a colonist to promise a few cows, they would in most cases be easily tempted to abuse their powers if opportunity offered. According to Kaffer usages, the person who loses property, must be prepared with an armed force of some kind or other to support his claim, otherwise the Chief who maintains no armed police of his own, cannot be expected to have it in his power to do prompt justice, even in the clearest case.

I have been thus particular in claiming my own original suggestions, which constitute all that is valuable in the treaties entered into with the border Kaffers, by Captain Stockenstrom, and for which so much credit has been claimed by those who wish to represent themselves as THE friends of the Kaffers. It would have savoured somewhat of common honesty, if the admirers of the treaties had acknowledged the source whence their materials were drawn; and it will perhaps surprise those who by a series of artful misrepresentations have been led to believe the Wesleyan Missionaries to be the advocates of the Commando System, &c., to find that the leading particulars of this "*new,*" "*humane,*" "*liberal,*" "*conciliating,*" "*just,*" and "*improved*" system of border policy; are actually taken from the recommendation of a Wesleyan Missionary, upon whom the *religious* periodicals of the day were bestowing the epithets of "*sanguinary,*" and "*truckling,*" at the very time, he and his colleagues were risking their lives to save the Chiefs and people of Kafferland from impending destruction.

We now proceed to examine these treaties, in reference to the arrangements and plans agreed upon, for the detection and punishment of thieves, and the restoration of property stolen from the Colony. These particulars which form the principal subject of the treaties, constitute at the same time, their great and incurable defect. The following are the principal causes of their inefficiency in reference to the prevention of theft, and the preserving of amicable relationship with the Kaffer tribes.

1st.—*The injudicious introduction of a local or fiscal regulation into the treaties*, has the *practical effect* of placing no small portion of the moveable property on the frontier *beyond the pale of legal protection.* Will it be believed, that in various specified cases, the Colonial Government disclaims all right of the recovery of property stolen, *and thus legalizes in such cases, a certain class of thefts from the colony*, for which it does not profess to demand reparation? *This limitation of the claim of the Colonial Government and its subjects to restitution, neutralizes all the good which might have resulted,* had even every other item in the treaties been in all respects unobjectionable.

The propriety of Colonial regulations calculated to check the carelessness of individual farmers on the frontier, is unquestionable. It was highly desirable that in certain specified cases, the Colonial Government should inflict penalties upon those whose remissness tempted the predatory habits of the neighbouring Kaffers, and thus exposed the property of other colonists as well as their own to daily loss; but such regulations ought not to have been inserted in a treaty between the Colonial Government and the Kaffer tribes. The matter concerned the Colonial Government alone, and the absurdity of making the Chiefs of Kafferland parties in the infliction of punishment upon careless colonists is obvious. Under whatever circumstances cattle &c. may be stolen from the colony, the guilt of the Kaffer thief and the ill effect of the example of his success, and impunity remain the same. It is impossible to conceive of a greater error in legislation than the plan adopted in this case, of punishing the carelessness of individual colonists, by leaving colonial property in the hands of the plunderers, and the effect of this absurd regulation is as injurious to the Kaffers as to the Colonists. It operates as a stimulus to the predatory habits of the former, from which of course the most careful of the latter suffer. It is the undoubted duty of the Colonial Government to claim restitution *in all cases* where the property of its subjects has been stolen from the colony. The right of the individuals who have lost cattle &c. to *full* compensation depends upon circumstances, concerning which the Colonial Government may very properly legislate.

The evils resulting from the insertion of these police regulations in the treaty, thus limiting the right of the claim of the loser to restitution, become almost insupportable, when the regulations themselves are taken into consideration. They are calculated to expose the Colonial farmers at all times to serious inconvenience, and compliance with them is in very many cases impracticable.

The 24th article of the treaty provides that the colonist who has lost property, in order to establish his claim to redress, must be able *to swear* " that the property when stolen was properly guarded, and in case of horses, cattle, or the like, that they were so guarded by an armed herdsman,"—" that if the robbery had been committed during the night, the property had been when stolen, properly secured in kraals, stables, or the like." Now these regulations press severely upon the conscientious colonist.*

---

* The following extract from a letter addressed to the local journal by Mr. J. Collett, a respectable sheep farmer on the Koonap will illustrate the practical working of this local regulation:

"I submit also that the circumstance of the unfortunate farmer being prohibited crossing the boundary at once when on the pursuit of his cattle spoor, and his being compelled to travel several miles first to report it, by which one whole day is often lost, and then to give over the spoor to the Kaffer police, does in reality not only deprive him of his best and almost only remaining chance of recovery, but his being compelled by the 24th clause of the treaty to make oath they were stolen under such circumstances as therein described, and which nine times out of ten he cannot do, effectually bar him from any claim whatever to compensation; and if nine farmers out of ten are unable to make the required oath, and if the Kaffers are

There are few cases in which a man can *swear* that at the time of the theft, his cattle &c., were "*properly guarded;*" the herdsman might be asleep, or he might have neglected his charge, to seek honey in the bush, or hunt for game; or from the nature of the country, part of the flock might have been concealed from view by jungles or ravines; this is no uncommon case, as from the scantiness of pasturage in some seasons in South Africa, the cattle &c., are obliged to cover a great extent of country while grazing. In some exposed parts of the frontier, the employment of an "armed herdsman" exposes him to almost certain death; the gun and ammunition being a temptation, even beyond that allowed to retain all cattle and horses but such as shall be sworn to, is it not, I would ask, virtually encouraging them to plunder the colonist? And is it reasonable to expect the Kaffers will ever, under a system so favourable, desist from plunder so long as there is a herd of cattle left on the frontier. The authorities may attempt to persuade them as they really have done that it is to their interest to be honest and refrain from stealing; but what avails preaching a doctrine to a Kaffer to which their own experience and practice give the lie. They know, to our sorrow and loss, that they are infinite gainers, and it must be more than mere words that will ever deter them from pursuing that employment which they have proved to be so profitable, and the prosecution of which is attended with so little risk.

"I would not, however, be understood to say, they always or invariably steal under cover of the treaty, that being contrary to fact. When they come out to plunder, they seldom or never return empty-handed; for if, after concealing themselves in the woods and kloofs with which our farms abound, and watching vigilantly perhaps for several days and nights, they do not get a favourable (I had almost said a lawful) opportunity of accomplishing the object of their errand, they will then resolve on some desperate attempt, and either break into some secure kraal at night, or seize the armed herdsman by surprize in the field, first secure his gun, fasten him most probably to some tree, and then walk off with all, or a selected part of the flock, as they may think fit or most expedient; then by the most refined stratagem, such as driving the cattle circuitous routes, over long grassy hills, through a particularly stony piece of country, and in a variety of other ways, they endeavour to elude and foil their pursuers, and generally effect a safe retreat with their booty. Nor does the proprietor of cattle stolen from out of a secure kraal, or taken from an armed herdsman, when he comes to make his report, find himself in any better position as to his claim to compensation, than his unfortunate neighbour who had not taken the so-called preventive caution, if he fails to bring the spoor to the boundary,—and it is those, and those only, who have had experience, who can form any idea how difficult and Herculean a task it is, in dry, windy weather, to follow on the spoor of cattle: and how often does it happen that after every precaution in the first place, and every exertion subsequently to bring the spoor to the boundary, the poor sufferer, either from unfavourable weather, or the spoor being obliterated by the spoor of other cattle, or perhaps from want of practice or ability, fails to bring it within a mile or half a mile, or it may be within 100 yards of the boundary line, and in which case his cattle or horses, whichever it may be, are, to all intents and purposes, irrecoverably lost.

JAMES COLLETT.

afforded by the plunder of the cattle : so far from being any security either to the herdsman, or the property, the arms he is furnished with are in most cases the cause of his death and the loss of the property. The Kaffers usually steal in companies ; they seize a favourable opportunity when the herdsman is off his guard ; secure his gun before he can give any alarm ; or if he see them and resist ; how can one or two men protect a herd of cattle from half-a-dozen desperate men ? The farmer may think himself fortunate if his herdsman can make his escape, and bring intelligence of the loss in time to follow the spoor before it be effaced. If the herdsman has been careless, and has left out of the kraal and of his master's cattle, &c., or neglected to secure the gate of the kraal, there is no redress, should any cattle be stolen ; for in such cases the owner cannot swear that they were "*properly secured*." Thus it happens that a large proportion of the cattle, &c., stolen from the colony are not legally recoverable, and are not claimed by the Colonial Government. To their great surprise, the Kaffers have found out that in a majority of cases, they may steal and retain the property of the Colonists with perfect impunity ; the irritation continually produced in the minds of the unfortunate and plundered farmers by the operation of this local regulation, and the injury inflicted on the habits of the border Kaffers, may easily be imagined.

2d.—The restrictions on the pursuit of stolen property, and other regulations on this subject, facilitate the escape of the thief or thieves, and oppose unnecessary obstacles in the way of the recovery of the property, even when the terms of the local regulations have been complied with.

Here it will be desirable to present to the reader part of the 23d, the 24th and 25th articles of the treaty, which embrace all the regulations referred to ; and which *seem* specially designed for the benefit of the thief, and to afford him every possible chance of escape ; that these injurious tendencies were not contemplated by the framers of the treaties is but poor consolation to the Colonists, who have suffered from the misconceptions and consequent errors of their rulers; injuries equal to any which could have resulted, on the monstrous supposition of the existence towards them of a feeling of positive malignity. In the following extract from the treaty, attention is particularly requested to the passages in italics:—

"23. But if such criminals or depredators, being pursued upon the spoor, *be not overtaken before they shall have crossed the line* occupied by the said Amapakati, the course agreed upon in the following article shall be adopted for the apprehension of such criminals or depredators, or the recovery of property carried off by them;—*aud on no occasion whatever shall any Patrol or armed party of any description, be allowed to cross the said line,* so occupied, for the said purpose.

"24. If any person being in the pursuit of criminals, or depredators, or property stolen by them, shall not overtake or recover the same, *before he shall reach the said line,* (provided he can make oath that *he traced the said criminals,* depredators,, *or property, across a particular spot on the said line,*—that the property when stolen was properly guarded, and in case of cattle, horses, or the like, that they were so guarded by an armed herdsman,—that the pursuit was commenced immediately after such property was stolen,—that if the robbery was committed during the night, the property had been, when stolen, properly secured in kraals, stables, or the like,—and that the pursuit in that case was commenced, at latest, early next morning), *such person shall be at liberty to proceed direct to the Pakati living nearest the spot,* where he can swear such traces to have crossed the said line,—*which pakati shall be bound at once to receive the statement, examine the traces, and, if the statement appear well founded,* use his utmost endeavour to recover the stolen property, as well as the perpretators pursued; and it will be at the option of the party pursuing to continue the search at once, under the guidance of the said Pakati, *provided he do not go armed, or accompanied by armed British Subjects,* or assist in any violence of any kind within the said territory. If the party pursuing shall thus, with the assistance of the said Pakati, or with that of the police, to be hereafter named, recover the property pursued, he shall be at liberty to proceed with the same, either to one of the said Agents, or to one of the military posts, most convenient to himself, in order to make, before such Agent, or officer commanding such post, a statement of his proceedings, and the quantity and nature of the property recovered, which statement he shall be liable at all times to be called upon to make oath to, after making which statement he shall be at liberty to carry off the said property, leaving the said Pakati or police to pursue the criminal, and to recover compensation for their exertions, by means of the Kaffer Chiefs and their councils, according to the Kaffer usage;—and the said contracting Chiefs do hereby bind themselves in all such cases to exert themselves to the utmost to cause the criminals to be apprehended and punished, as well as on all occasions to cause the said Chiefs and policemen to be equitably rewarded for their exertions.

"25. If, however, a party pursuing stolen property and depredators, in the manner specified in the foregoing article, shall deem it more safe, or convenient, or expeditious, to proceed to the nearest military post, he shall be at liberty to do so. *The officer commanding such post shall provide such party* (after he shall have stated himself prepared to make oath required in the said foregoing article) *with a policeman, who shall accompany such pursuing party to the spot where the said traces cross the said line, and examine the same with the assistance of the said Pakati, whose presence must be obtained.* He, the said pursuer, shall then, if he do not think fit or safe to follow the spoor further, or, having so followed the same, prove unsuccessful, proceed to the Resident Agent for the Chiefs, into whose territory the criminals and property were traced, and, before the said Agent, lodge his complaint upon oath, and, in case of lost property, swear particularly to the circumstances stated in the said foregoing article, and also the exact value of the property stolen, and not recovered. Unless this affidavit be made, the Agent shall take no further notice of the case; *but, as soon as such affidavit shall be made, the said Agent shall, if he have no reason to discredit the same, (he being at all times at liberty to demand further proof, and it being at all times the bounden duty of the party complaining to produce good and sufficient proof), to lay the case before the Chiefs of the territory*, into which the criminals and property were traced. And the said

Chiefs do hereby engage to call a council, and to enter into the strictest investigation, to cause the stolen property to be recovered, if possible, and the perpetrators punished. And the said Chiefs do further pledge themselves and engage, *that, if at the end of one month after the case shall have been laid before them, the said perpetrators or property shall not have been discovered, and, if it shall nevertheless have been clearly proved, before them and their said council, by the evidence of the said pursuer,* Pakati, *and policeman, or other proof, that the property was traced into their territory*, they, the said Chiefs, shall at once indemnify the person robbed to the full value of the property lost, *and no more*, and compensate the said Pakati and police for their exertions."

Here let us consider the facilities afforded by these regulations for the escape of the thief, and their inefficiency to the recovery of the property stolen. FIRST.—If the depredators "be not overtaken before they shall have crossed the line" (of boundary) further immediate pursuit is impossible; even if the thieves and cattle &c. be in sight, yet if once across the line, they are secure until the *Umpakati* (councillor) be seen; perhaps this man's kraal may be ten miles or more from the place where the *spoor* has crossed the line. This delay in the majority of cases, secures the escape of the thief and the loss of the spoor by rain, or by other cattle tramping out all traces in the immediate neighbourhood, so that it requires long and tedious search to find them again, even if found at all. The only method which affords a fair chance of recovering the property is expressly forbidden, for " on no occasion whatever, shall any patrol or armed party of any description be allowed to cross the said line, so occupied," " for the said purpose." *Secondly*.— Supposing property to be stolen, and the loser has *proof* that the cattle &c. are in a certain kraal in Kafferland,*

---

*The case of Mr. Robert Hart, of Somerset, is one illustration among many. In August, 1837, this gentleman lost upwards of 200 head of cattle, stolen in misty weather, from Somerset. "Just at that time one of the Kat River settlers having been plundered, had followed his cattle far into Kafferland, and on the Kei River, among the Kaffers under Tyali, had discovered some of the identical oxen which had been stolen from Mr. Hart as above stated. On receiving an intimation to this effect, that gentleman immediately dispatched a rela-

or have been seen to pass within the colony *towards* the boundary line; and beyond the colony in a direction leading *from* the boundary line; in this case, which one would suppose would constitute sufficient proof of the reality of the theft, the colonist can obtain no redress;" for he cannot " make oath that he traced the said criminals, depredators, or property across *a particular spot* on the said line; and lest by chance; common sense, and correct feeling, should tempt official men to look at the facts of the theft rather than the technicalities of tracing over a particular spot, it is expressly provided that, " unless this affidavit be made, the agent shall take no further notice of the case." From the rocky, slaty nature of the country, near extensive portions of the boundary line, the spoor of cattle, &c. is most frequently lost, and no one can possibly tell the "*particular spot*" where the cattle &c. have crossed the line; beyond the line at a short distance from it, where this sort of rock or slate ceases, the spoor may be usually traced, and its correspondence with the spoor on the other side proves its identity; but the treaty makes no provision for such local difficulties; the spoor must be traced over a "*particular spot*" which in very many cases from the nature of the soil, and from other accidental causes, is impossible.

THIRDLY.—The discretionary power permitted to the umpakati and policemen to act or not, (thus constituting persons generally of equivocal character a kind of judges in a case in

tive, accompanied by several natives, to the neighbourhood where these cattle were said to be secreted; and here accordingly they soon discovered amongst some large droves of Kaffer cattle, several of the animals in question. The Kaffers, however, no sooner learned the object of their visit, than they behaved in the most insulting and irritating manner,—drove off their herds of cattle to a distance, and used such menaces, that the party were glad to get back in a whole skin; though not before they had identified some 20 or 30 of the stolen animals. Of course, the Chief Tyali on being taxed with this robbery, and informed of the conduct of his people, appeared to be much irritated, and readily promised redress. Accordingly the cattle which *had actually been seen*, were returned to the owner; but the colonial authorities refused to sanction the levy of any fine for the robbery; or to afford Mr. Hart assistance in the recovery of the rest of his property; although he undertook to point out in the Kaffer kraals the identical stolen cattle, and hence, they are still retained by them —with the sanction of the colonial authorities."

which they are probably parties indirectly concerned,) by a necessary consequence, places the plundered colonist completely at *their* mercy. When the owner of stolen property having complied with all previous conditions, brings his matter to the umpakati; this man is to determine whether " the statement be well founded" or not. Or if the owner apply to a military post, a policeman (usually a Kaffer in colonial pay, and frequently of the same tribe with the thieves) is sent to examine the traces or spoor, with the assistance of the umpakati "whose presence *must* be obtained." In a subsequent stage of the affair, before reparation can be obtained from the Chief of the tribe into which the property is traced, the evidence of the umpakati and policemen is requisite, in order to substantiate the claim for redress. Now if the umpakati and policemen be dishonest, or in a league with the thieves, or supposing the thieves to be their relatives or friends, in which case the said umpakati and police would themselves according to Kaffer law, have to pay a portion of the fine levied on the criminals, what possibility is there of redress to the colonist? Let it not be imagined that this is supposing an extreme case.* In a

* That this is no unusual case, I have sufficient information to prove; as a specimen take the following instances from a letter of Mr. J. Collett above referred to: the evil might so far as the policemen are concerned be partly met by selecting them from Kaffers of a different tribe from that in which they were expected to be called to trace thieves. The expense of the Kaffer police is above £120 a month!! From December 1836 to June 1838, a period of 18 months, the rations, clothes, &c. for the police, amount to £2192 8s. 11d.; the far greater part of this money is spent upon the police attached to the Resident Agent of the Gaika family. It would be very desirable if the *detailed* expenditure of so large a sum, bestowed on so unimportant a class of inferior agents, were laid before the public. The saving to the Government, arising from the good conduct of Pato's people of the Gonokwabi tribe, may from this fact be estimated.

" One of the cases to which I have adverted, and the first I shall name, happened in this neighbourhood about four or five months ago, and for the correctness of which I hold myself responsible. A respectable man of the name of Mildenhall, lost out of his kraal by night 28 head of choice colonial cattle. The robbery was immediately discovered; the spoor of both cattle and Kaffers soon found, and successfully followed to the boundary line; report, agreeably to treaty, was accordingly made to the nearest post, Fort Beaufort, when the then commanding officer, Captain Armstrong, with great promptitude sent for the Kaffer police, and ordered them to proceed forthwith in company with Mildenhall to the spot where the robbers crossed the Kat River, and with the least possible delay follow the spoor into Kafferland: but which, to the astonishment of Mildenhall, and no doubt to the

great many instances, there is good reason to believe that the umpakati and police are themselves parties concerned, and their friends depending on their connivance, are the most daring and active robbers. FOURTHLY.—The latitude allowed to the agent to render assistance or not, offers the grossest insult to the colonial character. When the owner of the stolen property, *has made the requisite affidavit*, even then the agent

great annoyance of Captain Armstrong, they positively refused to do, stating as an excuse they were not compensated at all adequate to the efficient and arduous services they performed. They however, (after receiving threats from the commanding officer, and promises from Mildenhall) accompanied him, though evidently very reluctantly, to the boundary line, where on their arrival they contended (as is a common practice) it was not the spoor of the cattle in question, and sat very deliberately down for some time to smoke their pipes; but as the proprietor of the lost cattle insisted on its being the right spoor, (and which they too well knew) having traced it from his own kraal to the identical spot where they stood, they were ultimately prevailed on to take it up. They had not, however, gone many hundred yards, when they (the police) all agreed that as it was getting late in the day, they had better return again to Fort Beaufort that evening, and re-commence the pursuit the following morning; and which accordingly they did: thus giving the thieves ample time to effect their purpose by getting so deep into Kafferland as to insure their success; and the result proved exactly what might have been expected; they got successfully off with their booty, and notwithstanding Mildenhall lost 1 is cattle out of a secure kraal, followed the spoor to the boundary, gave it over to the police, made the necessary affidavit, and in fact complied in every particular with the absurd requirements of the treaty, yet he has never, up to the present moment, (although his loss was a heavy one) received any kind of satisfaction or compensation whatever!

"Another of the cases to which I allude (and for the sake of brevity this one must suffice) happened more recently. A Dutch farmer named Van Aardt, and who is my next neighbour, having had stolen out of a very strong kraal by night five head of cattle, followed the spoor as in the other case to the boundary line, made his report, affidavit, &c., got the police, brought them to the spoor, when, instead of following it up instantly as they were ordered, and as was their duty to do, they actually returned after a few hours delay back again to Beaufort, as though intending to give themselves no further trouble about the matter. Van Aardt, disgusted and exasperated at their bare-faced knavery, rode himself off to Beaufort, and reported the circumstance, when they, (the police) after receiving a severe reprimand from Colonel Somerset, (who happened to be there) returned again to where they had abandoned the spoor; but not, however, until they had allowed sufficient time for the neighbouring Kaffers to drive a large herd of cattle on the spoor of the five, and so completely obliterate the same, as to baffle all further attempts at pursuit.

"A young lad, an apprentice of Mr. Bear's, was sent to Fort Beaufort by his master on business, where on his arrival he turned out the mare on which he rode for a short time to feed, when to his surprise she suddenly disappeared. He immediately made diligent search, and being a clever lad, soon found the spoor of both the mare and the Kaffer who had stolen her, when he ran instantly back to the house where he had offsaddled, borrowed another horse, and, paying no regard to the treaty, pursued on the spoor of his mare, and with such expedition and success, as to get within sight of the thief, who on observing himself pursued so closly, sprang off, left the

may demand *further proof*, and the owner is bound to be provided with *good* and *sufficient* proofs that his allegations are true. The agent, if disposed, may thus treat the most worthy and respectable colonist as a perjured person, until he prove by the evidence of neighbours, &c. that his statements are true; the loser complaining to the agent, must furnish *good* and *sufficient proof*, until the agent " *have no reason to discredit the same.*" What constitutes good and sufficient proof is not stated, and what in the agent's opinion is such, no one can possibly opine. *He may* be profoundly skilled in the law of evidence, and *he may* be provided with tests adapted to the trial of human credibility; but this after all is doubtful: and we cannot help thinking that it would have been a much better arrangement had his duty to interfere been rendered imperative. If, in the prosecution of the inquiry, proof were elicited of the falsehood of the statements of the complainant, then the natural check on such unprincipled conduct would be a prosecution at the suit of the Attorney General for perjury. FIFTHLY.—The opportunity afforded the Chiefs and their councils of evading restitution is manifest, for even after the umpakati, policemen, and agent, have sat in judgment on the case, and decided in favour of the complainant, the theft must be again " *clearly proved* before them and the said council," before restitution is made. The degree of evidence which ought to satisfy the Chief and council, is no where stated. The other parties including the agent, may be satisfied of the justice of the complaint, and yet in the opinion of the Chief and council, the parties interested in being very sceptical and hard of conviction, the case may not be " *clearly proved*." Here room is left for a thousand quibbles

---

mare, and ran into a Kaffer hut. The boy coming up, first took possession of his mare, and then went to the Kaffer kraal to enquire for the thief, when one of them, (no doubt to screen the whole kraal from guilt) candidly confessed the thief was there, and pointed out the hut where he lay concealed; and who, should this prove to be but one of our *honest policemen* from Fort Beaufort, dressed in a check shirt and white trowsers; and I am informed this same man not only escaped punishment but is up to the present time employed as a policeman.

of which the clever Kaffer readily avails himself, and the chance is greatly against the colonist. What must the agent do? If he value his reputation with his superiors, he will do nothing; he will as a prudent man, see "difficulties in the case." Like the sagacious *official* Dogberry, immortalized by our dramatic poet, he "*may suspect by virtue of his office*" that the Chief is "*no true man,*" and that "*the less he meddles, or makes, with such kind of men, why, the more for his honesty,*" in the eyes of his official superiors.

3rd.—The *unjust and heavy responsibility imposed upon the Kaffer Chiefs*, is another leading defect in the treaties, and must have arisen from a total mis-conception of the nature of a Chief's authority, and the position in which he stands in reference to his people.

As the treaties now stand, the Chiefs are responsible for the restoration of cattle &c. traced into their territory: and *yet in consequence of the arrangements of that treaty, the thieves who have rendered the Chief responsible, are in most cases likely to escape beyond his jurisdiction, before he is aware of the theft.* This is sure to be the case if the thieves belong to another tribe.* For this annoyance (and to them

* The following instances among many, may be adduced in proof of the injustice inflicted on the Kaffer Chiefs by this system. Dinisi, one of the petty Tambookie Chiefs, has had to pay cattle to the value of 4,300 dollars, (£322 10) for 12 horses traced into his country. It can be proved that the thieves are not under his controul, but belong to Rili's country, on the Ameva, and had succeeded in passing undiscovered, through a thinly peopled part of the Tambookie district. Mapassa, another Chief of the Tambookies has had to pay 450 dollars, (£33 15) for four horses stolen by persons unknown; a shower of rain fell and effaced the spoor. In this case he was however by the native law *legally responsible;* but in another and more serious instance, the enforcement of the treaty will be attended with gross injustice. Some months ago, Matwa, (son of Gaika, residing in Makomo's country) headed a party of Kaffers and Tambookies, attacked the Fingoes on the Mancazana and carried off 120 head of cattle, bringing them through an uninhabited part of Mapassa's country; Mapassa managed to retake 27 head in the possession of his own people and restored them, but the other 93 head, which Matwa and his allies contrived to take through his country, it is not in his power to restore, since Matwa is supported by a powerful tribe. The Colonial Government hold Mapassa responsible, and intend to enforce payment, although from Matwa being nearer the inhabited part of the colony than Mapassa, it would be easier for the Government to recover the cattle from him; *but this the treaty forbids.* The reason why Mapassa submits to this injustice is this; he is not a powerful chief and is surrounded by enemies. It is therefore of the utmost importance to him that he stand well with the Colonial Government.

it is a serious annoyance) they may thank the absurd regulation restricting the immediate pursuit of the stolen property across the boundary line. The regulation that, "on no occasion whatever shall any patrol or armed party of any description be allowed to cross the said line (of boundary) for the said purpose," of following quickly after the depredators, is based on European notions of the respect due to the integrity of the territory of a foreign power. The Kaffer Chiefs and people have no such feeling, and in their intercourse with others, in tracing stolen cattle, no such respect (which to them appears ridiculous) is ever paid to the integrity of territory. *They* are accustomed to follow their cattle, &c. until they find a party legally responsible for them. According to the principles and usages of their domestic, as well as of their international law, the loser of property is expected, with the assistance of his friends, to act as his own police, and himself find out the thief or responsible person, after which, if the parties offending refuse to settle the matter to the satisfaction of the parties aggrieved; *then* the inferior Chief of that branch of the tribe, or in case of his not being able, the Chief himself and his council decide the case. *We* may arbitrarily constitute a Chief responsible for cattle &c., which we say and perhaps can prove, have passed into his country, but the Kaffers consider the responsibility of the Chief not to begin, until first the cattle, &c. have been traced to a responsible party, and compensation has been refused by the delinquent and the subordinate Chiefs. It is absurd and mischievous to make a Chief responsible beyond the extent of his constitutional power, which is the only proper measure of the degree of his responsibility. The utmost we have any right to expect from a Kaffer Chief is, that he will administer justice impartially on the principles of Kaffer law to English complainants, who have complied with all the previous formalities of that law. We have no right to bully or deceive the Chiefs into an agreement which they do not properly understand, and up to which they cannot act, without themselves suffering great injustice. To us the method of making the Chief personally reponsible may appear a "royal road to justice," but it can never be enforced without provoking a degree of irritation which will gradually prepare the way for another war. In our intercourse with a semi-barbarous people, it is desirable that we should as far as possible frame our legislation where *they* are affected, as far as possible on the principles of law and justice recognised and acted upon by *them*. Why should not the treaty recognize the Kaffer mode of proceeding in case of theft, as obligatory upon the colonial owner of stolen property? Let the colonist accompanied by his friends or servants follow his property just as a Kaffer would, until he had brought the *spoor* to a responsible party; and then let him quietly leave it, and let the agent take up the case and see that justice be done to the aggrieved party, according to the principles of Kaffer law; with this exception, however, the fines levied should be taken by the agent and applied to the payment of the Chief, friendly Kaffers, &c., and the colonial owner of the property stolen merely receive his own again. This to the Kaffers would appear perfectly equitable, whereas the plan of not following the cattle across the boundary, until the delay caused by the limitation of the treaty, has given the thief time to escape beyond the power of the chief rendered responsible by the said treaty, is *felt by them to be a grievance, against which they have seriously remonstrated*,* and it will be objected to, as occasions occur from time to time in which the hardship is felt more severely than hitherto. So far the treaties have never been seriously enforced; the executive of the colony has obtained such redress as it could by fair words, and has quietly put up with the losses

---

* When Captain Stockenstrom, then Lieutenant Governor, met the Slambie and Gonokwabie Chiefs on the Guanga in November 1837, Umhala asked why the patrols could not follow the cattle, since owing to the delay occasioned by the new plan, the thieves were beyond pursuit before the Chief was aware of the theft? On being informed that this could not be, since the treaty forbad it, Umhala replied "Then you are the best friend the thieves ever had." Intelligent Kaffers have repeatedly asked me why Englishmen, so wise in many things, are so stupid in reference to the measures taken in the pursuit of stolen cattle.

for which no redress could be obtained; but if a straight-forward Governor, were to imagine that treaties like all other agreements were valuable only as they were fulfilled, and were so rash as to apply that *test* to the treaties in question; he would find that he had unthinkingly embarked in an undertaking, the issue of which would compel him to a re-extension of British jurisdiction to the Kei, or to a complete subjugation of the Kaffer tribes. What man will dare to risk the chance of commencing such a war, until the evil of the plunder of the colony is beyond endurance, and then the unfortunate and impracticable arrangements of the treaties, oblige us either to suffer patiently the loss of property to the amount of some thousands sterling annually, or to commence another Kaffer war, the expences of which is well-known to the treasury at home, though the British public have only as yet been partially enlightened on the subject.

In concluding these brief remarks upon the treaties of December 1836, we may observe, that no one possessed of local knowledge can carefully examine the regulations affecting the recovery of stolen cattle, &c. without being convinced of the impossibility of effectually securing the property of the colonists, or the peace of the frontier; by a system which, while it restricts the activity of the sufferer and opposes a series of useless delays and hinderances in the way of his obtaining redress, at the same time imposes an unjust weight of responsibility on the Chiefs of Kafferland, equally irksome and annoying to them, as it is useless in reference to any practical results benefitting the colonist. If all the chicanery attributed to the most degraded branches of the legal profession had been put in requisition for the purpose of defeating the ends of justice, and of tempting the border Kaffers by tolerating a perfect impunity in theft, to become a nation of thieves; a better system for insuring such a result could hardly have been devised. Such are the treaties upon which Captain Stockenstrom. and the Colonial Office, rest their claims to the approbation

and the Colonial Office rest their claims to the approbation of a philanthropic public. All that is valuable and just is taken from the hints furnished by a letter of a Wesleyan Missionary. The gross mistake of intermixing police regulations with national treaties; the restrictive enactments neutralizing all the good to be anticipated from an efficient check upon the predatory habits of the border Kaffers; and lastly, the verbosity, tautology, and consequent obscurity of the language employed, (the sense being so lost in a wilderness of words, that it is difficult to discern the meaning) these belong peculiarly to the individuals who framed the treaty.

It now remains to consider the *practical working* of Captain Stockenstrom's new system. If in its actual results it could have been proved to have considerably lessened the depredations of the Kaffers on the colony, and had communicated an additional feeling of security to the Colonists, and their natural allies the Fingoes, and friendly Kaffers of the Gonokwabie tribes; then, in spite of all the fault to be found with its details, we should be compelled to bestow a measure of praise, justly due to its authors and administrators. In investigating these partial results, *there can be no mistake*, as the question is purely one of fact, based on arithmetical calculation.

From December 1836, to the end of December 1837, during which period the "*safe, secure*, and *efficient* system" of Captain Stockenstrom was in full operation, the moderate calculation of losses actually reported (besides the numerous cases not reported) amounted to 384 horses, 2,403 head of cattle stolen, besides 24 murders. The estimated value of this property thus stolen, amounts to about £8,000, which is no small tax to be paid in twelve months by the recently plundered Colonists to their Kaffer neighbours. For the months of January and February, 1838, I can find no returns; but the plunder continued at the same ratio. From March, regular returns of cattle, &c. stolen, together with the number recovered, were directed to be published by the new Governor, Major-General Napier.* Up to this period we have those official accounts for six months, *three of which have been marked by peculiar energy and activity on the part of the Colonial executive, in consequence of General Napier's firm tone, and decisive measures;* and these results for six months singularly confirm the accuracy of the estimated losses of 1837.

1838.	STOLEN.						RECOVERED.					
	HORSES.		CATTLE.		SHEEP.		HORSES.		CATTLE.		SHEEP.	
Month.	Rec.	Irr.	Rec.	Irr.	Rec.	Irr.	Rec.	Irr.	Rec.	Irr.	Rec.	Irr.
March,	5	36	57	35	1	..	5	12	50	4	1	..
April,	13	24	284	230	2	8	5	1	153	39	..	1
Arrears,	..	36	..	37	..	6	..	..	..	..	..	..
May,	1	71	72	247	1	5	1	3	35	46	..	..
June,	13	24	59	61	..	101	5	..	28	3	..	..
Arrears,	..	20	..	26	..	..	..	..	..	..	..	..
July,	2	5	14	61	..	25	..	7	5	11	..	..
Arrears,	..	..	..	..	..	..	..	12	..	56	..	..
August,	8	20	68	63	..	..	4	..	30	..	..	..
Lost,	42	246	554	760	4	144	20	35	301	159	1	1
Recov.	20	35	301	159	1	1						
	22	211	253	601	3	143						

Thus it appears that the total loss of property for six months of 1838, including that which is *reclaimable* by treaty, and that which, according to the heading of the government returns, has been "robbed from the colony, taken across the frontier, and not reclaimabel,"—is as follows:—

233 Horses,
854 Head of Cattle,
146 Sheep. Value about £4,000.†

*In these official returns *not one* instance occurs of cattle traced to the Gonokwabie tribe, under Pato, Kama, and Kobus Congo; the principal thefts appear to have been committed by the people of Makomo, Tyali, Eno, and Botman.

† This analysis is framed from the *official* monthly returns. It is much to be regretted that these returns are not more clearly arranged, so as to present at one view the state of the cattle account with the Kaffers. By *my* estimate the balance of cattle, &c. claimed according to treaty on the 1st of August was 18 horses, 215 cattle; but the government estimate is

We may, therefore, on undoubted data, calculate the regular plunder of the frontier Colonists under the *new* and *improved* system at the amazing sum of £8,000 per annum. With the exception of 1834, which was a year of licence, at no period previous to the late war has the colony been plundered *during peace* to so great an extent; and it should be remembered that the present inefficient and worse than useless system, has not the merit of dispensing with the expense of a large military force. On the contrary, the number of troops on the frontier, is about three times the number previous to the war, and the expenses annually

11 horses, 198 cattle, making a difference of 7 horses, and 17 head of cattle. Probably 7 horses and 17 head of cattle have been retaken; but of this, there is no account in the published return. If we deduct them from the estimate in the text; the cattle, horses, &c. due by the Kaffers 1st of September, will be as follows:—

Horses.	Cattle.	Sheep.	
15	236	3	Reclaimable by treaty, but not yet recovered.
211	601	143	Not reclaimable.
226	837	147	Value about £3,900

As this ratio of depredations had been going on from the beginning of Captain Stockenstrom's administration, up to his leaving the colony, and has only been checked by the vigorous measures of Sir George Napier; we need not wonder at the following illustration of the little confidence entertained by the monied interest and by the agents of the Orphan Chamber in the Cape, as to the value of landed property on the frontier.

Cape Town, 5th June, 1837.

Sir,—I am requested to make application by ———, of Albany, in behalf of several persons there, to know if you will be inclined to advance loans of money on first mortgage on landed property in that district, (particularly in Graham's Town and Bathurst), the parties being willing to abide by all the usual regulations of the guardian fund.

I have the honor to be, Sir, your obedient Servant,
(Signed,) J. C. CHASE.
To C. BURTON, Esq., Master, Supreme Court, Orphan Chamber Jurisdiction.

Master's Office, July 21, 1837.

Sir,—In reply to your letter of the 5th ult., requesting to know, on behalf of ———, for several persons in the Albany district, whether I am inclined to advance loans of money on first mortgage of landed property in that district, I have to acquaint you that the Committee of the Guardian Fund deem it unadvisable at present to entertain any applications for loans of money from the frontier districts.

I have the honor to be, Sir, &c.
C. BURTON, Master.
J. C. CHASE, Cape Town.

At present, (Oct. 1838) confidence is partially restored, and the natural superior advantages of the Eastern frontier are again attracting capital. Landed property has risen in value a little; and should a just and decisive administration afford the requisite security, there can be no doubt but that this part of the colony will soon rival Australia, especially in the article of Wool.

incurred and paid by the British government have been raised from 30 or £40,000, to about £200,000; besides an additional civil establishment to the amount of nearly £5,000 per annum paid by the colony.

In many instances *the vigorous enforcement* of even ill-advised plans conceals their deficiencies, and the activity of the executive compensates for the neglect or ignorance of an inexperienced or incompetent legislature. Had Captain Stockenstrom's treaties been enforced in the cases for which the treaties had provided; this, although affording but an imperfect measure of protection, would have satisfied the Colonists that the Government was able and willing to protect its subjects; and the Kaffers would have been convinced that the licence allowed by the treaties, was merely the result of a mistake in minor arrangements, and not the consequence of timidity or indecision. *But the treaties were never enforced* for the protection of the colony or its allies. So far as the recovery of stolen property is concerned, or the protection of our native allies; the stipulations of the treaties may be considered as a dead letter. In a majority of cases where the provisions of the treaty had been fulfilled by the Colonists, the stolen property traced, and the period of one month allowed to the Chiefs had elapsed, no redress was even then obtained; fair promises and the usual excuses were made, a few worthless cattle were returned, and the loser tired of the trouble and loss of time gladly gave up the concern. In fact, the enforcement of the treaties was impossible, unless the Colonial executive had chosen to provoke another war; for the Chiefs and their councils could not see the justice of being made responsible for thefts in cases where the activity of the Colonists, if unrestrained by the treaties would have obtained redress at an inferior tribunal. If the Colonial Government *will* tie up the hands of its subjects, and thus place impediments in the way of the recovery of their property, that concerns the Colonists; the Kaffers have no desire to interfere with the local arrangements of their neighbours; but the Kaffer Chiefs and their people will not be responsible for the results of our folly; and this ridiculous scheme of forcing upon them the adoption of European notions and usages of international law, will ever prove in practice a complete failure, and in no case can it be enforced without the risk of a war.*

The most serious instance of the inability of the new Lieutenant-Governor to enforce the provisions of his own treaties, occurred in the beginning of August 1837, when the Fingo settlement in the ceded territory near Fort Peddie, which had been declared by the treaties under British protection, was attacked by a party of Kaffers under the Chief Siyolo. Five hundred head of cattle were seized from those poor refugees who were living in imagined security, relying on the promised protection of the Colonial Government; the Fingo Chief was stabbed in the presence of the Resident Agent who had gone to remonstrate with the assailants on their breach of the treaty; an English Corporal and ten Fingoes were killed on the spot, and eleven were severely wounded.* This attack had been preceded by the murder and ill usage of several Fingoes in the neighbourhood; their cattle were frequently taken

* General Napier attempted to enforce the treaty when on the frontier, May, 1838. Three clear cases of cattle due according to the treaty by Botman, a petty chief, were reported to him *by the parties suffering loss.* The resident agent was severely reprimanded for his neglect; and Botman was informed that, unless the cattle were forthcoming *in ten days,* an armed party would be sent to make seizures to the amount due. Before the time expired, a number of old maimed cattle, by no means equal to the value of the property lost were sent in, *and gladly accepted,* as General Napier had meanwhile discovered that the strict enforcement of the treaty would have produced an alarming excitement, and perhaps a general war. Another case, in which Messrs. Simpson & Stanton clearly proved the loss of a herd of cattle traced into Kafferland,|is about to be settled; not by making the Chief pay the amount for which he is by treaty responsible, but by a draft on the *Colonial Treasury*; which is to be repaid by the sale of cattle recovered from the Kaffers, and not claimed by the owners; and this eventually brings the compensation for losses out of the pockets of the Colonists themselves.

* As an instance of the little reliance to be placed in the statements respecting the peace of the frontier contained in Captain Stockenstrom's organ; the *Commercial Advertiser,* we may state that the very week the news of this aggression reached Cape Town, the Editor states (12 Aug.) "The Colonial frontier is *perfectly* quiet."

away, and their women beaten and plundered while working in their gardens, within sight of a British Fort! When the Resident Agent sent to complain to the parties thus acting, his messengers were insulted, and told that the Fingoes were *dogs;* things which had no business with cattle. No steps were taken by the Colonial executive, to demand redress, from which the Kaffers naturally inferred (and as the event proved justly) that no protection would be afforded the Fingoes, notwithstanding the treaties in their favour; and that they might be plundered with impunity. It was the conviction of the weakness of the Colonial Government, *and a general impression in Kafferland, that the Lieutenant-Governor was desirous of getting rid of the Fingoes* that led to this daring, successful, and unpunished outrage. The Lieutenant-Governor on visiting the scene of action, endeavoured by every means to prove that the Fingoes had been the aggressors, and had provoked the attack, but on finding that his statements in justification of the plunder and murder of British dependants could not be corroborated by independent witnesses; he was obliged to admit that the Kaffers had broken the treaty, and for this he demanded reparation.* In about a month, 74 head of miserable cattle were sent to Fort Peddie, as payment for 500 taken away, and *the Lieutenant-Governor acknowledged himself satisfied.* This unfortunate truckling to the robbery and murder of the people of a tribe solemnly declared to be under British protection, sealed the fate of Captain Stockenstrom's new system of border policy. The Kaffers were emboldened to insult a Government, which its executive had rendered in their view, so contemptible; and the Colonists, even the most sanguine, lost all confidence in the continuance of peace or security. Through all Kafferland the moral effect of this unpunished plunder and murder of the Fingoes, was most injurious. In Faku's

* If the Colonial Office will grant a copy of Captain Stockenstrom's despatch to the Secretary of State for the Colonies, relative to this transaction, I pledge myself to disprove every assertion criminatory of the Fingoes, by unanswerable documents and undoubted evidence. Will no independent member of the House of Commons move for an inquiry into this affair?

country, nearly 300 miles further up the coast, I was informed of the whole particulars, long before the news arrived by our regular post. The most merciless ridicule by the natives, of the conduct of the Lieutenant-Governor, accompanied the statement of facts; and the natural conclusion was drawn, that in the late war the Kaffers had been victorious, and had compelled the Colonists to sue for peace, and restore to them their country again.

That a system which the experience of twenty months (up to September, 1838) purchased at so dear a rate, had proved to be so useless in reference to the benefical results anticipated from its opertion, should have been permitted to continue without the modification at least of those particulars which were injurious to its practical efficiency, is one of the many evils of which the Colonists have a right to complain, as resulting in part from the unmerited obloquy, which in the mother country has been thrown upon their character. The unreasonable prejudices of the British public, in which the Government appear to parcipate, renders a fair hearing for the statements and views of the Colonists almost impossible. Had there been the slightest probability that the case of the frontier inhabitants of the Cape would be fairly brought before the Legislature, and receive ordinary and dispassionate attention, no Colonial functionary would have dared to persevere with such determined pertinacity in upholding a system which the results of every month's experience proved to be so ruinous to the interests of all parties concerned. The calculations of tyranny are usually incorrect; but this case forms an exception to the ordinary rule. The Colonial executive knew the vantage ground on which it stood, and the strength of its position. It guarded itself from all inquiry, by its tact in identifying its measures with the liberal and philanthropic aspirations of the people of England; this merit, which has no foundation in truth, it assumed to itself; and the bigotted violence of *a certain class of its Colonial opponents*, has more than any other cause served to confirm the public in the delusion. By this means, a series of measures, which in their natural consequences must of necessity prove destructive to the *best interests*, and perhaps to *the very existence of the Kaffer tribes*, (as well as the Colonists) have been the subjects of approbation in Britain, from their imagined efficacy in preventing the recurrence of the injustice of bye-gone ages, and of conserving the liberty and independence of the original proprietors of the soil!! Time will be requisite to remove the delusion; meanwhile the Colonists must submit to suffer the ill effects resulting from having suffered impressions so injurious to their character to remain uncontradicted so long, that they are now received and reasoned upon as undoubted truths.

The delusive system of Captain Stockenstrom has been supported by a talented portion of the Cape press, and to this circumstance we may attribute the continuance of the delusion in the Cape, and in Britain, respecting its real nature and tendencies. The Cape *Commercial Advertiser*, a paper distinguished by the ability of its editor, as well as by its consistent and powerful advocacy of religious institutions and liberal principles, was at once the organ and the defender of Captain Stockenstrom's administration. By this means a very respectable portion of the Cape public were led to form opinions in reference to the affairs of the eastern frontier the very reverse of truth, and similar impressions through the same widely circulated medium were conveyed to the press of our native land; and thus it has been generally supposed, that the new system worked well, that it bade fair to remove and prevent every occasion of collision between the Colonists and Kaffers, and that it had answered in every respect the anticipations of its benevolent friends and advocates.

Before Captain Stockenstrom entered upon his duties the *Commercial Advertiser* stood fairly committed to support his measures. As soon as intelligence of his appointment reached the colony, the versatile editor, who had been *almost* though *reluctantly* convinced of the benevolence and justice of the system of Sir Benjamin D'Urban as administered by Colonel Smith, began to indulge in glowing anticipations of the benefits which would result from Captain Stockenstrom's administration, although, of course, a perfect stranger to the instructions Captain Stockenstrom might receive in reference to the regulations of our frontier intercourse, and the nature of our future relationship with the Kaffer tribes. Under whatever system that might be adopted, Captain Stockenstrom was in his opinion, to be the political saviour of the country; this is apparent from the following paragraph; " The Colonists may rest assured that we have seen the last of our Kaffer wars; we advise our friends, the public, to prepare themselves for peace and plenty. Nothing is wanted but the presence of the Lieutenant-Governor to consolidate an efficent system, and terminate for ever the irregularities from which so many wars have sprung."—*Commercial Advertiser*, *July* 1836.) The flattering visions of hope thus freely indulged were not likely to be willingly given up, and hence the editor was more easily led to place implicit confidence in the demi-official flattering statements respecting frontier affairs conveyed to him by certain correspondents, whose names, although carefully concealed from public view, are, in spite of their anonymous disguise, well known. That these individuals, profitting by the *new* and *improved* system, may have reasons for defending it, is no criterion by which its merits can be determined. In consequence, however, of such *ex-parte* and prejudiced statements, in which the hopes and wishes, rather than the experience of the writers, must have been embodied; the editor of the *Commercial Advertiser* during the whole of the year 1837, a period of unprecedented insecurity and plunder of frontier property, during which some thousands of the Dutch inhabitants had quitted the colony to seek for peace and security among distant tribes of barbarians; was induced to write the following series of remarks on the state of frontier affairs, which display at once his ignorance of the actual position of things, and the sources whence his apocryphal information was drawn: "All is quiet in Kafferland."—"We hear nothing of hostile inroads or Kaffer depredations."—"For the last four or five months our intelligence from the frontier bears evidence in favour of the order of things now *firmly* established in that quarter."—"We hear of no agitation, disturbance, robbery, or theft; the Lieutenant-Governor's reign has been one of *unvarying* tranquillity on the part of the people on *both sides* of the border."—"The news from the frontier is of the most pacific character."—"*Profound* tranquility is the telegraph from the whole frontier this week."—"We receive by every post the most satisfactory accounts from Kafferland."—"We shall have little to say in future of the new system administered by Captain Stockenstrom."—"From the frontier we continue to receive assurances of peace and tranquillity."—"By letters from the eastern frontier we learn that peace and quietness reign on that border and Kafferland."—"All remains tranquil."—"Our accounts for several weeks past may be summed up in the words of our correspondent,—'such tranquillity has not been known for many years.'"

In spite of all these delusive announcements, it can be clearly proved that during the year 1837, this year of "unprecedented tranquillity," under the firmly established rule of the Lieutenant-Governor, property to the amount of £8,000 was taken from the frontier districts of the colony by the Kaffers.* And yet, in the very face of this detailed account, which has never yet been invalidated, the *Commercial Advertiser* of January 1838, thus boldly supports the deception which *facts* had so completely exposed. "We announce that the account between the Kaffers and the

* I am satisfied that this is a moderate estimate of the average annual loss sustained by the colony from Kaffer depredations under the new and improved system; the calculation made for 1837, is confirmed by the official returns for six months, of the year 1838, which give an average result of about £8,000 per annum, as the total amount of loss for that year, should the following months correspond with the preceding six months. See pp. 96, 97.

Colonists for the last twelve months has been equitably adjusted, and that probably for the first time there exists no balance against either party."—*(3rd January, 1838)*
"Relying on what we consider a good authority, we feel assured that the peace and security of the frontier have been as well provided for as circumstances would admit, during the past year."—*(27th January, 1838.)*

When however the published official returns for the months of March, April, May, and June 1838, and the presence of the new Governor on the frontier, placed some check on the continued publication of demi-official falsehoods; the editor then reluctantly admitted the unpleasant truth which it was impossible any longer to conceal, "By private letters we learn, that 'the country within the Kaffer boundary (that is Kafferland itself) continues undisturbed: 'but the Kaffers,' says the writer, 'have been stealing beyond anything I have ever witnessed; and they manage to get the cattle across the boundary without the authorities or the police being able to bring the spoor to the line, and consequently there is no redress.' Our correspondent adds, 'I am sorry to say, the continued drought is likely to retard agricultural operations; the waters within the colony are becoming very weak, and grass in Kafferland is scarce.'—This may in some measure account for these *intolerable depredations*, that is for their *unusual amount* and frequency."

The credit due to the *Commercial Advertiser* as an authority on the state of the frontier may now be estimated by any unprejudiced enquirer. The testimony it gives, is simply the echo of two or three individuals who have *weighty* reasons for praising a system by which *they, and they alone,* are benefitted. We cannot help admiring the talent of the editor, his unwearied advocacy of liberal and enlightened measures, and his consistent support of the interests of religion and humanity; and we may gratefully commend his zeal for the prosperity of the colony in the introduction and furtherance of local improvements; but pledged as he is to a *party*, and *to partial views* on this question of border policy, and grossly deceived as he is by the incorrect nature of the intelligence conveyed to him;—his opinions and authority are of no weight in a matter, in which local knowledge, personal experience, and dispassionate feelings, are requisite, in order to arrive at correct conclusions.

Captain Stockenstrom left Graham's Town, 9th August 1838, *on leave of absence*, and his successor, Colonel Hare, the Acting Lieutenant-Governor, shortly arrived from the Cape, and entered upon the duties of his office; thus the Government of the Eastern Province was administered by Captain Stockenstrom for a period of about one year and ten months.

NOTE IV.

HINTS FOR THE IMPROVEMENT OF THE PRESENT SYSTEM OF BORDER POLICY.

Whatever may be conceived to be the comparative merits of the two plans of border policy, the only remaining questions of practical utility, are these.—How can the present system be rendered more efficient? How can we preserve inviolate the *principles* of the treaties, and at the same time obviate *in detail* their many and serious defects? The treaties of the 6th December 1836, having been ratified by the British Government, must be maintained, but some alteration in their details, calculated to prevent the injustice which is at present experienced alternately by the Colonists and Kaffer Chiefs, (owing to the enforcement of sundry injudicious stipulations) are absolutely necessary, and may reasonably be expected from the wisdom and justice of the British Government.

There are, however, two preliminary measures, which would tend much to facilitate the carrying into effect any proposed amendments. These are *first*,—the vesting the office of Lieutenant-Governor, in the hands of an individual competent from his military rank to take the supreme military, as well as civil command on the frontier. *Secondly.*—The receiving the Gonokwabie tribe, under Pato and Kama, as British subjects, on a plan similar to that adopted by Sir Benjamin D'Urban.

In reference to the first of these measures, it must be observed, that the defence of the frontier being the main business of the Lieutenant-Governor, a mere civilian in the possession of that office, labours under all the disadvantages which we may easily suppose would be experienced by a *civil* Governor of a fort or garrison town. No one will dispute the fact, that a military man is generally as competent as any other professional individual to discharge the duties of a civil Government. There may be advantages on the side of the civilian, resulting from experience previously acquired in the legal or civil departments in Britain, but are not these more than counterbalanced by his incapacity for the military command of the colony? In times of difficulty nice questions too frequently arise as to the respective powers and jurisdictions of the civil Governor and military commandant, which prove extremely detrimental to the public service; these would be obviated by the concentration of both offices in one competent individual, and surely in the present state of the British Army, there can be no difficulty in finding individuals possessed of the requisite military rank, combined with every other suitable qualification for the important office in question.*

The *second* preliminary measure recommended, viz, the reception of the Gonokwabie tribe under Pato and Kama, as British subjects, is due to their exemplary conduct, for a period of 15 years.† Hitherto, so far from being *distin-*

---

* Much of the indecision which characterised the brief administration of Captain Stockenstrom, no doubt arose from his not possessing the full command of the military as well as the civil power. From my firm conviction of the impossibility of his being able to act with sufficient promptitude, in the critical state of affairs, I took the liberty of strongly urging upon him during a short interview at Wesleyville, in December 1836, the necessity of demanding either an extension of authority, or an acceptance of his resignation. To those who object to a military man as a Governor, merely *because he is a soldier,*, I recommend the perusal of a splendid article in the " London and Westminster Review," for January 1838, page 367; an article too long to quote, and which would be spoiled by an abridgment.

† This was desired by them before the war of 1834—5, and a petition was sent to the Colonial Government formally expressing their wishes. Pato and Kama have sense enough to perceive that some alteration in the Kaffer system of government, is requisite in order to preserve their people as a

guished and *rewarded*, as the faithful friends and allies of the Colonial Government, they have received far less attention than other Chiefs, whose notorious turbulence and bad faith, have rendered *a hollow friendship and a predatory truce with them*, a desirable purchase. It has been too much the unjust and mistaken policy of the Colonial Government, to undervalue and neglect its allies, in order to conciliate those whose troublesome enmity it desired to propitiate. This policy arose from no ill will towards the former, but simply from the position in which the executive has been placed. The Governor of the Cape colony is sent to administer its affairs for a brief period, (not less than three, and not more than six years); the maxims of expediency adopted by his predecessor, are of necessity his guide in the beginning of his administration; and the same maxims are continued as principles of action, even when his experience proves their fallacy, because he considers that towards the close of his official career, it would be absurd to hazard untried schemes, involving himself in responsibilities in the adoption of plans, the carrying out of which must be left to his successor. His object is therefore to finish his term quietly. Hence the courting of enemies, whose restlessness is feared, and the neglect of friends whose fidelity may be relied on. It is now time that this truckling expediency should cease to influence the councils of the Colonial Government, and it is with pleasure I record the first symptoms of a return to a more manly and honest policy. On the arrival of General Sir George Napier on the frontier, a supplementary treaty was entered into with the Gonokwabie tribe under Pato and Kama, in which the Fingoes were also included. By this treaty, these tribes were recognized as British allies, and received under British protection, (19th June, 1838) and there can

---

nation, and to secure the possession of their lands, and their progress in civilization. In December 1836, they *strongly* objected to the treaties imposed upon them by Captain Stockenstrom, wishing (as they said) for no change; but they were at length almost compelled to accede to them, being threatened with a loss of their Chieftainship!! i, e. of their being treated as Chiefs by the Colonial Government.

be no doubt that this decisive act contributed much to the *subsequent comparative* peace of the frontier. Let this measure be followed up by a formal reception of these tribes as British subjects, with certain limitations suited to their present social state. We have in India different codes of law applied to the different classes of our subjects there. Why cannot we have a modified system of Kaffer law for our Kaffer subjects? In a political point of view, the announcement of the Gonokwabie and Fingo tribes having been received as British subjects, and placed on a perfect equality as regards their territorial and legal rights with the other subjects of the Colonial Government, would produce an impression favourable to the continuance of peaceful relationships on the frontier. Eventually these tribes, having become subjects, might be partially armed as an irregular militia, bound to serve when *necessity required* for the defence of the colony; and thus the employment of British troops, with the exception of those requisite for garrison duty, might be in a great degree dispensed with. By a judicious system of this sort, the expense of at least one regiment might be saved; and should a war unhappily be forced upon the colony by the other tribes; the Gonokwabie and Fingo militia, assisted by a few European officers, selected from the Colonial farmers, would be found to render far more effective assistance in putting down aggressions, than double the number of regular troops. On the fidelity of the Gonokwabies the utmost reliance can be placed. The Chiefs are now as honestly attached to the British Government, as any native born subjects in Britain. For fifteen years the Gonokwabies have remained in peace with us; all the youth of the tribe therefore have been accustomed to regard the Colonists as their natural friends. In such a state of things there would be no risk in furnishing a portion of this tribe with arms, on the reception of which the Chiefs would become responsible for their production at fixed times and places, for the inspection of a proper officer; the expense of the muskets and ammunition, together with some honorary and distinctive badge to be worn by the militia when in service, and the cost of a few head of cattle to be slaughtered on occasions of musters, reviews, &c., would be trifling when compared with the present enormous force maintained as a *peace establishment*, and which, after all, is miserably adapted for the bush fighting, and wild irregular warfare, in which it must occasionally engage.

The alterations in the details, and other arrangements resulting from the treaties, and which appear highly necessary in order to their practical efficiency, are as follows:—

I. *The dismissal of the Kaffer police*, which, at present, is of very questionable utility, and the necessity for which will be superseded by the addition of the proposed alterations. This police costs about £120 per month; from 1st Dec. 1836, to June 1838, the expense for rations, &c., was £2,192. 3s. 11d.; and in the estimates for the year 1838, the sum of £1,500 was voted for them; thus, about £1,500 per annum would be at once saved to the Colonial Treasury by abolishing this force.

II.—*Some modification of the regulations respecting thefts.*

1st. Let the restrictions on the right of recovery of stolen cattle be rescinded, and confined to the necessity of simply proving *the property to be stolen by Kaffers*, and *traced into* or *found in* Kafferland. Any local regulations punishing the carelessness of Colonial farmers can be framed by the proper authorities irrespective of the treaties.

2nd. Annul the regulations which prevent *the immediate* pursuit of stolen property across the line of boundary;— allow the Colonist to act as the laws of Kafferland permit

* No one acquainted with the country and the habits of the Kaffers, can entertain the notion that this would give the Colonist any chance of making reprisals, and thus settling the affair by force of arms, instead of appealing to the regular Kaffer judicatories. No small party of armed farmers would dare to attempt this, as it would in all probability lead to the sacrifice of their own lives. The Kaffers being accustomed to assemble in great numbers with wonderful celerity, at any given point, could easily cut off their retreat into the colony. The Kaffers are a very different people from the timid Hottentots, or wandering Bushmen; and the overlooking this difference has led to manifold errors on the question of the Border Policy.

the Kaffer to act under similar circumstances. Let the Colonist go with a limited number of friends, (armed, of course, if they choose),* and having traced the *spoor* to a responsible party, there leave it,—proceed next to the agent, and place the affair in his hands; taking care, however, that immediately on crossing the border, a messenger be sent to inform the Umpakati (stationed according to treaty) of his errand. It will be the duty of the Umpakati to inform his chief of the circumstance, and the agent will see that the Colonist has justice done to him *according to the usages of Kaffer law.**

3. On receipt of the cattle and fine, let the agent deliver to the Colonist the *value of his property and no more*; the fine received can be applied by him to the chief and his council, and to other friendly and influential parties. By this means the Kaffers would see that the Colonial Government simply desired justice in the remuneration of the Colonist, and the punishment of the Kaffer thief; and by a judicious distribution of fines, the agent would be enabled to secure an interest in the council which would much facilitate the discharge of his duties.

4. If the *spoor* of cattle be traced into Kafferland, but not brought to a responsible party, then let the responsibility of the chief, and his council remain as provided in the treaty; but if the spoor be traced into the territory of a chief, and by his people carried fairly into the territory of another chief, let the first chief who, by the terms of the treaty is responsible, have the assistance of the agent's influence, and if necessary, of a patrol, in order to enforce restitution from the parties who have rendered him responsible. By this means the many instances of gross injustice,

* Missionaries residing in Kafferland find no difficulty in obtaining justice *according to Kaffer law*, but they carefully avoid receiving any thing beyond the value of the stolen property; and would rather be actual losers, than even *appear* to gain by the punishment of the thief. The fines are usually given to the persons employed in tracing the *spoor*, to the Chief &c. On one occasion a Missionary declined enforcing the customary fine; the Chief said to him, "If you pay my people for thieving, don't trouble me again." Soon after his cattle were again stolen; no one was willing to follow the *spoor*, or in any way assist, inasmuch as the active agents in the former case had received no remuneration. When the *third* case of theft occurred, the worthy man wisely refrained from interfering with the due course of Kaffer law.

occuring under the present system towards the chiefs on the *immediate line* of frontier will be avoided. Some of these cases are detailed in a preceding page, (see page 91). This patrol would never be needed, except when the thieves belonged to small parties of banditti inhabiting fastnesses in the mountains, and under the controul of no chief. Where there exists a proper chief and council, the formal demand of the British agent backed by an appeal to the treaty, and a resolute determination to enforce the provisions now recommended to be appended to it, would be sufficient to secure redress. The reasons on which the recommendation of these alterations is founded, have been already stated in NOTE III; which is devoted to the consideration of Captain Stockenstrom's system of border policy. If these changes be made, the system will work *more* equitably for all parties, and if enforced by a vigorous and active executive, *may, for a time,* preserve the peace of the frontier. *No solid peace,—no stable security can be expected from any plan which contemplates merely the regulation of our external relationships with the Kaffers*. Comprehensive plans of a christianizing and civilizing tendency, adapted to work efficiently on the whole body of border Kaffers, can alone afford a sufficient security against the continuance of petty depredations, and the recurrence of lamentable inroads, similar to that which signalized the year 1835.

It is an error however to suppose that the prevention of theft depends *merely* upon the adoption of an efficient system of regulations with our Kaffer neighbours. More than half of the evil results from the want of a Colonial police, and can only be met by the establishment of a regular and efficient local constabulary force in each Field-Cornetcy; this subject will be discussed in the following NOTE.* In addition to this, every encouragement should be given for the re-occupation of the farms on the immediate line of frontier. A respectable farming establishment is as useful as a small military post, in reference to frontier defence,

* NOTE V, Vagrancy and its remedies, &c.

and the detection and prevention of theft. If the farms bordering on Kafferland were freed from all taxes on stock, and from the payment of quit-rent, and a small monied premium were allowed the occupier from each male above 18 years of age capable of bearing arms, residing upon the farm, and ready to act on being called out by a proper authority; there can be no doubt that all these farms would be occupied, and they would of themselves form a line of defence, which would much contribute to the security of the colony. Some have proposed the rendering of the present line of boundary *impassable by cattle*, (excepting on the usual lines of road which may be at all times easily guarded) by improving the *natural* obstacles afforded by the high banks of the Fish River, and by building a stone wall where the banks of the river afforded no such barrier. Much no doubt might be done by this means to throw such difficulties in the way of successful cattle lifting, as would quite indispose the most adventurous Kaffer from making the attempt. The expense of a stone wall nine feet in height may be estimated at the very highest at four shillings and six-pence, per yard square; each yard in length would be equal to three of measurement, and thus cost thirteen shillings and six-pence: one mile would be £1,188, and if 50 miles were found necessary, the sum of £60,000 would cover the expense. This sum might be borrowed by the Colonial Government in England, or perhaps in the colony, at four per cent. and a small additional tax, or the reduction of some useless expense, would pay the interest and a part of the principal every year. Provided the quarrying and carting of the stone were performed by convict labour, of which the prisons of the colony unfortunately furnish an ample supply; one half of the expense would be saved. If such a wall were built, there would be some justice in making the Chiefs bordering upon it, responsible for cattle brought into their country, since this would be impossible except by the connivance and assistance of their people in making the requisite breach; and in most cases cattle would be so quickly followed, that time would be wanting for so laborious a task. The saving recommended in the disbanding the Kaffer police, amounting to £1,500 per annum, would pay three-fifths of the interest of the money borrowed, and the immediate effect in raising the value of landed property would be felt by every proprietor in the colony.

The establishment of regular official communications, between the Colonial Government and the Tambookie and Amapondo Chiefs, Vadanna, and Faku; would tend to give the executive a commanding influence on the frontier. These distant chiefs are too far from our borders to feel any interest in plundering the frontier farmers. They have uniformly manifested a friendly disposition, which has been tested by trying and difficult circumstances. If the good offices of the Colonial Government were employed for the preservation of peace between these chiefs,* and a frequent communication were kept up in the interchange of messages, trifling useful presents, &c.; the effect would be most beneficial in convincing the border Kaffers of the ne-

* The present state of the Tambookie and Amapondo country loudly calls for some interference on the part of the Colonial Government. Between these two important tribes, both of which are our *tried* and *proved* friends, there exists at present a hostile feeling, which manifests itself in continued mutual petty aggressions, and occasionally breaks out into open war. The Wesleyan Missionaries at Clarkebury, Morley, and Buntingville, have at different times succeeded in preventing an open rupture; and had their influence been zealously backed by a *strong word* from the Colonial Government, much misery and bloodshed might have been saved. To the Rev. Samuel Palmer, of Morley, no small credit is due, for the manly intrepidity, patient courage and meekness of wisdom by which, in the midst of war, he has been enabled to preserve his flourishing and important station in peace. The Colonial executive appears to shrink from any more intercourse with the powerful native tribes than it can possibly avoid; this is a short-sighted policy. A Colonial influence on the Bashee and Zimvoobu is the most efficient method of keeping the clans on the Keiskamma in awe. Since writing the above; news has been received of the destruction of the Tambookies, and part of Rili's (late Hinza's) people by Faku and Capai. The immediate cause of this inroad was an attack made upon Capai a few months ago by the sons of Eno, and other Chiefs of the Gaika family. It is strange that the Colonial Government could not interfere to prevent an attack of this kind by petty chiefs on their frontier, which in its consequences must have been expected to prove injurious to the Tambookies *our friends and allies*, who have been repeatedly promised protection on account of their fidelity during the late war. Had the New Province been retained and the system of regular intercourse with Faku, &c., commenced by Colonel Smith been continued, the Colonial Government might have kept all the country as far as Natal in peace. (October 1838.) Such is the anxiety of Faku to stand well with the Colonial Government, that a *word* sent last June from General Napier would have saved the Tambookies, and prevented the misery of starving thousands.

cessity of remaining at peace with the colony, which had secured such powerful friends in their rear. By thus maintaining the balance of power in Europe, many aggressions are prevented, and there is no reason why a similar line of policy in South Africa should not be attended with equal success.

To conclude: any system recommended, or adopted for the management of the Eastern frontier will need, for the present, the support of a large military force. It is much to be regretted that such should be the case, and that the revenue of Britain should, after thirty years possession of the Cape colony, have to be applied to pay for the defence of its subjects against a few naked semi-barbarian hordes. Every acre in the Cape colony has already been paid for by the British Treasury, at a rate equal to ten fold its actual value.* Such are the fruits of Colonial mismanagement. Under a judicious system of colonization, the Eastern frontier need not have cost the mother country one farthing. It is now too late to amend the past; but surely experience will teach wisdom for the future. Let no time be lost in preparing the Cape colony for self-government.† Divide the colony

* In the Parliamentary papers of 1838 No. 361, there is an abstract of the Commissaries' accounts of the payments from the several military chests in the following colonies, from April 1st, 1836, to March 31st, 1837, amounting to £1,732,627. Of this sum so large an amount as £313,410. was spent on the Cape of Good Hope, and chiefly on the eastern frontier. At present the expenditure cannot be much less, neither is there any probability of its speedy reduction.

† A beginning was made in 1834, by the appointment of a Legislative and Executive Council for the Cape; the privileges and powers of the non-official members of the former were, however, seriously abridged in 1838, by orders from the Home Government, sent out with the present Governor, Sir George Napier. Municipal regulations have been recently granted, and Municipalities have been formed in the Cape, Graham's Town, and other villages. So far as I can judge, from what may be observed in Graham's Town, *they work well*. Young beginners in legislation for local objects may naturally be expected to blunder a little; but *there must be a beginning*, and to defer that beginning to half a century hence, would only postpone the evil without avoiding it. Apply this reasoning to the subject of a Representative Assembly; the local parliaments of the eastern and western province might not equal the British House of Commons, or the Roman senate, but they would understand their own *local affairs*, better than the most enlighted senators not possessed of such local knowledge. In such an assembly there would doubtless be exhibited much prejudice, ignorance, and party feeling, (from which indeed other and higher assemblies can boast no exemption) but

into two governments, with a representative assembly and legislative council for each; then, after a while, let the entire expense of the defence of the frontier be equally borne by each government, since both the Eastern and Western divisions are alike concerned in the integrity of the Eastern frontier. When colonies have to pay for the troops *required* for their defence, they will manage to do with a comparatively small number, and expedients will be devised not only for *efficient* but *unexpensive* security. The natural advantages of South Africa, and especially of the Eastern province, are so great, that provided security be afforded, capital finding profitable employment will rapidly flow in, and the increased wealth of the community arising from the full developement of the resources of the country will enable them to bear the charges attendant upon their civil government and their military defence. But this cannot be expected, unless the inhabitants have a voice in the management of their own concerns, and a check upon the expenditure of the money raised from their taxation. It is not my intention to do more than merely allude to this important topic. Indeed, no reference would have been made to it, but from my full conviction that the evils arising from the ignorance of the Home Government as to these local affairs, will never be removed, until by repeated discussions in a free

then there would also be a fair share of good sense and correct feeling; and the *discussions* on important matters of Colonial policy would do more towards placing the Home Government in possession of correct information, than all the hundreds of despatches annually received from Colonial Governors. The practicability of the thing is soon settled; there are towns and villages to send *burgesses*, and a slight sub-division of the districts would form counties, from which members, representing the farming interests, would be sent. A constituency is already provided in the persons liable to be called on to serve on juries. For a Legislative and Executive Council in the eastern province there would be the Lieutenant-Governor, the next in command, the Secretary to Government, the Agent-General for Kaffer affairs, (at present in obeyance), and the resident Judge, or head legal functionary, who, in case of the separation of the eastern province into a distinct government, would no doubt be appointed; and two or three experienced gentlemen of ability and character, might easily be pointed out as very well suited to act as non-official members. The appointment of a Representative Assembly would have no small influence in stimulating a taste for literature in the country districts; many would begin to read regularly the report of debates in which *their* members took part; in which *their* interests were freely discussed; and in which taxes were imposed which *they* must pay; and thus the newspaper would be the pioneer of literary taste.

and representative assembly, the sense of the respectable portion of the Colonists is brought to bear on questions vitally affecting their interests, and thus forced on the attention of the British public and Legislature. So long as the Cape public has no acknowledged organ by which it may communicate its views as a community to the Home Government, it must expect to be misunderstood, misrepresented, and misruled. And on the other hand the British Government and nation, in return for the privilege exclusively possessed by them of thinking, acting, and legislating for the Cape colony, must be prepared to expend about £300,000 per annum on a peace establishment, with an occasional charge of half a million or more for the expense of a Kaffer war.

NOTE V.

VAGRANCY AND ITS REMEDIES.

The Cape colony is supposed to contain 65,000 white inhabitants (Malays included), 35,000 emancipated apprentices, 18,000 free coloured people, and 32,000 Hottentots. The white inhabitants are the capitalists of the country, and with some few exceptions, the sole proprietors of the soil; the apprentices, free coloured people, and Hottentots, are generally speaking only acquainted with agricultural employments, except in the neighbourhood of the Cape, and on some large establishments where the apprentices (late slaves) are frequently trained to the exercise of mechanical trades. It is calculated that about 8 or 10,000 of the Hottentot and free coloured people are wandering over the country, having no *regular* employment, occasionally compelled by hunger, or induced by the desire of obtaining intoxicating liquor, to work for a few days, but chiefly living without any *visible* means of subsistence on waste lands, and in the neighbourhood of towns and villages. The flocks and herds of the farmers are the main support of this mass of idleness and vice. In a country so thinly peopled, and with such large farms; it is difficult at once to detect the loss of a cow or a few sheep, and yet more difficult to obtain evidence sufficient for legal conviction, even in cases otherwise morally certain. But even if the evidence be sufficient, the Magistrate may be so far removed, that the farmer finds it prudent to put up quietly with the loss, rather than throw away his time and money for a mere nominal punishment of the criminal. So lax is the practice of the Magistracy in reference to theft, that in cases where a thief has been clearly convicted of slaughtering a valuable Saxony ram worth £30, the punishment awarded has been imprisonment for 10 or 20 days, comfortable lodging and a plentiful supply of food at the public expense; after which the thief invigorated by rest, and furnished with favourable reminiscences of a prison life, is again let lose upon the industry of the country.

So many individuals consuming what they do not assist to produce, would be felt as a serious evil any where, but in a poor and thinly peopled country like South Africa, the burden is almost intolerable. Besides the pecuniary loss experienced by the farmer, his family is exposed to insult and alarm during his frequent necessary absence, from parties of wandering vagrants, demanding food from his unprotected household; his servants are tampered with and too frequently induced to connive at depredations on his property. The *industrious* portions of the *coloured* classes, are equally if not to a greater extent sufferers with the farmers. Should they accumulate a little property and obtain permission (as in such cases they readily do) to reside with their stock on a spare portion of an extensive farm, which the proprietor does not need for his own grazing, in this comfortable state they are immediately surrounded by crowds of needy friends, and relations, their property is quickly consumed, and they are reduced to beggary. By this means, the unrepressed vagrancy of the colony, prevents the rise of a respectable middle class of coloured people, for after repeated efforts, an industrious man, who has long struggled to raise himself and family in the scale of respectability, finds from the peculiarities of his social condition that this is impracticable, and he too often succumbs to his hard fate. I have met in the course of my limited experience with dozens of instances of natives industrious, ambitious of rising, and possessed of no ordinary shrewdness, of whose lamentable histories the above is an abstract. Europeans not being able to estimate the power and influence which the natural custom of sharing all things in common has over the Hottentot mind, are apt to judge harshly in such cases, and attribute to extravagance and thoughtlessness, the prodigality which has been the unavoidable result of the poor man's position in reference to the social habits of the community to which he belongs. The Hottentot has no select class of his countrymen to go to, when he has raised himself above a servile condition; there is as yet no nucleus of respectability to which he can cling, and where he would find usages and notions in full operation, tending to the conservation of property, and stimulating to its increase, by the necessary exertion requisite to support an improved style of living. Thus he naturally falls back upon the mass of his countrymen, and his degradation is the inevitable result. The Kaffers, Fingoes, and Bechuanas in the colony, are not so much exposed to the injurious effect of this national custom as the thoughtless Hottentot is; and the national trait of covetousness so visible in the former classes, comes in to the aid of civilization, and renders them more likely to form the small beginnings of a future respectable coloured population.

How to avoid this evil of vagrancy, is a question which would puzzle the wisest and most dispassionate. The difficulty is increased by its having become a party question. Some of the Colonists contend for the severest restrictive measures, others for measures less severe; while a few are of opinion that the evil will gradually disappear with the present or succeeding generation; that the present inconvenience must be patiently borne; and that it is better so to do, than to incur a serious taxation to meet the expenses requisite for the carrying into effect any plan of employment and support for vagrants, which would be rendered absolutely necessary by the enforcement of an act for the suppression of vagrancy. So far as the interests of the Colonists *alone* are concerned, perhaps the opinions of this party are correct; the evil will in a great measure cease in the following generation, but it will be from the awful decrease of the coloured population from starvation, intemperance, and disease. *To save them some decisive steps are requisite.* The great, and to me overpowering objection to any law on the subject is this; the enforcers of the law, those in all cases entrusted with its execution, would be of one class of the community, and would frequently be persons not well disposed to the other class, which the law principally affected; and the evil would be yet further increased, inasmuch as the class thus affected would be that which is distinguished by a colour, and physiognomy, associated with degradation, servitude, and disgrace. Under such circumstances, it is to be feared that no provisions or guards could prevent a vagrant act from being in many cases an engine of oppression, as it would be carried into effect principally by individuals who, from their hereditary prejudices, ought not to be entrusted with power over the liberties and rights of the coloured population. Were the laws of the country framed and administered on the principles of a pure despotism, by an irresponsible executive, which looked merely at present convenience, regardless of the future consequences of its measures on the character and habits of the community, the evil of vagrancy might soon be removed. But in legislating for *a free people*, we must not look merely to the removal of present and pressing evils, but also to the remote consequences of our measures, in their probable influence on the training and character of a community of free men, on whom in a few years the duty and privilege of self-government, and the working of free institutions, will devolve. Laws which tend *to force* the labour of the lower classes, and restrict their freedom of action within narrower bounds than those of other classes of the community, even if administered without any glaring abuse, tend to perpetuate the evils of the social system, which they were framed to remove, and are, therefore, as inexpedient as unjust.

Much, however, may be done towards remedying the evil of vagrancy, without in the least interfering with the liberties of the colored classes. The appointment of an additional number of magistrates, and the extension of the power and jurisdiction of the magistracy—the establishment of an efficient system of local police or constabulary force; and an improved prison discipline would leave little to be desired, so far as the protection of property is concerned.

1st.—*The appointment of an additional number of Magistrates, and the extension of the power and jurisdiction of the Magistracy.* Let the most respectable and intelligent farmers in each Field-Cornetcy, be appointed Justices of the Peace, for their respective vicinities. Two or three forming a quorum might be empowered to settle disputes between masters and servants,—enforce the performance of contracts, aud punish summarily petty depredations and other offences. By the extension of the power and jurisdiction of the courts of the regular salaried magistracy; the time, expense, and delay occasioned by the turning over so many unimportant cases to the Circuit Courts, would be avoided. Nine-tenths of the prisoners sent to the gaol are committed for petty thefts which ought to have been immediately punished by the local justices, by which means the colonial treasury would have saved the expense of supporting a number of prisoners; and the complete demoralization of the criminal, the natural consequence of a prison life would have been prevented. To prevent the abuse of the powers thus conferred on the local magistracy, all the proceedings and decisions of their courts, should be recorded and published in the Gazette, and also be regularly brought under the cognizance of the judges of the Supreme Court.

2nd.—*The establishment of an efficient system of local police or constabulary force.* No police worthy of the name exists in the colony, except in Cape Town. Why cannot the

Magistrates of each Field-Cornetcy, (supposing such to be appointed) be empowered to assemble the inhabitants at stated periods, and impose a rate for the support of such a police force as the necessities of the Field-Cornetcy might require? Why cannot the Field-Cornetcies be formed into parishes or municipalities, and make local arrangements for the protection of property, &c.? The system of centralization is now carried to such an extreme, *that the repairs of a town clock,* and the minutest items of local expenditure require to be gravely discussed in the Council chamber. Hence the Colonists are in the habit of looking in all cases to the Government, and are apt to expect from its measures, results which can only be anticipated from their own energetic exertions in their several local spheres. Farmers on a distant frontier are tempted to imagine that the *whole* attention of the Executive, ought to be specially directed to the protection of *their* property from vagrants and robbers, and that it is not too much to expect that half the revenue of the colony should be devoted to that *one* object. These unreasonable expectations are in a great measure the result of the state of complete dependence upon the central Executive, in which they have been trained for generations past. Let the policy of the Colonial Government be completely changed in this respect. Form the Field-Cornetcies into self-governed parishes or municipalities, charged with the duty and obligation of meeting as far as possible their local expenditure and local defence: the inhabitants would then understand the practical difficulties in the way of rendering an extensive and thinly peopled country as secure as England. On the other hand they would have all the protection they were willing to pay for; and by an economical expenditure of their resources, would obtain all their circumstances required. So far as a police is concerned, the expense would be trifling; coloured men placed under a European inspector, would be easily procured at a cheap rate, and if their diligence were stimulated by pecuniary rewards for the apprehension of offenders, foreigners without passes, &c., they would prove very efficient.

3rd.—*Improved prison discipline.* Prison discipline of any kind is almost unknown in the Cape colony; and yet the cost of the judicial establishment, the police, prison expenses and support of convicts, in other words *the direct charge on the colony on account of crime,* amounts to about £50,000 per annum, or one third of the gross revenue of the whole colony. The question will naturally be asked; Why cannot convict labour be made applicable to useful perposes, whether in public works or in private undertakings, in a country where labour is in demand, and is generally procurable at a dear rate? The answer is, those who pay the money for the support of convicts, &c., have no check upon its expenditure, and no share whatever in the management of their own concerns. Individual Governors, Magistrates, &c., may patriotically strive to introduce reform in this branch of the public service, but the evils to be remedied are so entwined with other abuses, the growth of years, that nothing short of an entire remodelling of the whole frame of the Government, will be likely to work a thorough cure. Such is the present state of the prisons that confinement is no punishment; the convict receives higher rations than the British soldier, he feeds on the best food, and his appetite is stimulated by an agreeable variety in his weekly bill of fare; his health is tenderly cared for, and he is generally kept in perfect idleness. There is certainly a show of employing a portion of them in the public works, but this is a mere shew; the work done is under no interested inspection, and one would think that the opportunity of allowing the criminals a comfortable airing, and a sight of their former friends and associates, were the main things aimed at in the regulations which profess to make their labour available for the public good.* This state of things ought not to be. Surely, prison discipline may be so managed that its subjects may leave the prison at the expiration of the

* I am informed that recently some improvement has taken place in this respect; and that in Graham's Town especially, the labour of the convict is under proper inspection, and is usefully directed in road making, &c.

allotted period; not worse than when they entered, and without any desire to experience its severe but salutary training again.

By such decisive steps, many of the evils arising out of vagrancy will be alleviated; but the destruction of vagrancy itself, and the removal of all its consequent inconveniences, must result from other measures of a very different character, which have for their object THE ELEVATION OF THE SOCIAL CIVIL AND MORAL CONDITION OF THE BLACK AND COLOURED POPULATION OF THE COLONY.

It cannot be denied that with the increased trade and wealth of the colony, the physical comforts of the industrious portion of the Aborigines have also increased; few of the Hottentot race are met with who are not clothed in some fashion or other with European garments. The Kaffers, Bechuanas, and Fingoes, in Graham's Town, who are in the weekly receipt of wages averaging those of respectable labourers in England, are generally distinguished by their superior style of dress, as well as by their industry and aversion to intoxicating liquors. But while there has been a manifest improvement in the condition of the *industrious* portion of the colored people since the promulgation of the 50th Ordinance; it must also be admitted that the immediate effects of that measure have been anything but beneficial to the majority of them. No one can compare the general *r*espectability and comfort of the Hottentots in a farmer's service, with the squalid poverty and wretchedness of the miserable beings, who since their emancipation from forced contract service may be found congregated in the villages of the colony; to these the change has proved injurious in every respect, Do we, therefore, object to the measure, or would we alter it? By no means. The fault of the 50th Ordinance, is its *imperfection* as a measure of justice to an injured people. That it removed some restraints under which the population laboured, that it established the claim to be considered as free citizens of the colony, and thus tacitly admitted the injustice to which for two centuries they had been subjected, we readily admit. This sort of justice cost the Colonial Government nothing beyond the trouble of compiling the document so pompously termed, "*the charter of Hottentot freedom.*" Like all half measures which aim at alleviating symptoms rather than effecting a thorough cure, it has failed to answer the sanguine expectations of benevolent men, and the reason of this failure is obvious. The Hottentots had only one-half of their wrongs redressed; they were restored to liberty and freedom of action, but they were not placed in the possession of land or other property, as some compensation for the whole colony and the numerous flocks taken from their ancestors. By the domination of the Colonial power, their primitive form of government had passed away, and their social system suited to their simple condition had disappeared with it. Under such circumstances it was the bounden duty of the Colonial Government to use every effort towards placing the Hottentot population in situations where the social edifice might, in part, be re-constructed, and where removed from the temptations of large towns, small communities would, by degrees under judicious superintendence have been fitted to undertake the responsibilities of free citizens. In a word, the state was morally bound to place itself *in loco parentis* to a people its subjects had plundered, and by long confinement in a state of pupilage, had, in part, unfitted for the exercise of self controul. From this neglect of duty all parties suffer to this day. The Hottentots are generally sinking deeper and deeper in the scale of being, in consequence of their exposure to the temptations and vices of a town life. The Colonist suffers from their incurable vagrant habits, at once the result and the cause of idleness and vice, And the Colonial Government has to pay a greater sum annually in prisons, and in police expenses, than would be necessary if properly applied to place every Hottentot in the country in the enjoyment of a location amply sufficient for the supply of his wants.

The existence of so much misery among the Hottentot population, assumes a serious aspect when viewed in connection with the increased mental cultivation of that injured race. For 40 years the Missionaries of the London Society have laboured assiduously among them. A large proportion of the Hottentots have been brought under religious teaching, and no small number have made considerable progress in the elementary branches of literature. With increased cultivation, there has naturally arisen a keen sense of the wrongs of their ancestors, and a deep feeling of the practical injustice under which they labour, owing to the influence of the social prejudices of the great mass of the white Colonial population. Under such circumstances it is impossible for men to be otherwise than discontented. Those who are under decidedly religious influence may restrain the expression of their feelings, but *they* nevertheless feel, and those who are under no decided influence of the kind, hesitate not to give vent occasionally to sentiments indicative of the strong feeling of dissatisfaction which pervades the whole community. We must not be surprised at this. It is the natural consequence of the intellectual advancement of a people once too degraded either to feel or understand their claims on the justice of the Government. And now that they begin to feel, we must not wonder that vague imaginings of anticipated good, and extravagant expectation as to present benefits, are the characteristics of their inexperienced speculations. They are not satisfied with their present position, *neither ought they to be*. Now is the time for a wise Government by a measure of *practical justice*, to give a beneficial direction to the new feeling which has been created. It should open a way of escape from the pressure of want, and furnish a field for the profitable exercise of industry, and thence would arise opportunities for the employment and gratification of individual talent and ambition. By this means, the evils to be anticipated from a wide spread and deep rooted feeling of dissatisfaction among the Hottentot population would be avoided. One common interest would be a bond of union among all classes of Colonial society. The coloured classes participating in the general prosperity of the colony, and sharing the enjoyment of local patronage, would feel themselves identified with the interests of the colony, and the stability and security of its political institutions. In the furtherance of this desirable end, the following plan is recommended to the consideration of a benevolent public and a provident executive.

1st.—Let the Colonial Government immediately take steps towards acquainting itself with the *actual* condition of the Hottentot population. By the assistance of the agents of the London Missionary Society, as well as through the medium of the Field-cornets and Civil Commissioner of the districts, information may be obtained of the exact number of the Hottentots, distinguishing their sex, married or single, infirm or able bodied, the extent of their property or stock, their character and previous habits, their necessities, &c. These statistical details would prove of considerable assistance in framing plans of a *practical* nature for their immediate relief and future progressive improvement.

2nd.—An estimate should be made of the capabilities of the Kat River Settlement, of the lands granted to Mission institutions, and of unoccupied lands in the possession of the Colonial Government; this estimate should be made by a *practical farmer*, who would be able to state how many Hottentot families might yet be located, and what assistance would be necessary towards enabling them to commence cultivating the ground, with a fair prospect of obtaining a subsistence.

3rd.—It would then be seen, what further land was requisite for the location of the Hottentot families yet unprovided for. Very probably the sum of £20,000 would purchase land of the best quality for cultivation and grazing, sufficient to locate the remaining Hottentot population, as well as provide a few cows or goats according to the nature of the land for grazing, agricultural implements, seed, oxen, &c., for the assistance of the poorer settlers. But if even £30,000 were necessary, this sum might be borrowed on the credit of the Colonial Government at four per cent interest; and a fund for the discharge of the same with the interest annually due, might be provided from savings in the police and gaol expenditure, as well as from the increased revenue which might be anticipated in a few years from the additional number of profitable producers and consumers thus added to the population of the colony. Or if necessary there can be no doubt but that the British Government would make a grant towards effecting so desirable an end, provided proof were afforded of the good faith of the Colonial Government and the practicability of the scheme itself.

4th.—The Hottentot locations should be situated on spots convenient for cultivation, and if possible where irrigation is practicable. Each location should comprise at least 50 families: in some cases 100 or 150 families might be located together. A native school-master attached to each location, and a Missionary appointed to conduct the religious services and superintend the schools in every two or three locations would be requisite. The London Missionary Society would readily appoint suitable persons, provided the Colonial Government would furnish the means of supporting them by an annual grant, which is as justly due to the religious claims of the Hottentots as to those of the Boors, Scotch, and English settlers.

5th.—For the due Government of these native settlements, advantage might be taken of the provisions of a recent ordinance, authorising the erection of municipalities when such is the desire of the inhabitants. Bye laws might be framed to guard against the injurious effects of canteens, idle and desolate vagrants, &c.

6th.—In order to carry those desirable measures into effect, a commission might be appointed, consisting of an officer appointed by the local Government, and two or three Missionaries well known to the Hottentots as their friends, and possessed of influence over them. Nothing can be effected without the hearty co-operation of the Missionaries, but *with this*, no obstacles are too difficult to be overcome.

7th.—In case land suitable is not procurable in this colony to supply the wants of the whole Hottentot population, it would be desirable to negotiate for the purchase of lands on the northern and north eastern frontier from the present claimants. From the Winterberg to the Orange River there are extensive wastes of uninhabited country, entirely unsuited to the habits of the Tambookie population but well calculated for the establishment of Hottentot settlements. A trifling extension of the boundary of the colony by purchase or treaty would be no disadvantage compared with the benefits resulting to the colony from such settlements placed there.*

8th.—Considering how much the prosperity and security of the Cape colony depends upon the social improvement of its coloured population, it might perhaps be desirable for an officer to be appointed for the special purpose of carrying into effect and watching the operations of such plans as may be adopted for the furtherance of this desirable object. Such an individual corresponding through the Colonial Government with the Home Government, could not fail of doing much good, provided he were competent for the discharge of his duties. Every new Governor, and almost every inferior authority commences his administratration with a *profession of zeal for the improvement of the aborigines*, and nothing is done. By the appointment of

* Should the Colonial Government decide upon the settlement of the vast unoccupied tracts of the interior, by emigrants going forth under the direction and controul of responsible officers, according to the plan proposed in Note VII, then the claims of the Hottentots and other civilized aborigines, would undoubtedly be considered as of *at least* equal importance with those of any other class of Colonial subjects. In this case money would be wanted not for the purchase of lands, but for stock, seed, agricultural implements, and temporary support.

an individual *with nothing else to attend to*, perhaps *something* may be at least *attempted*.

So far as the Hottentots are concerned, the duty of providing for *their* being placed in circumstances favourable to their progressive improvement plainly devolves in justice upon the Colonial Government. Nothing can be more clear than *their* claim to some recompense for the injustice of bye-gone ages. It is impossible to restore to them the *whole* of what they have lost, whether in land or other property; but it is hoped that the measures recommended, if carried into effect, would remove present misery, provide against further future degradation, and would tend to place the Hottentot not merely on a footing of *legal* equality, but would also afford him a fair chance of attaining to an actual *social* equality with the rest of the Colonial community.

There is another class of coloured people in the colony, who, though they have no claim on the *justice* of the Colonial Government, yet, as forming a most valuable class of its subjects, possess no small claim upon its *politic* consideration. These are a number of Kaffers, Bechuanas, Fingoes, emancipated prize slaves, &c., who by industry having acquired property in cattle and money, and by long residence in the colony have become aware of the value of the possession of legal rights and the security of property, consider themselves as Colonial subjects since they never intend to leave its territory. These require land on which to form small agricultural villages, and for this they would be able to pay on the usual terms. But there are difficulties in the accomplishment of this object: *first*, they are aliens, and an ordinance would be requisite to permit them to become proprietors of landed property: *secondly*, land is usually sold in large farms of from 3,000 to 6,000 acres, at prices varying from £300 to £1,000 and upwards; a farm of such an extent is far beyond the wants or the means of individuals of this class. A combination of the means of forty or fifty individuals is the only plan by which such a purchase could be made, and this union would require the friendly aid of an intelligent European towards rendering it effective. The Rev. W. Shaw, of Graham's Town, who is well acquainted with this class of the coloured people, is of opinion that there are in the neighbourhood of Graham's Town, in the district of Albany alone, two or three hundred individuals who might be immediately settled in small villages, they themselves *ultimately* paying every expense. An advance of money on legal interest for a few years would be all that was requisite from the Colonial or British Government, and this could be secured as a mortgage on the land purchased. The subject has been frequently discussed and carefully examined by Mr. Shaw and myself during the last 18 months; and a plan was arranged for bringing the subject in the shape of a formal proposal before the Colonial Government and the British public; the circumstances of the colony however in our opinion rendered some delay expedient: but it is to be hoped that something may speedily be attempted for this interesting class of coloured people. Considering that within a few months 35,000 slaves will be freed, it is highly desirable that the number of small independent proprietors should be increased, and thus a tangible object be presented to the ambition of the liberated slaves, a something within *their* reach, to which by the industry of a few years *they also* may attain.

It may be desirable briefly to enumerate the advantages resulting from the carrying into effect the plan here recommended of locating the Hottentot population, and a respecttable portion of the other coloured classes.

1st.—A numerous and increasingly powerful body of the people would be attached to the soil by the enjoyment of a property in it. These would have a *stake* in the colony, and would thus have an *interest* in its protection from foreign aggression, and in the execution of the laws framed for the protection of life and property. They would supply the want so much felt, of a class of small proprietors, producing articles of consumption neglected by the more extensive grazing farmers. Nothing gives a man such keen perceptions of the rights of property, as the possession of property by himself: and thus if 20 or 30,000 people could be placed on a right system in this happy position, there would be so many citizens eventually gained to the colony, in lieu of so many vagrants, &c., careless of its interests because deprived of a fair chance of sharing its prosperity.

2nd.—Native settlements of the kind proposed, would furnish a most valuable supply of labourers to the neighbouring farmers, because, consisting of a respectable class of men, the supply could be depended upon, as the cultivation of their own locations would not occupy all the time of the settlers, and they would gladly embrace the opportunity of earning a little ready money at intervals. Under the judicious management of sensible missionaries or lay agents, all the useful and necessary arts connected with rural life might be taught to the young, and afterwards practised to the manifest advantage of themselves and the neighbouring farmers.

3rd.—Facilities would be afforded for religious instruction as well as for secular branches of education. So long as the coloured population are almost wholly scattered on solitary farms, or demoralized in large towns in the neighbourhood of canteens, we cannot expect much improvement in the mass; but if placed in more favourable circumstances, removed from temptation, and religious instruction be used in humble dependence on the Divine blessing, we may reasonably expect no small measure of success, and that a religious and industrious peasantry will be raised up, the pride and the strength of the colony.

Two objections occur to me, as likely to be made to the plan proposed in the preceding pages.

1st.—It would tend to keep the coloured races a separate and distinct class. I would observe, that peculiarity of colour and degraded habits have made them so; and that poverty, vagrancy, &c., will keep them not only a separate, but also a degraded people. Ordinances and Acts of Parliament can only give a legal equality; an assimilation of habits, &c., can alone produce a social equality. It is only by raising the coloured people to the rank of free proprietors, and exhibiting them in the light of an industrious and respectable class, that the prejudices arising from associations of inferiority and slavery can be effaced. At present the coloured people cannot mix on equal terms with the white population, and for a good reason, they are not *socially* equal. When they become so, there will be few obstacles in the way of their gradual amalgamation.

2nd. The second objection is, that it would draw away too much labour from the usual occupations, and thus prove injurious to the prosperity of the colony, and especially of the farmers. If this could be proved, it would be an argument, not for refraining *to do justice*, but for carrying the plan into effect gradually, so as to allow time for the places of the labourers to be filled up, as they are drawn away to the new settlements. But I am persuaded there is labour more than sufficient to supply the demands of the Colonial farmers, even if the whole of the Hottentot population, and the more respectable of the other coloured classes were settled as proposed. It is not the want of labourers which we have any cause to fear, *but the indisposition to labour arising from the absence of adequate motives to impel the labourer to regular exertions*. If settlements were in existence, where the coloured men might enjoy the accumulated savings of labour in the society of friends and equals, this would stimulate the coloured people to seek labour with avidity; especially if at the same time an active magistracy and an efficient police, checked the tendency of the idle and dissolute to fall back upon a vagrant and dishonest mode of existence.

Other objections may be started to the plan proposed,

and perhaps in bringing it into practical operation many of its details might require some modification ; but the safety of the colony absolutely requires the adoption of the great principle of "JUSTICE TO OTHERS, MERCY TO OURSELVES," here advocated. The colony cannot afford to allow the execution of such a plan to be impeded by trifling obstacles. *The next generation will see either a happy, contented, coloured, rural population, or a servile war.*

There are many who feel a strong repugnance to the interference of a Missionary in *secular* arrangements, even for the benefit of the distressed remnants of once powerful and populous tribes, reduced by our national injustice to poverty and degradation. Carry (say they) the Gospel to these outcasts, and this of itself will produce every desirable result. The application of this principle in other cases is acknowledged to be absurd. An efficient ministry by no means supersedes the necessity of *sound* legislation. No one is less disposed than myself to underrate the value of a preached Gospel, apart from the influence of which no legal mechanism, however skilfully constructed, can work well. Christianity is a great moving power; the social machine in South Africa especially is so clogged and impaired, that it is difficult to bring the *power* to work upon it. The vicious and unhealthy state of the civil and social condition of the bulk of the population, tends to neutralize almost all the good effected through the instrumentality of moral means and religious influence. In spite of every obstacle the Gospel partially prospers, and among other beneficial results, it has done, and is yet doing, much towards opening the eyes of no small number of intelligent Colonists, to perceive the radically unsound condition of Colonial society as at present constituted, and hence many of them feel willing to make any reasonable sacrifice towards applying an immediate remedy. While we rejoice to recognize in the christian ministry a *divine* institution for the spiritual benefit of the family of man, we would not forget that the "*powers that be*" are also of *divine* appointment for a specific purpose, that they may be "*a terror to evil doers, and a praise to them that do well.*" Hence as christians we may look to a wise legislation on christian principles, in connexion with the direct preaching of the Gospel, as so many means by which *the All-wise God* dispenses his blessings upon mankind. And "What God hath joined together, let no man put asunder."

A brief notice of an abortive attempt of the Colonial Government to form a few settlements of Hottentots along the eastern frontier, together with the failure of the *forced* location of a part of the Fingo tribes in the Zitsikamma, naturally claim a place in the consideration of this subject.

In the year 1837, Captain Stockenstrom (the Lieutenant-Governor) established about six parties of Hottentots along the Fish River, as appendages to the nearest military posts, and professedly under the inspection of the commanding officers. Rations were allowed, and supplies of arms and ammunition granted them, that they might be ready to act as a militia if needed. Meanwhile Captain S., and other benevolent individuals furnished them with *goats* and a few other necessaries, and sanguine anticipations were entertained of the success of this experiment. An appeal to the benevolence of the British public was made through the medium of the London Missionary Society, and in the pages of several religious periodicals. Judicious individuals acquainted with the unsuitable localities chosen for the site of these settlements, and aware of the neglect in the selection of suitable persons to take the lead, and exercise some controul over the others, as well as of the almost total want of the capital requisite for the purchase of stock and agricultural implements, anticipated the complete failure of the scheme. In fact it met with no countenance even from some of the most ardent friends of the Hottentot race, as the precipitancy with which the measure was hurried into execution, and other suspicious circumstances led to a pretty general conviction that the object of the undertaking was not so much the benefit of the aborigines, as the influence it would have upon public opinion at home. Let not the public at home be deceived. It is not by settling heterogenous masses of Hottentots on waste lands, (chiefly such as no European farmer has ever thought worthy of acceptance) and then leaving them to cultivate without either stock or farming implements; that the debt of the colony can be paid. Of some of their locations I can speak from personal acquaintance, as well as from information received from judicious individuals, in the habit of visiting them frequently.

At KAFFER's DRIFT, OLD POST, there is about 4,000 acres of land, some of it tolerably fair both for cultivation and grazing. In June 1837, a party of Hottentots were settled here; 100 goats were given to them, which all disappeared in about six months, owing to the *brandt sickte,* a disease which immediately seizes such animals when placed on sour grass farms. The party are allowed rations of one pound of meat, and one pound of bread each man, and an additional half-pound of meat for such as have wives. Rations are regularly drawn for 26 men and 20 women. Very few of the men are to be found on their locations, and when enquired for, the usual answer is they are hunting, &c. Some time ago two of this party were detected in a theft, 100 miles from their location. In fact they are compelled to wander about the country to seek for subsistence, as their rations are barely sufficient for the women and children. The whole of the land under cultivation does not exceed an acre and a half, which would not produce one week's consumption for the party. This is one of the best sites of any on the Fish River for a native location, and an industrious party, placed under an intelligent superintendent and furnished with a few cows, and working oxen, ploughs, seed, &c., might succeed in ordinary seasons.

Near FRAZER's CAMP, two parties were stationed. One under Tonjes Perciner has now five men, with women and children left. These have made small gardens, but having no plough or seed, cannot cultivate extensively so as to secure a livelihood. The other party, under Piet Louw, has two men with women and children yet remaining; their location is less favourable for cultivation, and is in just the same situation as the other, and from the same causes. That attempts so ill arranged, and not followed up by a judicious superintendence should fail, is not to be wondered at, and is no argument against the success of plans of *practical* not *party* benevolence.

The history of the forced settlement of a portion of the Fingoes on the Zitzikamma, is another specimen of the mismanagement of the Colonial executive, for which however less excuse can be made.

It was deemed expedient, on the cession of the neutral territory to the Kaffers, to remove such of the Fingoes as had been settled near the Chumie and Block Drift. Pato and Kama, the Chiefs of the Gonokwabie tribe, were quite ready to receive them, and grant them lands on the sea coast, where their industrious habits would have ensured a subsistence; and the Wesleyan Missionaries would have been able to protect them, through their influence over Pato's people. The Colonial Government were aware of the willingness of the Chiefs of the Gonokwabie tribe to accede to any arrangement for the security of the Fingoes, and the presence of a Missionary on the spot afforded the means (which the Colonial Government *professes* to value) of communicating religious instruction. A Missionary deservedly popular with the Fingoes (Rev. J. Ayliff), and peculiarly calculated to secure an influence among them, was accordingly appointed to Wesleyville, near which the Fingoes were to have been located, in accordance with an almost positive promise on the part of Captain Stockenstrom. When however the removal took place, it was not to Wesleyville, a place suited to the previous habits of the Fingoes, but to the Zitzikamma, *a tract of country which the experience of a century had proved to be utterly worthless* for such a purpose. Here the Fingoes were unwillingly located, their cattle, goats, &c., soon died, and cultivation did not succeed. When General Napier, the newly appointed Governor, arrived on the frontier in April 1838, under the influence of incorrect information, he expressed his opinion of the entire suitability of the locations, and his determination to support them. In October, however, experience having convinced him of the necessity of removing the Fingoes from so unsuitable a locality, directions were sent for them to settle near Fort Peddie, where the great bulk of the Fingo races are already placed, and where, under the protection of the Fort, and of the Resident Agent, they may live in peace and prosper.* From these specimens of the mistakes committed by the Colonial authorities, it is to be hoped that in the event of any grant of public money being made for the specific purpose of purchasing lands for the aborigines, that a careful check will be exercised upon its appropriation, and that no waste useless lands, the property of the Colonial Government, or of favoured individuals, be palmed upon the Commissioners, as suitable for the location of Hottentots or other coloured people.

* It is but justice to Captain Stockenstrom to state, that his reason for desiring to remove the Fingoes to the Zitzikamma, was understood to be, his wish to remove them to a considerable distance from the border, the Zitzikamma being at least two hundred miles within the Colonial boundary. He appears to have thought that troubles must arise from the Fingoes being settled in the immediate vicinity of the Kaffers. But the greater part of these people were already permanently settled by a treaty of his own, in a district around Fort Peddie, adjoining the Kaffer territory, and they cannot be removed without their own consent; besides, in a good state of things there surely could be no difficulty in the Colonial Government securing protection for the remaining clans of Fingoes, when they were offered lands, as a free and independent people, within the territory of a friendly border tribe; the Fingoes and the tribe offering them an asylum, being the natural allies of the colony.

NOTE VI.

EMIGRATION OF LARGE PARTIES OF COLONISTS BEYOND THE COLONIAL BOUNDARY.

For some years past there have been *occasional temporary emigrations* of parties of the Colonial farmers beyond the northern boundary, in consequence of long droughts which have compelled them to emigrate in search of water and pasturage for their flocks.* But no general movement of a large portion of the Colonial population with the avowed purpose of abandoning the colony, ever took place previous to the year 1836. Within the last two years, about 5,000 Colonists, (women and children included) chiefly Dutch have left the colony, and are now residing beyond the Orange river in a north-easterly direction, as far as Port Natal.

The motives which induced this emigration, and the feeling entertained by the emigrants towards the colony, may be gathered from the following letter of Mr. Peter Retief one of their leaders, addressed to the Governor of the Cape.

* In 1834 it is stated that 1,500 Colonists, including women and children, servants, &c., were during a part of the year grazing in the Griqua conntry, others in the direction of the banks of the Kei.

"The Undersigned, Conductor and Chief of the United Encampments, hereby

"HUMBLY SHEWETH,—

"That as subjects of the British Government, we, in our depressed circumstances, repeatedly represented *our grievances* to His Majesty's Government; but in consequence of finding all our efforts to obtain redress fruitless, we at length resolved to abandon the land of our birth, to avoid making ourselves guilty of any act which might be construed into strife against our own Government.*

* The following remarks by the editor of the *Graham's Town Journal*, (9th August 1838) bearing on the subject of emigration from the colony, may be considered as a fair specimen of the opinions of the most reasonable and dispassionate Colonists. If the language be deemed *strong*, there is unfortunately too much reason for employing it:—

"This emigration is one of the most extraordinary proceedings of the present day; but strange and extravagant as it is, it was foreseen, and the Government distinctly warned of it long before it took place. Ignorance, therefore, on the part of the authorities, cannot be pleaded, seeing that this caution stands recorded in a public despatch from the Governor of the colony to the Colonial Minister. And what, we may ask, would have been the consequence, had this migration not have taken place? Why, in all probability, a similar scene would have been presented here to that which has been witnessed in the Canadas. *The whole country might, and it is very probable would, have been torn to pieces by intestine commotions; and the British Government, instead of having merely to defend the frontier against the incursions of the Kaffers, might have been necessitated to send hither an expensive armament to put down rebellion, as well as a costly commission to pacify opposing interests, and to bring the country again into a state of quietude.* The outlet to the north and east has been a safety-valve to the colony, and there is every reason to believe has actually saved the Government a large expenditure of public money.

"We have watched this emigration carefully from the first, and have been at some pains to bring under the notice of the public its whole course and progress. Whilst, however, *we have viewed the measure as one marked by extravagance, and as fraught with certain suffering and disaster to those engaged in it*, we could not, in conscience, declare that the inhabitants, and more especially the frontier farmers, were without any just cause of complaint. *Their grievances have been made known to the Government,—a deaf ear has been turned thereto; and the Colonial Minister, instead of adopting that line of policy which would have restored confidence, and have smoothed down that asperity of feeling, the natural consequence of again seeing the country laid desolate by an irruption of savages,*—all the ordinary pursuits of industry suspended,—the husbandman called to quit his home, and to take the field against the common enemy, leaving his family in numerous instances dependant on charity for first necessaries,—*has taken exactly that course which has tended most effectually to cause exasperation*, and which has led so many hundreds of valuable hands to plunge, with the recklessness of despair, into the trackless wilderness, and to place themselves beyond the pale of civilization.

"It would be monstrous to suppose, that the Minister of the Crown *intended* to produce this result, or had any idea of the bearing of these measures which he had resolved to adopt. *We firmly believe that in the choice of a Lieutenant-Governor to administer this province, as well as in the policy pursued towards the neighbouring tribes, it was conscientiously thought that the*

"That this abandonment of our country has occasioned us incalculable losses,—but that, notwithstanding all this, we cherish no animosity towards the English nation.

"That in accordance with this feeling, commerce between us and the British merchants will, on our part, be freely entered into and encouraged; with the understanding, however, that we are acknowledged as a free and independent people.

"That we have understood with deep regret that nearly all the aborigines and tribes by whom we are at present surrounded, have been *instigated* to attack us; but that although we find ourselves in a position to confront and defy all our enemies, we nevertheless humbly request your Excellency, as far as it may be in your power, to use your authority and influence to repress such hostilities, in order that we may not be compelled to shed the blood of our fellow creatures, as has recently been the case in consequence of the attack of Masselikatse upon us.

"That we trust soon to convince the world, by our conduct and deeds, that it is not, and never was, our intention unlawfully to molest any of the native tribes; but that we, on the contrary, set the highest value on universal peace and good will among men.

"That, finally, we confidently hope that the British Government will permit us to receive all such claims and demands as may be lawfully due to us in the colony.

"I have the honour to be, Your Excellency's
obt. humble Servt.,
"(Signed,) P. RETIEF.
"Sand River, July 21, 1837."

The grievances alluded to were the annoyances to which they were exposed in the colony from vagrancy, the want of due protection from the Kaffers, owing to the injurious

most unexceptionable measures were taken to secure the public interests, and to gain the public approval. Whether this has, or has not, been the result, the official returns, after two years' experience of the plunder of the colony by the Kaffers, testify in language which it is impossible to misunderstand or gainsay. The Government have been deceived—most palpably and egregiously deceived—and the consequences are the present state of public feeling, and the misfortunes, and suffering, and absolute destruction of so many of our fellow colonists.

operation of Captain Stockenstrom's treaties, and the loss sustained by them in the emancipation of their slaves. One third of the appraised value was all that was awarded as compensation by the British Government, and this instead of being paid in money on the spot, was paid in London, and thus the Colonial farmers, principally Boors, unacquainted with the details of business, were compelled to employ mercantile agents to receive their awards, for which they had to pay at the rate of 12 or 16 and in some cases 20 per cent in commission, charges, &c.

In projecting this emigration, the parties concerned entertained no doubts of the legality of their proceedings; and this view of the case was supported by the public press and by the express declaration of the Lieutenant-Governor.*

. * In the report of the Aborigines Protection Society, May 1838, surprise is expressed that no steps were taken by the Colonial Government to repress the emigration.
"The intentions of the emigrant Boors to abandon the colony, and the spirit by which they were actuated, having been so long known to the Government at the Cape, it has been thought by the committee somewhat anomalous, that no decisive local measures appear to have been adopted with the view of checking them in the first instance, and especially after receiving intelligence of some of the evils inflicted on their border tribes by these intruders. Nor can it be passed over without serious animadversion, that, in not a few cases, these emigrants it is feared, have taken with them, under whatever pretence, many of the apprentices, to be still retained in slavery—even of those for whom they had received their share of the twenty millions sterling compensation money."
It was the opinion of a high legal authority that the emigration might have been checked by a simple proclamation, prohibiting the exportation of live stock, cattle, sheep, &c., the *food of the country*, without a special permission from the authorities. A few apprentices have left the country with their masters, and the *council* of the emigrants has decreed that they shall receive their full freedom at the specified period. In justice to the Boors, the following extract from Instructions to Commandants ought to be generally known as indicating some regard for native rights.
"9. The Commandant and his Field-cornets will take the utmost possible care that no servants, of whatever colour or class, are ill-used ; as he will be bound immediately to report the guilty parties, without any distinction, in order that they may be punished according to the laws provided under this head.
"10. The Commandant will also take particular care that no person possesses himself by violence of the children of Bosjesman or other aboriginal tribes, that he does not entrap them in an unlawful manner, nor take them away from their parents or relatives, nor keep them in his possession, Any person offending, to pay a fine of not more than one Hundred Rix dollars, and not less than Fifty Rixdollars ;—neither will it be permitted for any person unlawfully to molest any tribe or people that may be met with on the journey."
With some of the principal Boors concerned in this emigration, I am per-

In the *Commercial Advertiser* of the 10th September 1836, the following observations are found. "Emigration in itself is no crime. It should not be committed in secrecy, as if it were a crime. If properly conducted the emigrants will carry with them the sympathy of all their fellow subjects, and be assured of the good offices of the British Government on their behalf, whenever they could be perfectly exerted." Captain Stockenstrom (the Lieutenant-Governor) in his reply to an address from Uitenhage (printed in the above paper of the 14th September 1836) observes, "It is but candid at once to state, that I am not aware of any law which prevents any of His Majesty's subjects from leaving his dominions, and settling in another country, and such a law, if it did exist, would be tyrannical and oppressive; nor could we wish to prevent our brethren from bettering their condition."

It was the intention of the emigrants to proceed far into the interior, with a view of settling in the neighbourhood of Delagoa Bay, but at some distance from the coast where a considerable extent of fertile country previously explored by one Louis Treckard was known to be vacant. Aware of the vast extent of unoccupied and unclaimed country to the north-east of the Orange river, in the direction of Delagoa Bay and Port Natal, they never anticipated any hostile collision with the native tribes, and in their circumstances, hampered as they were with wagons, large flocks of cattle and sheep, helpless women and children, the contemplation of any aggressive measures would have been the height of madness. Entering into friendly relationships with the Chiefs of the Bastards, Bechuanas, Abasutu, and Mantatees, they passed along the Caledon river towards its source, unmolested by the native tribes in whose country they were

sonally acquainted, and know them to be truly pious and humane men. Much as I in common with others, regret the step they have taken, we should regret if the abuse heaped upon them (by certain party writers, who pander to popular ignorance and prejudice, both in the Cape and in Britain) should in its irritating tendency, tempt them to forget to exercise the forbearance and humanity, expected from their known character.

travelling. The Zulu Chief Matzilikatzi, who had recently destroyed a large portion of the Bechuana tribes formerly residing near Kurrichane, incited by the hope of plunder, sent out a marauding party, which falling by stealth upon a small party of Boors encamped at least 300 miles from Matzilikatzi's territory, destroyed the women and children, killed the few men left on guard, carried off the cattle and sheep, and burnt the wagons. This unprovoked attack brought on that Chief a signal and deserved punnishment, to the great joy of the oppressed relics of the Bechuana tribes.* As the emigrants drew near the pass in the Qua-

* The following incorrect statement appears in the report of the Aborigines Protection Society, May 1838.

"The case of the destruction of the tribe of Zoolas, under the government of Moselakatzi, by the emigrant Boers, has awakened a deep interest in the minds of the Committee. A comprehensive view of the case has been communicated to the society in the shape of an extract from a journal drawn up by Captain Harris, of the Honourable East India Company's service, and sent from the Cape of Good Hope to this country, to Dr. Hodgkin, by that eminent friend of humanity and distinguished ornament of science, Sir John Herschel. From this document it appears that the number of emigrants amounted to 5,000 or 6,000 souls, including 1,600 men capable of carrying arms; that on their way towards Port Natal, they had entered the territory of the warlike and jealous Chieftain, Matzilikatzi, in a way that led to hostilities, and the infliction of much misery and suffering on both parties.

"Later accounts convey the intelligence that sanguinary conflicts had continued, that the tribe of Aborigines under Matzilikatzi, had been entirely defeated and routed, and the Chieftain himself compelled to seek safety in an ignominious retreat, with a few followers, to a ravine in some distant mountain. The American Mission commenced among this tribe, under very favourable and promising circumstances, has been of course annihilated by the retirement of the Mission families from a spot where no longer any natives remained to receive their instruction.

"In the case of Matzilikatzi, it is important to keep in view that although he commenced the attack on the emigrants, they had most unjustifiably placed themselves in the position of enemies, making an inroad on his territories. Since they had not merely entered his country without his permission, but by a route which he had utterly prohibited, under the known determination to consider all as invaders and enemies, who entered his country by that route. In order to secure himself against hostile and sudden invasion from that quarter, he employed armed parties of his soldiers or police to examine and scour this part of the country. A body of these armed subjects of Matzilikatzi fell in with a party of the emigrants, whom they, of course, attacked, and over whom, by superiority of numbers, they easily obtained a victory. This created on the part of the emigrants, a thirst for revenge. A cry for war was raised—blood was demanded—the friends of the conquered party, reinforced by others from the colony, flew to arms—attacked the principal camp of the Chieftain Matzilikatzi, and nearly destroyed the whole, leaving a fearful demonstration of their reckless disregard of all native rights, and their resolution, as civilized men, not to yield the palm for ferocity and revenge to uncivilized tribes or pagan warriors."

Here it may be observed 1st, that the Boors never entered the territory

thlamba mountains (or Drackenberg range) which separate the country of the Zulu Chief Dingaan from the Bechuana country, it was determined that a small party under Mr. P. Retief, should visit that Chief to treat with him for the purchase of the unoccupied country extending from the Tugela to the Umzimkulu river. The following account of subsequent events is from the pen of Mr. Boshoff, who visited the emigrants in May, June, 1838.

" Retief, deceived by the crafty Dingaan, placed such implicit confidence in his friendship, that we doubted not, and soon persuaded his whole party, that Providence had opened a door for them, and that they would be able to live contented and safe in the immediate neighbourhood of Dingaan's people. Accordingly, in January last, they decended the Draakberg, excepting Uys, who, not content with the form of government established by Retief and Maritz, and having had some personal disputes with the latter, he and his party kept back on this side the " Drackenberg."*

" As soon as Retief had executed his commission by compelling the Mantatee chief Sikonyella to restore the property of which he had plundered Dingaan, according to agreement with him, he resolved upon a second visit to Dingaan, intending to take with him a party of 200 men, supposing that by the warlike appearance of such a body of mounted men, the Zoola chief would stand in some awe of them, and that he would then have such respect for them, as at

claimed by Matzilikatzi, and if they had, their right would have been just as good as his, he having only *recently* taken possession of the country he occupies by first plundering and murdering the timid Bechuanas. 2nd. The American Missionaries never had any prospect of usefulness while residing in Matzilikatzi's country; during the three months they were there, no natives were allowed to attend their religious services. 3rd. If the Boors had succeeded in completely destroying the power of Matzilikatzi, they would by so doing have conferred a great benefit upon the cause of humanity; and the poor Bechuanas, whom his tyranny had reduced to the lowest degradation and misery, have as great a claim on the sympathy of the British public as a mere horde of robbers and brigands. If this statement be a specimen of the general accuracy of the *facts* presented to the public by this society (which under impartial management might be productive of good) I anticipate but little advantage from its efforts. The American Missionaries present on the spot fully vindicate the Boors from any blame in this unfortunate transaction. The conduct of the Chief Matzilikatzi called by the Kaffers Umzillikazi, was the less excusable, since he had actually entered into a treaty with the colony, through the medium of Dr. Andrew Smith in 1834.—*(See the last volume of Parliamentary Papers.)*

* Retief, Maritz, and Uys, were the principal leaders of the Boors. Landtman, Rudolf, and Potgieter, also possessed considerable influence.

least to consider it his own interest to keep the treaties which he had in part made, and which Retief was then going up purposely to ratify. On the other hand he thought Dingaan would look upon it as a great honor to himself, he being passionately fond of dances and warlike exhibitions and exercises. Maritz, however, and some others who could not forget the conduct of Umselikatsi, were inclined if not to doubt Dingaan's friendly intentions, at least to give him no opportuntiy of executing any sinister design ; and they therefore, told Retief candidly that they disapproved of his intention, and that they feared the Zoola tyrant would not let slip an opportunity of striking a blow, when he found them too confident of safety, trusting themselves in his hands in his own kraal, and amidst the Zoola nation. Mr. Maritz even went so far as to offer to go himself, attended only by two or three men, observing that 'if they were destroyed it would be quite enough.' By this time they had received some vague and varying reports that Dingaan had greatly altered with respect to the Emigrants after Retief had left him on his first visit. Most unfortunately, however, Retief was not to be shaken in his confidence in Dingaan's friendship and goodwill ; but as so many objections were made and apprehensions entertained, he declined issuing an order for any one to accompany him, but left it to such as might volunteer for the purpose. In the beginning of February 1838, he left the encampments of the Emigrants—who were already beginning to separate into small parties about the Blaauw Krans and Bushman rivers—his partly consisting of 70 persons, 30 servants and 200 horses. Notwithstanding the warnings and cautions Retief and his party received, Dingaan so well knew how to deceive them, and to gain their confidence so completely; that he inveigled them within an enclosure before his house, unarmed too, just as they were up-saddling to depart, and massacred in cold blood every living soul of them, not allowing one to escape to tell the horrid tale ! *

" As the time fixed by Retief for his return had elapsed, and rumours were spread about that a Zoola—talking across the river at one of the encampments to another then in the service of the farmers, had said that all the white men were dead ; as also that a large party of the Zoolas had been seen together on the other side

* For particulars of this event, see the journal of Rev. F. Owen (then residing at Dingaan's kraal) in the following pages.

of the Tugala, a small patrol was at length sent out over the Tugala into Dingaan's territory, pretending to be hunting buffaloes; and as they actually took their course towards the spot where Dingaan's army was then encamped behind a hill, and had approached to within a few hundred yards, an old Zoola met them and enquired what they were looking for, and upon being told that they were hunting, he pointed in a different direction, where he said there were many buffaloes. But as they still persisted in going on, the Zoola went before them, and strenuously insisted upon their taking the direction pointed out by him. Here, again, they were unfortunate enough, with a view to avoid suspicion, actually to suffer themselves to be turned about. On their return a report was made, of course, that they had discovered nothing, and the people were once more persuaded that there was no cause for apprehending any danger,—nay more, those who still inclined the other way were laughed at and accused of cowardice. Early in the morning of the second day after the return of the patrol—on a Saturday morning—the hour was come when all should be undeceived. The Zoolas, who by their spies had mixed frequently with the farmers, and who knew their position so well that they could execute their bloody purpose to their utmost desire, began to attack both the encampments, situated at the Blaauw Krans River and Bushman's River, about ten miles asunder, at the same moment. The attack having been begun a little before day-light, many of the farmers at the out-posts were butchered before they awoke; and others only just opened their eyes to close them again for ever! As day began to dawn, the Zoolas were perceived at some of the scattered wagons,—they had surrounded them, and the cries of women and children were heard mingled with the report of the few shots that were fired now and then; but the word "mercy" was unknown to these miscreants. *Not even satisfied with stabbing their welted broad spears into the bosoms of unresisting women, or piercing the bodies of the infants who clung to them, they cut off the breasts of some of the women, and took several of the poor little helpless babes by the heels, and dashed their brains out against the iron bands of the wagon wheels.* So perfectly taken by suprise was the encampment that not a few of the parties in the vicinity; upon hearing the few shots fired, were congratulating themselves on the circumstance, thinking that Retief and his party had at last returned, and were firing a salute. No preparation for defence was made until daylight enabled them to see the approach of the ferocious enemy. Then every one flew to arms, and a resolute resistance was made. Parties of three and four, in their night clothes, were seen to defend themselves with success against whole Zoola regiments,—the women assisting in carrying about ammunition for the men, and encouraging them. A little son of Mr. Maritz, about 10 years old, was repeatedly told by his mother to go and hide himself, but he as often replied " I see no place where to hide myself, give me the pistol and let me shoot too." Small parties of three, four, and five, were now coming in from all directions; and at the Bushman's River the savages having at last been repulsed by less than 50 men, they fled precipitately through the river, which was rather swollen, and being fired upon as they crossed the river up to to their breasts and chin in water, hand-in-hand to support each other, many were drowned and shot.

" At the Blaauw Krans they were also repulsed, but the farmers after pursuing them a short distance, had to return to their wagons, which they brought together to form a close camp, and then to search for and attend to the wounded, which fully occupied them that day. On the following day Mr. Maritz, at the head of about 50 men, resumed the pursuit of the enemy, but as they had been left unmolested for the greater part of the previous day, they succeeded in carrying off to a safe distance over the Tugala the greater part of the cattle, between 20 and 25,000 head, as also some sheep, and the goods plundered at the wagons. Maritz only recovered what was still on their side of the river; and wherever his little band appeared the enemy fled without offering any resistance. At the river they found a large body of Zoolas endeavouring to drive cattle and sheep across the stream, but upon being attacked they rushed into the water, and here again several were shot and many more drowned. It was now about dusk, the river greatly swollen, and the few fordable places dangerous in the extreme. Maritz and his party therefore, with tears flowing over their cheeks, were compelled to leave their property in the hands of the enemy, and to return to their wagons. This day search had again been made for the maimed and wounded, and several found, but of these very few indeed were in such a state as to afford any hope of their recovery. To hear of the number of wounds inflicted upon some who have recovered, is incredible; one child who had received 30, and a woman 22 assegaai-wounds, are still living, though injured for life. It is believed that about 500 Zoolas fell on this occasion, besides the wounded and those that were drowned. At one place about eight or ten families, the Rensburg's and Pretorius's, were driven from their wagons to the top of an adjoining hill, which was only accessible from two sides. Fourteen men here stood in their defence against a whole Zoola regiment, the number of which encreased to about 1,500. Repeated assaults were made for about an hour, but the gallant little party as repeatedly drove them back until at last their ammunition failed, and no hope was left. But providentially at this critical moment two mounted men came to their assistance, and made their way to the top of this hill through the line of the Zoolas, and upon learning there that the ammunition of the party was almost expended, they undertook at the most imminent peril of their lives, to force their way back to the wagons, from whence they safely returned at full speed with an ample supply. All this was done in less than five minutes, and as the firing now began with greater vigour than before, the Zoolas retreated, and as a few more burghers arrived, they were soon put to flight, leaving on that spot about 80 killed." [On reckoning the number killed by the Zoolas at Blaauw Kranz, it appeared that 40 men, 56 women, and 185 children had been murdered, also 250 of their native servants. In a subsequent attack, Piet Uys and ten men were killed by the Zoolas.]

"The emigrants are now (June 1838) encamped at the Tugala and Bushman's rivers, by parties of from 50 to a 100 wagons, and have commenced ploughing at the latter, and other places. They must frequently, from necessity, expose themselves to great danger; and it is feared, that if the enemy should take advantage of their situation, and they should be off their guard, fresh disasters may yet befall them. There are altogether about 1,000 wagons, 640 men, about 3,200 women and children, and say 1,260 blacks. It is also calculated that they have still about 300,000 sheep, 40,080 head of cattle, and 3,000 horses, including mares and colts, consequently, with the exception of those who have been plundered by Matzilikatzi and Dingaan, and such as had gone thither wretchedly poor after having sustained severe losses by the late Kaffer invasion, still there are many in tolerably good circumstances; but the necessities of the poor already begin to press heavily, and there is not one who has the credit of having done in this respect so much as Maritz."

The particulars of the death of Mr. P. Retief and his party are thus detailed by an unexceptionable eye-witness, the Rev. F. Owen, of the Church Missionary Society, in the following extract from his journal, beginning February 2, 1838:—

"Feb. 2.—Dingaan sent for me at sun-set to write a letter to Mr. Retief, who, with a party of Boers is now on his way to the Zoola capital. The letter was characterestic of the Chief; he said, 'his heart was now content, because he had got his cattle again;' (some cattle which Mr. Retief had recovered for him from Sinkoyella, another Chief, as the condition on which Dingaan would grant him territory) he requested that the Chief of the Boers would send to all his people, and order them to come up to the capital with him; but without their horses; he promised to gather together all his army to sing and dance in the presence of the Dutch, who he desired would also dance; he said he would give orders that cattle should be slain for them in every place through which they passed on the road; *and he promised to give them a country.*" I asked how they could come without their horses? He said, "tell them that they must bring their horses and dance upon them in the middle of the town, that it might be known who can dance best, the Zoolas or the "Abalungo," the general name given to white people The Dutch will be too wise to expose themselves in this manner.

" 3rd.—Large parties of Zoolas in their war dress were yesterday evening entering the town. This morning when we were at family prayer, the unusual sound of muskets was heard from the west; this proved to be the arrival of the Boers, who presently entered the town on horseback, with their guns in their hands. An immense concourse of Zoolas were present to receive them. The deputation, in number about 60, brought back the cattle which they had received from Sinkoyella. The Boers immediately shewed Dingaan the way in which the Boers danced on horseback, by making a sham charge, causing the air to resound with their guns. This was something the Zoola Chief had never witnessed. In their turn, the Zoolas exhibited their agility in dancing.

"6th.—A dreadful day in the annals of the mission! My pen shudders to give an account of it! This morning, as I was sitting in the shade of my wagon reading the Testament, the usual messenger came up with hurry and anxiety depicted in his looks; I felt sure he was about to pronounce something serious, and what was his commission. Whilst it shewed consideration and kindness in the Zoola monarch towards me, it disclosed a horrid instance of perfidy, too horrid to be described towards the unhappy men who have, for a few days, been his guests; but who are now, alas, no more! This news came like a thunder-stroke to myself, and to every successive member of my family as they heard of it. The reason assigned for this treacherous conduct was, that they were going to kill him! That he was anxious for my reply; but what could I say? Fearful on the one hand of seeming to justify this treachery; and on the other, of exposing myself and family to probable danger if I appeared to take their part. Moreover, I could not but feel it was my duty to apprise the Boers of the intended massacre, whilst certain danger would have ensued, I apprehended should I be detected in giving them this information. However, I was released from this dilemma by beholding an awful spectacle! My attention was directed to the blood-stained hill, nearly opposite my hut, where all the executions at this fearful spot took place, and which was now destined to add sixty more bleeding bodies to the number of those who have already cried to heaven for vengeance. "There," said one, "they are killing the Boers now." I turned my eyes, and beheld an immense multitude on the hill, about nine or ten Zoolas to every Boer, were dragging their helpless unarmed victims to the fatal spot, where those eyes which awaked this morning to behold the cheerful light of day for the last time, are now closed in death. I lay myself down on the ground; presently, the deed of blood being accomplished, the whole multitude returned to the town to meet the sovereign; and as they drew near to him, they set up a shout that reached the station, and continued some time. Meanwhile, I, myself, had been kept from all fear for our personal safety; for I considered Dingaan's message to me as an indication that he had no ill designs against his missionary; especially as the messenger had informed me, that Thomas Halstead, an Englishman, from Port Natal, the Boers, interpreter, was to be saved; nevertheless, fears afterwards obtruded themselves upon me, when I saw half a dozen men with shields sitting near our hut, and I began to fear, lest we were to fall the next victims. At this crisis, I called all my family in, and read the 91st Psalm, so singularly and literally applicable to our present condition, that I could, with difficulty, proceed with it. I endeavoured to realise all its statements; and though I did not receive it as an absolute provision against sudden and violent death, I was led to Him who is our refuge from the guilt and fear of sin, which can alone make death terrible. We then knelt down, and I prayed, really not knowing, but that in this position, we should be called into eternity. Two of the Boers paid me a visit this morning, and breakfasted only two hours before they were called into another world! When I asked them what they thought of Dingaan, they said, "he was good;" so unsuspicious were they of his intentions. He had promised to assign over to them the whole country between the Tugala and the Umzimvooboo Rivers; and this day the papers of transfer were to be signed. I have seen by my glass that Dingaan has been sitting most of the morning in the middle of his town since the dreadful affair. An army in several divisions collected before him. About noon the whole body *ran* in the direction in which the Boers came. They are, I cannot allow myself to doubt, sent to fall unawares on the main body of the Dutch, who are encamped near the head of the Tugala; for to suppose that Dingaan would murder this handful, and not make himself master of the whole number, with their guns, horses, and cattle; would be to conceive him capable of egregious folly; as he must know that the other Boers will revenge the death of their countrymen. Certain it is, as far as human foresight can judge, we shall speedily hear of the massacre of the whole company of the Boers; or what is scarcely less terrible, wars and bloodshed, of which there will be no end, till either the Boers or the Zoolas cease to be. To Dingaan's message this morning, I sent as guarded a reply as I could; knowing that it would be both foolish and dangerous to accuse him at such a season, of perfidy and cruelty. Moreover, as his message to me was kind and well intended, shewing a regard to my feelings, as well as my safety, I judged it prudent and proper to thank him for it.

7th. "I did not give an adequate idea of carnage yesterday, I omitted to state that several of the Boers had children with them under eleven years of age, as I am informed, and all these are slain! They had likewise their Hottentot servants, and all these were slain, and also, besides their interpreter and his servant, the number of slain must have been nearer 100 than 60.

9th.—My interpreter returned to-day to my great joy; the King sent for him soon after his arrival, and gave him a very plausible account of the late affair; he said, " if he had not dispatched the Boers. they would have fired upon him and his people before they left." The perfidious tyrant gave the following account of the manner in which they were seized. He invited them all into a cattle fold, to take leave of him; his people were then ordered to dance, and forming themselves as usual into a semi-circle, they approached nearer and nearer to the Boers, till he gave the command for them to seize hold of the unsuspecting victims of his jealousy. In the confusion their interpreter was seized contrary to his wish."

After a mock trial, in which Mr. Owen's servants were compelled to bear witness against their master and Mistress, Dingaan having extorted a wagon and other presents; permitted them to depart on the 10th, and on the 14th they arrived at Port Natal, from whence they eventually sailed for the colony.

The following particulars of the journey of Mr. Boshoff, from the colony across the Drackenberg range to Natal, will be interesting, as it describes a tract of country previously unknown.

" Our party left the Nieuw Hantam on the 30th April 1838, and on reaching the Orange River found it greatly swollen by rains in the interior. The fords were utterly impracticable for wheel carriages, except by floating them across; and by this process, which occupied one whole day, we at length reached the opposite shore. On the 31st April we stopped at the first Griqua or Bastard farm-house, the residence of a person named William Nielson. This man is superior to the generality of these people. His residence is about an hour and a half with a horse wagon from the Orange River. He has much land under tillage, and we are informed, that he is the only individual among Kok's people who cultivates land to such an extent, as not only to supply himself, but to have a surplus for sale to the Colonial farmers. He has built a neat little cottage expressly for the accommodation of travellers and strangers; and a day seldom passes without visitors, either traders or Boers, with both of whom he appears to be on the best and most friendly terms, although one would suppose that if any of the Griqua Bastards had cause to complain of annoyance by trek-boers old Nielson must be the greatest sufferer. The main road runs across his place, and every day such visitors pass his door either backward or forward. Here we met with the two Italians and a woman I mentioned in my former communication, returning from the camp of the emigrants, having travelled the whole distance an horseback. These persons gave us such an account of the dangers we were likely to encounter before we could possibly reach the farmers, whose situation was also described as so imminently perilous, that we began to entertain apprehensions that even should we be so fortunate as to be able to make our way through the numerous and strong posts of the enemy, yet there was very little probability of our being in time to render any effectual assistance to our unfortunate brethren. But the greater the danger was described, the more determined were my brave companions, Joubert and his little party, to proceed.

"The journey from thence to Moroko's station, a distance of 25 hours from the Orange River, was travelled so slowly that we did not reach it until the 11th May. A body of 200 men was expected here on the 12th from the Riet and Modder Rivers, on their way to join the emigrants; but instead of that number only two arrived. From Nielson's place to the sources of the Modder River, we saw but three places which exhibited any traces of occupation. On one spot there was a small house half finished, and on the other two structures something resembling the habitations of men, one grade in civilization above the savage tribes, and even these were in a dilapidated state. *This unoccupied country is about* 100 *miles in breadth, and it abounds in pasturage and water for millions of sheep, and thousands of large cattle.* It is claimed by Kok's Griquas, and it is said that his right thereto was fully acknowledged by the Lieutenant-Governor on the occasion of his meeting their Chiefs and principal men, on his visit made some short time ago to the frontier. They were then told that if they could agree with the farmers, they might allow them the use of these lands, upon payment of rent; and as these people do not require one-*fiftieth* part of the rich pasturage abounding in that extensive waste, several of them have rented out large tracts of land to Colonial farmers for six, eight, or ten years, and longer.

"We visited several of the farmers who are settled there, and they seemed quite happy. They appear to know little, and indeed not to care much, about what is going on in the colony. They have few servants; but these give them little trouble by bad conduct, as where they find it necessary they punish offences, without any fear of vexatious law-suits in consequence The servant aware of this, gives very little trouble; he respects his master's authority, and in general conducts himself in a very exemplary manner. Few of these farmers sow corn or cultivate gardens, for want of running water or strong fountains for irrigation. They obtain wheat, Indian and Kaffer corn from the [Platt Berg] bastards occupying the tract of country called "Newland," and also from Maroko's people, [Thaba Unchu] for money, or in exchange for cattle and sheep. They do not trouble themselves about politics; and as they can readily sell or exchange their slaughter oxen at the rate of Rds. 50 per head, cows at Rds. 20, and wether sheep at Rds. 4 or 4½, without the trouble of going any distance to market to dispose of them, and as the traders not only purchase their cattle, but supply them at their own doors with every thing they require, they seem to be content. There are no complaints of cattle stealing, instances of which are very rare. Vagrants are very few indeed, except a small party now and then of wandering Bushmen and Corannas may be considered as such. Independently of these advantages they enjoy a privilege highly valued by the grazier, viz., that of changing the pasturage frequently, which, without any expense worth mentioning, tends to cause an increase of their stock to an extent of 200 per cent. beyond that within the colony. I believe these persons still pay their taxes; at least, many of them repair to Colesberg for that purpose, and also to get their children baptized, and hence they consider themselves as still within the jurisdiction of the Colonial Government. During the whole of our journey from the colony to Natal we only met with two parties of Bushmen. On our way thither we fell in with a small company of six, and on our return with another consisting of eleven persons, and we heard there were but very few of those people in that part of the country.

"Throughout that district, and for a distance of fifty miles beyond Moroko's territory, there is abundance of game. The pasturage from Moroko's country to the———and river, a distance of 90 miles, or 18 hours, is a mixture of sour and sweet grasses. With the exception of a few mountains, the Sand river was the first running stream we found after crossing the Riet river, and both of these are weak and inconsiderable. Still there is no scarcity of water, as for the whole of that distance there are along the road a number of large pools of good fresh water, so that the traveller is sure to find a plentiful supply of water every day, however short the stage he may make.

" From the ———— and river to the top of Draakberg, also about 90 miles, the country presents an irregular surface, and the pasturage is sour. On the Draakberg we crossed several running streams ; the largest is the Eiland's river, and which is much such a stream as the Hex river. All the way from the New Hantam to the Draakberg, the country is destitute of wood, and the traveller is compelled to collect cow dung for the purposes of fuel. From the New Hantam to the Riet river, our course was north-east, thence to Moroko's due east, thence to the Vet river, a distance of 35 miles, again north-east, thence to the Eiland's river, again east, and from the Eiland's river down the Draakberg to the emigrants' camp south-east.

",On the 19th May we descended the Draakberg with six wagons and a cart, and reached its base in an hour and a half. Some parts of the descent were so steep that we were compelled to chain two wheels ; but upon the whole the road is not very difficult. From the foot of the mountain to Port Natal the distance is computed at 42 hours with horse wagons (210 miles). In the winter the cold is as severe on these mountains as in the Sneeuwberg; but on descending into the level country it is as temperate as in the Camdebo; and as you approach Port Natal it becomes still warmer. On the 4th of June (nearly the middle of winter in this latitude) we saw in the garden of a native, under the Stinkhoutberg, a distance of between 50 and 60 miles from the coast, Indian corn, of luxuriant growth, in full blossom, together with tobacco plants, and pumpkins, and calabashes, all uninjured by frost. At Natal we partook of two large dishes of Indian corn in a green and unripe state.

" On the whole the climate is healthy and so mild that two crops of almost every kind of grain may be reaped in a year. The soil is a dark mould, deep, loose, and very fertile. Indian corn has been often found in the fields of the natives of such vigorous growth, that a man on horseback, standing in his stirrups, could not reach the top of the plant. This grain, as also Kaffer corn, pumpkins, and tobacco, are grown without irrigation. It is is said that from September or October to March, and sometimes to April, rains are so frequent that the highest hills may be so successfully cultivated. Independent of this, however, there is such abundance of water, both by rivers and springs, that by means of irrigation a hundred times more produce might be raised within the comparatively small tract of country over which I travelled from the Draakberg to Natal than in the whole of the eastern province. But as irrigation does not appear necessary, with very few exceptions, it appears certain, that were there sufficient population, the whole country might be converted into corn-fields and plantations.

"We crossed in our progress several beautiful rivers, the largest of which are the Tugala and Umgani. The first resembles the Breede River, near Swellendam, or even lower down, and the second is not much inferior in magnitude. In rainy seasons I have no doubt they are navigable for large boats for a considerable distance. The other rivers are, the little Tugala, the Bushman, the Umbooti, the Umzalak, the Umlas, and several other streams, resembling in size and volume of water, the Berg River, the Hex, or the Zonderend, and some rather smaller. All these streams have their sources in the Draakberg, at a distance of from 15 to 30 miles higher than where the road crosses the range. In many places they are capable of being led out without any other expense or labour than merely making a channel to conduct the water.

"From the character of the soil and climate, I have no doubt but that every kind of fruit-tree which grows in the colony will flourish there. I have seen bananas, dates, a specie of medlar, and some others, growing wild,—as also a sort of cane, and Spanish reed, which are also indigenous.

"Timber for building purposes, wagon making, &c., is every where to be had. The country is hilly, like that in the neighbourhood of Swellendam or George; but it is quite open, the wood only growing along the margin of the rivers, and in the kloofs. Near Port Natal, for 15 miles from the shore, it has, however, the appearance of a continued forest.

"Coal is found at the Sand River, between the Great and Little Tugala Rivers, and at the Blue Krans River. We dug up some near the road between the Tugalas, of which I brought home with me a small quantity. This was taken from near the surface, and proved on trial to be coal of second or third rate quality. We also found a small piece of coal on the shore, about a mile east of the entrance of the Bay of Natal; but this might have been washed on shore from some vessel. However, there is no doubt but that the country in the vicinity of Natal produces abundance of this valuable article.

"The pasturage is extremely rich and very healthy for large cattle and sheep. The whole face of the country is thickly clothed by a great variety of grasses, growing from one to *eight* feet high. It sometimes for many miles in extent has more the resemblance of corn fields than grazing ground.

"Elephants, elands, buffaloes, and wild boars, are found in this part of the country; but animals of prey are very rare. After we descended the Draakberg we never saw so much as the footmarks of a jackall, wolf, lion, or other noxious animals. Sheep are permitted to graze at a great distance from the camp day and night, and are uninjured.

"The cattle, sheep, and horses, excepting such as have been much used, or kept close to the camp, look very healthy, and are in excellent condition. The farmers state that they have had no diseases amongst either cattle or sheep all the time they have been there. The horse sickness, however, similar to that known in the colony, is also prevalent there.

"The roads are smooth and good, although the country is not level. Stones are rarely met with, except in the bed of rivers.

"Since the death of Retief, and subsequently of Uys, the form of government amongst the emigrants has undergone some changes, and they have had several meetings to discuss, alter, and mature the system. These discussions have arisen out of the difference which existed between the respective adherents of Uys and Martiz. The former presented at last a memorial to the general council, stating, that for various reasons they could not submit to him as their magistrate, and praying that another individual might be appointed to preside over them. The council acceded to this, and accordingly appointed in his room a person named Badenhorst. The council consists of 24 members, who are elected by the people. It holds supreme authority, makes laws and regulations, appoints to all offices of trust and power, such as field-commandants, field-cornets, and wardmasters, and hears and determines upon all matters of importance.

"Mr. Maritz holds, in conjunction with the office of magistrate, the appointment of chief commissioner, or president, and as such has the charge of all public monies, regulates the receipts and expenditure, and in other respects has the same authority, and discharges similar duties as the civil commissioners within the colony. The magistrates alone have jurisdiction in petty civil and criminal case; but where the interest at stake amounts (I believe) in civil cases to the value of £7 10, and in criminal to a fine of £5, or imprisonment for one month, he is assisted by six heemraden. From these decisions there is no appeal. This court has, however, jurisdiction, with appeal, in case of higher value and importance. In criminal cases, however, where the offender is liable to the punishment of transportation, or whipping, and hard labour for more (I think) than six months, as also to the punishment of death,—for the trial of such offences a court is held, at which the magistrate within whose jurisdiction the crime is committed presides as judge, and a jury of 12 men, called " gesworenen," is impannelled to heare and decide on the evidence given. No death warrant can be executed until it has received the *fiat* of the general council, or " volks-raad," which also decides all cases in appeal, and exercises the power to remit fines and punishment. This council holds monthly sessions, and oftener when necessary, when one of its members sits as president.

" The Laws of Holland, as they are recognized in this colony, are followed by them, except in matters of a purely local nature, when the general council promulgates such regulations as may be necessary, or gives instructions to the respective officers according to circumstances. The members of council, and also their present magistrates, have been elected for one year only; and they deem this period, and the laws and regulations now in force, as sufficient to the exigency of their present circumstances; but they contemplate making many changes when they shall be peaceably settled. They are, however, greatly in want of an efficient head—of one properly qualified in every respect to direct and guide them, and who, unconnected with any party, may acquire the confidence of all. They feel this want very much, and it is generally thought that were such a person raised up, he would soon remove all party feeling, suspicion, and jealousy from amongst them, as well as prevent ambitious men from creating dissentions, which, though frequently of a trifling nature, have too often caused much annoyance, and brought them into great difficulties. Such disputes might have been the cause of great misfortunes had it not been for the forbearance which has been very generally manifested, by which party spirit has been prevented from degenerating into personal hatred between themselves. They have exerted themselves on all sides to remove the causes of disagreement, as soon as known, and to reconcile the disputants if possible. On the whole I found the people peaceably disposed, well behaved and orderly. During our stay among them we did not hear of a single instance of quarrelling or fighting between either man or woman, although it was feared by some, as wine and spirits had been obtained from Port Natal, such disorders would take place. Nor did I meet with an individual intoxicated, although while I was there brandy was for a few days retailed in the camp, and notwithstanding I saw some there who when in the colony were addicted to liquor, and were there very disorderly when under its influence. The emigrants in general are still decently, though some rather poorly, clothed. Not a child did I see in rags, or naked; but there are many among them, chiefly widows, who have been ruined by Dingaan, who subsist on the charity of others.

"Divine service is publicly performed thrice on every Sunday, and also on Wednesday and Saturday evenings. The officiating minister in one camp is Mr. Smit, formerly a missionary. He was elected to the sacred office he now fills during the time of the late P. Retief, and he still acts as the pastor of a considerable number of the emigrants, and is of great use to them. During the week days he catehcises the youth, while Mrs. Smit instructs the younger children. Every day Mr. Smit is actively engaged in the duties of his calling, and he is highly esteemed by his congregation. In the other camps Messrs. Stephanus Marits, Charel Cilliers, and some other persons perform divine service. Every morning and evening the sound of family devotion is heard in the tents in all directions. Prayer meetings are also frequent.

"There are many who will not acknowledge Mr. Smit as their pastor, he not having been ordained. Such persons marry their sons or daughters by means of a civil contract made before the magistrate. Their children they leave unbaptized, waiting in the hope that their repeated applications for a minister will be attended to; if not by their own countrymen, at least by some foreigner of the same religious persuasion.

"They have established several schools, but the parents complain that the want of accommodation prevents the teachers from receiving so many pupils as they might otherwise instruct. Others are compelled, in consequence of the paucity of servants, to take care of their parents' cattle; and of course, the education of these is much neglected. In some instances, parents instruct their own children.

"*There are not a few slave apprentices with the emigrants; but it has been determined by council that these shall be set at liberty on the 1st December, the same as in the colony.* The emigrants do not seem to have the slightest idea of entering into any slave trade whatever, and are even offended at a question on the subject being put to them. They say, " We are not averse to the emancipation of the slave,—the colonists never introduced the slave trade, the European government forced it upon us,—what we complain of is, that our slaves have been emancipated by England under a promise of full compensation, whereas, we have scarcely received one-third of their value."

"*They are most anxious to remain on friendly terms with the colony;* but if you begin to propose to them their return, argue as to the causes of their emigration, you soon find yourself in the back ground; you must submit to listen to a long catalogue of grievances, and which they state have driven them to take the step they have done; and they appear fully determined to run any risk, and to suffer any privation, rather than to submit again to the same annoyances."

By subsequent news from Natal, it appears that in an

attack upon Dingaan's people, most of the English residents have been killed, including Mr. Bigger; jun., a respectable young merchant, and John Cane, well-known as one of the oldest residents at Natal. The American and English Missionaries found it necessary to return to the colony. Maritz, the principal surviving leader of the Boers, is also dead. Meanwhile, the Colonial Government has exhibited some signs of a determination to interfere and take possession of Port Natal. It is reported (Oct. 1838) that 100 soldiers are about to be sent immediately. For the last fourteen years, the occupation of Natal as a preventive measure, as well as on account of other important advantages connected with it, has been pressed upon the attention of the Colonial Government; and now, when all the evil anticipated from its non-occupancy, has been effected, and many thousand lives lost, the necessity is acknowledged.— (*See Bannister's Humane Policy, Appendix, p.p.* 1 *to* 106. For full information respecting Natal, *see Isaac's Travels in South-Eastern Africa,* 2 vols. 12mo.—*Journal to the Zoola Country by A. F. Gardiner,* 8vo.—*Introduction to the Narrative of the Kaffer War, by the Editor of the Graham's Town Journal,* 8vo.)—Important effects *for good* or *for evil* will result from this emigration of the Colonists beyond the Colonial boundary. The attention of the executive will now be *unwillingly* drawn towards the distant tribes of the interior. Statesman-like measures, suited not only to meet present emergencies, but anticipative and preventive of future evils ought now to characterize the policy and proceedings of the Colonial Government. It is fully admitted that *something must be done.* What ought to be done, will form the subject of the following NOTE.

NOTE VII.

BRITISH CONTROUL OVER EMIGRATION BEYOND THE COLONIAL BOUNDARY, INDISPENSABLE FOR THE SECURITY OF THE ABORIGINES.

The following extracts from a letter of Captain Stockenstrom's to the Colonial Secretary, (dated Stockholm, 5th November 1834, and published in the evidence Abor. Com. pp. 117 123) forms a suitable introduction to the discussion of this subject. They contain a fair statement of the case of the emigrant Boers, and suggest the only efficient mode of remedying the evils of an emigration, which the Colonial Government cannot restrain.

" For the last six years migrations of Colonists beyond the boundary, have recommenced. I have more than once ordered them back, and seen the order obeyed; but during the last year of my residence in the colony, I again found numbers of these emigrants out of the colony, and believe that many more were preparing to join them from various causes. This must prove the source of much mischief, for though there are among them many well diposed men, there will necessarily be many bad characters who will not scruple (if even the others should) to follow the system by which their forefathers became possessed of land; and the present tenants when ejected, will increase the number of plunderers, and be unmercifully destroyed. With the Griquas and Corannas these emigrants must soon come in collision; and if they should become strong enough to dispossess those who have peaceably settled and and have gradually consolidated themselves into a useful community, they will bring a very dangerous enemy upon us; at any rate, the Griquas and Corannas stand on no more ceremony with the Bushmen and their land, than the emigrants will, and between the two parties, the savages will soon be homeless, so that from one extremity of the frontier to the other, a constant ferment will be kept up.

" Having thus to the best of my abilities laid open to you the existing evils, I will humbly attempt in compliance with your 8th and 11th propositions, to submit to your judgment, which I consider the best remedies in our present predicament. These appear to me to consist in strict justice, as far as such is still possible, by permitting no aggressions on the part of the neighbouring tribes against the colonists to go unpunished, provided you have ascertained beyond all doubt who the aggressors are, and run no possible risk that you make the innocent suffer; and by punishing with the utmost severity, every injury done by the Colonists to those neighbours, as if it were done to ourselves; nay more, those tribes should be understood to have the right to deal with such aggressions according to their own laws, if they found them committing the injury in their country, and their possessions should be held by us as sacred as those of any of His Majesty's subjects." (pp. 120 121)—" But in order to enable the Government to act steadily upon these principles, some steps must be taken to restore order beyond the limits of the colony, where *an unlimited field for European philanthropy and civilization is to be found.*

" On the northern frontier, you have *an extensive community, ripe for good and for evil.* If left to themselves, open to aggressions on one side, and with the temptation of weaker tribes easily overpowered on the other, it is to be feared that in spite of the best intentions of some of the leading men, and all the efforts of the Missionaries, they will retrograde. Whilst under our protection, which I believe they would most readily adopt, if extended upon liberal and just principles, they would vie with the Kat River settlement in improvement and in usefulness.

"I am aware that here the great objection against the extension of the colony, stands in the way; but the population is spreading itself, and has been doing so ever since the middle of the seventeenth century, in spite of the Government. If the Boers migrate beyond the frontier in great numbers, (which I fear they will) who is to bring them back? they tell you they are doing nothing illegal in withdrawing from a country in which they have no room for their flocks, and do not feel themselves comfortable, and that if you cannot extend the protection of your Government to them, they are ready to forfeit it; and those who talk of fetching them, or forcing them back by means of the Griquas, understand neither the nature of the people, the country, nor the question, or are certainly not averse to scenes of bloodshed. *Nor have I any desire to shut up the whites within certain limits* for the benefit of any particular class, *whilst all equally encroach.*

" *The disposable land in the interior is of unlimited extent*, and the white man will have his share do what you will, (the history of any colony proves this); but the question is, *whether he shall be allowed to go forth without controul*, dispossessing the natives, destroying them upon the least resistance, *and the Government follow when the mischief is irremediable*, as has been the case heretofore; or *whether, the Government shall take the land, prevent anything being taken, but what the natives choose to part with*, taking care that they be amply indemnified, that this indemnification be applied to their advantage, and that extensive tracts be reserved for their own support, in which they should be protected upon an equal footing with the most privileged classes; and in which I do not despair, the means might thus be provided to reclaim those who have been forced into a marauding life, and for whom, otherwise, there appears no other lot in store but extermination. I am, of course, alluding to those tracts adjoining the colony in which there are only wandering disorganized hordes to be found, and into which our emigrants find such easy access; for with those nations who can controul and protect themselves, I would only maintain the most amicable treaties, watching closely our borderers, who would then be under our check in the treatment of, and dealings with such nations." (p. 121.)—"Whether such an undertaking would require the immediate supervision of some high authority on the spot, I hardly consider myself competent to judge, for as I must admit that I feel strongly on the subject, I may not be totally free from bias." (pp. 121, 122.)

This document which must be admitted to be unexceptionable in point of authority, establishes the following facts beyond dispute:

1st.—That, the emigration of the Boers arises, in part, from the influence of natural causes (as well as from the existence of prejudices and dislike to Colonial control); and that this disposition to wander and reside, and even settle beyond the boundary, will continue so long as the colony is affected by long droughts, and while large tracts of unoccupied country invite emigration.

2nd.—That it is impossible to prevent this emigration by the employment of the Griquas, or any other coercive methods; and that those who fancy this possible, are both ignorant of local difficulties, and not averse to scenes of bloodshed.

3rd.—That, nevertheless this emigration conducted by private individuals, free from all legal controul, is sure to prove injurious to the native tribes, to the emigrants themselves, and to the colony.

4th.—That, the Colonial Government has the choice of two plans, *the interfering now and preventing the evils* which must arise from irregular and unauthorized settlements in the interior; or *to interfere eventually under most unfavourable circumstances, as soon as all the mischief possible has been effected.*

5th.—That to legalize and regulate the emigration of the Colonists would be no injury to the natives, seeing that *there is abundance of land unoccupied in the interior*, and might be over-ruled to answer a variety of important and beneficial ends.

The fact that there is abundance of land unoccupied, either from the want of native population,—from the unsettled state of the country,—or from the unsuitability of certain tracts to native habits and tastes, is a most important one in connexion with the question of legalizing and regulating emigration. If this be the case, the right of the Colonist to occupy, is on a par with that of the Griquas, Bastards, Tambookies, Kaffers and Zulus : and it would be unjust, as well as impolitic, to attempt " to shut up the whites within certain limits, whilst all *equally encroach*." The extent of this vacant land cannot well be shown on a map, as it lies in extensive but detached portions. Perhaps the following description may be understood by a reference to Arrowsmith's Map of South-Africa, (latest edition.)

No. 1.—Draw a line from the Winterberg to the sources of the Umtata, and thence to the Zimvubu, where it is crossed by the 31° south latitude (in the map). Another line extending from the Taaibosh Berg, along the Stormbergen, as far as the source of the Zimvubu river, almost parallel with the first line. These boundaries (which may be easily found on the map) enclose a fine country above 200 miles in length and 70 in breadth, which is *almost en-*

tirely uninhabited. Near the Colonial frontier, a few of Mapassa's Tambookies occupy a small portion of the country, but even there, such is the paucity of population that the kraals are 10 miles apart. This country abounds in water and good land both for cultivation and grazing, but is too cold for natives, and never has been permanently settled by them.

No. 2.—Between the Stormberg range and what is called Stockenstrom's River, there is a tract of country about 150 miles long and 40 broad. Its western boundary near the colony is the Stormberg River. *This country is also unoccupied, except here and there a few Bushmen kraals.*

No. 3.—Between the lower branch of the Orange River, and the Alexander, Riet or Modder River, is a tract of country which Mr. Boshoff states to be unoccupied, about 100 miles in length and breadth, " abounding in pasturage and water for millions of sheep and thousands of large cattle." This land is said to be claimed by a party of the Griquas: their claim stands on the same grounds as that of the Colonial farmers. However as the land is not occupied, the Colonial Government might easily arrange this matter and do justice to all parties. At present many Dutch farmers are settled here, of whom Mr. Boshoff gives an interesting account.

No. 4.—The immence country extending from the parallel of 29° south to 25° south, containing within its bounds the sources of the Caledon, Donkin, Ky Gariep, Mapoota and Elephant Rivers, *is almost entirely uninhabited*: partly owing to the country being unsuitable to native habits, partly from there being no people to occupy it, the original inhabitants having been destroyed by the Fitcani in 1822-5, and by the Zulus under Matzilikatzi in 1830-4. The extent of this country, which has never been properly explored, cannot be accurately estimated: it is at least 240 miles long by 150 broad.

No. 5.—From the Zimvubu to the Tugela River, and from the sea to the Quathlamba or Draakenberg range, there is a beautiful country well watered, admirably suited for cultivation and grazing, which may be estimated at 200 miles long and 100 broad. Excepting near the Zimvubu, where part of Faku's and Capai's people are now residing, and near Port Natal where a few thousand Zulu refugees did reside, under the protection of Europeans settled there: *this country is unoccupied.* Formerly it was well peopled, but the original inhabitants have been mostly exterminated by the Zulus under Chaka, the predecessor of Dingaan.*

No. 6.—On the east coast, from the Umtata to the Umgazi River, a distance of about 28 miles (in a direct line) and inland about 50 miles, there is another section of unoccupied country. In my journeys between the Wesleyan Mission Stations of Morley and Buntingville, I have had occasion frequently to ride over it, and in different directions. It is a most beautiful tract, well watered and wooded. Faku and Capai have destroyed and driven out the few inhabitants who recently occupied a portion of it near the Umtata. An European settlement in this section of country would prevent Faku and Capai from making their continual murderous inroads upon our friends and allies the Tambookies. Faku would willingly part with the land for a reasonable consideration. It is said that the Umtata mouth forms a good harbour, if so, its situation about half-way between the colony and Natal, points it out as a suitable intermediate port, from whence supplies could be conveyed into the interior, and the productions purchased by the traders be shipped for the colony or for Natal.

The whole extent of the unoccupied country, which might be taken possession of without injuring a single native, partly as unclaimed by any tribe, and partly by purchase or treaty,

---

* Faku claims the country as far as the Zimkulu, and provided he were secured from the Zulus, would probably choose to reside between that river and the Zimvubu.

amounts to 87,000 *square miles, or* 55,680,000 acres. The greater part of this land is far superior to the average of the grazing land in the colony, and is much better adapted for cultivation, (the country described in the 3rd paragraph excepted). If it were allotted in farms of 6,000 acres, the usual size of good grass farms in the colony, it would thus furnish room for 10,000 families of Boers, which reckoning children and servants, is equivalent to a population of 100,000 souls. If the colony which contains within its area so many deserts incapable of supporting any population, averages *one* to a square mile, there can be no doubt but that the countries in question would in a few years support *three* or *four* within that space.

Let it be clearly understood that the settlement of these tracts of country beyond the limits of the colony, is a question which circumstances *force* upon the serious consideration of the Colonial and Home Government. *If possible*, it would be highly desirable for the present Colonists in the Cape, (as well as those who have left it) to be confined within its legal boundaries. Half the energy wasted on new enterprises, if spent on improvements in the old colony, would develope resources as yet unthought of. But it is in vain to contend with the obstacles in the way of a dense population, presented by the fact, that, *beyond the boundary there are* 87,000 *square miles of unoccupied fertile territory*. The tastes and habits of the Dutch population are decidedly in favour of extensive grazing farms, and so long as there is opportunity *at any risk* of indulging this taste, they will apply to no other employment. When the 87,000 square miles are fully occupied, and further extension prevented by the legal security afforded to the native tribes by treaties expressly acknowledging their territorial rights, and minutely defining their boundaries, *then*, and *not till then*, we may expect the application of capital and skill towards increasing the natural capabilities of the soil, and thus enabling it to support a dense population. Meanwhile the emigration *will go on*, and *no power on earth can prevent it;*

and the question is, whether it shall go on uncontroulled under irresponsible guidance, or whether it shall be regulated in such a manner that the evils anticipated from the experience of the past shall be neutralized, and the influx of European and Colonial emigrants be rendered productive of benefits not only to themselves but to the native tribes around them, and to the general interests of civilization and christianity in South Africa.

The benefits derivable to the natives themselves from the settlement of Colonists *under legal controul*, and *on a well-regulated plan*, on the *waste* and *unoccupied* lands of the interior, are obvious: providing however that *law accompany civilization*, and not as heretofore *follow tardily after it*. It enters into the essence of every just and beneficent scheme of colonization of unoccupied lands, that the rights of the neighbouring natives be previously minutely defined and solemnly secured by legal enactments, and that no alienation of their territorial possessions thus defined be permitted *on any pretence whatever*. This great principle being secured, the following advantages to the natives of South Africa would result from the judicious settlement of the unoccupied tracts in their vicinity.

1st. The destructive wars which almost annually destroy thousands of lives, and expel the weaker tribes from their possessions, thus preventing the growth of settled and civilized habits, would be effectually checked. While we admit the evils arising from the unjust system of European colonization, involving as it does encroachment on the territorial right of the natives, and in some cases causing their extinction, we must not forget that a similar and more summary, and if possible more cruel process of encroachment and extermination is constantly going on among themselves. Had not the Dutch Colonists opposed an obstacle in the way of Kaffer aggression, no doubt the Hottentot races would have been exterminated by the former people; and had it not been for the terror inspired by the commando of 1828, sent from the colony to protect the Kaffers from the Fitcani and Zulus, these more warlike and barbarous tribes would ere this have desolated Kafferland. Within the last thirty years, at least sixty populous and powerful tribes have been exterminated by the Mantatees, Fitcani, and Zulus. The process is yet going on, and should even the Zulu power on the north and east be broken, and rendered incapable of maintaining its career of oppression, there is sufficient reason to believe that other powerful tribes in the interior, now dwelling to the north-west of Delagoa Bay, and as yet only known by report, would gradually advance in a southerly direction, to re-commence a similar career of bloodshed and desolation. This is not mentioned by way of extenuating European crime, but as suggesting a hope that after contributing our share towards the extinction of the native tribes, we may now, under a just system of colonization, contribute to their conservation. By the occupation of the waste and unoccupied lands by Europeans, exterminating wars and predatory inroads of the marauding tribes would be prevented. For instance, the occupation of the tracts numbered 1, 2, would put a stop to the mutual predatory inroads of the Abasutus under Moshesh and the Tambookies and Kaffers; the occupation of the tract numbered 3, would check the Bergenaars and Corannas, whose murderous attacks on the Bechuanas are very destructive. If the tract numbered 4, were thus settled, there would be no opportunity for Zulu inroads on the Bechuana tribes, and the occupation of the tract numbered 5, would screen the Amapondos from the same dreaded enemy. Again, if the tract numbered 6, were in the possession of Colonists, the Tambookies would be secured from Faku and Capai. The security thus afforded to the several tribes, and the stability secured by this cession of warfare to the labours of Missionaries, together with the gradual declension of warlike habits, would powerfully assist the advance of civilization and the progress of christianity.

2nd.—A field would be opened for the full employment of the labours of the natives, on terms advantageous to them. The new Colonists would require labourers as herdsmen, &c., and the young men from the adjoining tribes would gladly engage their services for one, two or three cows annually. Opportunities for the profitable employment of the numerous class of natives who possess no property of their own, are much wanted. A young man has no other means of obtaining a few cattle, than by stealing, or serving a very long and indefinite period at a Chief's kraal. Hence war, which affords a chance of procuring a few cows, is always popular with the young, who have nothing to lose and may gain. The capital and enterprise of the Colonists would thus open a field for the profitable exercise of native industry. In the same manner as the frontier Kaffers have become rich from the security afforded by the vicinity of the colony, and from the profitable market opened for their labours, so would the other tribes participate in these advantages from being placed in similarly favourable circumstances.

3rd.—Frequent and intimate intercourse with the Colonial settlements would exercise a civilizing influence upon the native tribes. I am aware that this has been doubted, and that the intercourse of Europeans with uncivilized nations has been considered as always productive of ruinous consequences to the latter. It is freely admitted that the unchecked and lawless intercourse of seamen with the inhabitants of New Zealand and the islands of the South Sea, and the settlement of run-aways in those islands, have proved most injurious. It is also true that the advance of European settlements has produced eventually equally injurious consequences, and from obvious reason. In the progress of these settlements *the territorial rights of the natives have been disregarded:* their lands have been obtained by violence, deceit, or by payment of a fictitious price, and thus deprived of their property in the soil, *they have not been in circumstances to reap the advantages which had they retained their landed property would have accrued from the additional value communicated to that species of property, by the capital and industry of Europeans.* Thus deprived of their means of subsistence, they have been compelled to serve the Colonists from the necessity of their circumstances, without having any controul over the wages of their labour. *But where the lands of the natives are not encroached upon, the occupation of a territory in the vicinity by Europeans possessed of capital and industry, and controlled by law, cannot but prove a powerful auxiliary towards their civilization.* A taste for European comforts is created, the simpler agricultural impliments, rough tools, and cooking utensils begin to be valued, and at length become necessaries. The warm blanket supplants the ox hide, and a shirt is found a convenient and cool article of dress in the heat of summer. A market is opened for mats and other simple articles of native manufacture. There is a regular demand for labour at prices, which although quite reasonable to the European capitalist, are a great advance beyond anything in the power of the native to acquire elsewhere. By becoming acquainted with European notions as to civil Government, the administration of justice, the punishment of crimes, the security of property, the possession of the utmost degree of *personal liberty* and freedom of action, coincident with the supremacy of law, and the existence of a vigorous executive, the native mind is expanded, and useful lessons are acquired. Neither are these lessons without their due influence on the practical working of their own systems. Men who have once resided with Europeans seldom submit to the oppressions authorised by the customs of their respective tribes, the evils of which are apparent to such from their experience of a different order of things elsewhere. This intercourse with Europeans is an advantage, not unalloyed however by incidental evils. But in the progressive march of Nations towards improvement, these evils must be encountered: they are the trials and tests to be gone through in the progress of moral and intellectual advancement. If we can devise means to check the encroaching spirit of European adventure, and regulate upon principles of justice the intercourse between civilized and uncivilized man; if we can spread efficient Missionary agency in every quarter where that intercourse is carried on, so as to neutralize as far as possible its evil tendencies, and render its beneficial capabilities more available, *then* we may hope that christianity, with the attendant advantages of civilization in its train, may commence in South-Africa a march of triumph going forth "conquering and to conquer."*

In accordance with this view of the case, the opinion of the Committee of the Aborigines Protection Society (see Report May 1838) is thus expressed, " It seems to be an opinion founded rather on past experience than on any essential principle in the nature of the case, that the coloured races must inevitably perish as civilization and christianity advance. Whatever past facts may be, and unquestionably they are painful enough, they are not evidence that no better scheme of colonization can be found compatible with the safety and improvement of the Aborigines. We cannot admit the doctrine that the establishment of a civilized community in the neighbourhood of uncivilized tribes, *must*

---

* The following extract from an able though sanguine writer, is appropriate:—" If we, the civilized, could not physically exist in the same land with the barbarian and the savage, without destroying them, it would be a paramount duty to discourage the extension of colonies; but history, early and recent, where the civilized have been just, shows all men to be capable of improvement; and the same experience also shows, that doing justice is the grand means to ensure the amelioration and the mutual safety of the most dissimilar races. The opinion of our inevitable hostility with our neighbours and weaker subjects abroad, must consequently be rejected; and so long as it is open to us to cease from being wilfully unjust in our daily relations with them, we must not dispair of raising the most simple to the true point of political well-being,—a state of self-protection.—(*Bannister's Humane Policy, preface,* p. vi.)

The remarks of the Editor of the *Graham's Town Journal* on *colonization*, are also deserving of notice here. "We think it may also be admitted that civilized governments in general have not paid sufficient attention to this important subject, and that much may be done to soften down and ameliorate those evils which have too often been the consequence of collision between civilized and uncivilized communities. To think, however, of preventing such intercourse altogether, would be just as rational as to attempt to check the ebb and flow of the ocean by a mound of sand. Hitherto civilized governments have tardily *followed* emigration, and to this simple cause may be attributed most of the mischief of which we now complain.

" Let existing governments, then, learn wisdom from experience, and instead of lagging far in the rear, take the lead, and by authority check and discountenance those evils which they cannot entirely prevent or eradicate.

be injurious to the latter, without supposing something extremely defective and improper in the regulations and principles of the former. Let these be corrected, and the evils must be diminished."

If the subject under consideration were the propriety of establishing a colony in a distant inhabited part of the world, of which we possessed comparatively little knowledge, and could not therefore be assured that our new estalishment would not of necessity prove injurious to the natives, it would be our duty to hesitate, to make further enquiry, and in taking the necessary steps towards accomplishing our design, to guard against inflicting an injury on those with whom our scheme must bring us in collision. The most important question in such a case is forcibly stated by the Rev. J. Beecham (in his pamphlet previously quoted, p. 21) to be, "Whether it is possible to construct a system of colonization which shall properly respect the rights of the Aborigines, and effectually promote their interests, as well as those of the Colonists themselves. The formidable difficulty which lies at the very threshold of all such attempts, is that which arises out of the question respecting the transfer of lands. How ignorant and barbarous people can be supposed to have knowledge and understanding sufficient to bargain for the sale of their lands, on something like equal terms with the Colonists; or how the Colonists are to raise funds ample enough to enable them to pay what will be the actual value of those lands to the natives themselves, when they bargain to understand the uses to which they may be applied,—is one of the questions of most difficult solution with which the subject of colonization is clogged."

This " question of most difficult solution" does not interfere with the proposed plan of colonizing *waste and unoccupied* lands, most of which are unsuitable for native settlements, and none of which can at present be settled by them, owing not only to the want of the requisite population, but also to the absence of security arising from the constant wars in which the tribes are engaged with each other. *Most of these lands have never been inhabited in the memory of man*, and if there be small sections of country which in the event of security being produced by European influence, the adjoining natives might desire to claim as their original possession, or as desirable for pasturage, &c., there exists no necessity either for taking that land heedless of their claims and wishes, or for purchasing it at an extravagant price: there is room enough for all and to spare. If it be stated, that by occupying these waste lands, we take away the country which seems naturally provided for room for the future increase of the present population, I would observe, that unless security of life and property can be established, there is no chance of the increase of population. South Africa has been peopled some thousands of years, and its history appears to have been that of the extermination of one race by another, and to what extent this process has been carried we cannot tell. It is going on now, checked however by Colonial influence. *The evil can only be remedied by the establishment of civilized settlements in the unoccupied tracts before pointed out; and the advantages resulting to the native tribes from the protection and peace thus afforded them, would prove of incalculable value to their present and future peace and prosperity.*

However unwilling the British and Colonial Government may be to enter upon so onerous an undertaking as the proposed occupancy of the *unoccupied country* between the old colony and Natal, there can be no doubt that within a short period the necessity of Colonial jurisdiction and the consequent legalization of the settlement of Colonists beyond the present border will be *so pressing*, that no other alternative will remain. The sooner the legal authorities interfere, the better for all parties, and *more especially for the nations bordering on the lands occupied by the emigrants.* In the next NOTE various suggestions as to the principles and details of the plan which ought to be pursued in the settlement of these territories, are respectfully offered to the consideration of the British and Colonial Government, and of all other parties concerned.

NOTE VIII.

PRINCIPLES OF COLONIZATION ALIKE BENEFICIAL TO THE MOTHER COUNTRY, THE COLONISTS, AND THE ABORIGINES.

The FIRST principle to be kept in mind, in order to maintain a sound and healthy system of colonization is, that *the pecuniary obligations of the new colony should be entirely borne by its own resources.* Nothing will better check wild schemes or splendid plans unsuited to an infant state of society than the *practical* application of this principle. The civil and military establishments must be on a scale bearing some proportion to the probable means of the colony for the repayment of the sums advanced for their support. Thus a burden will be saved to the mother country, and the colony itself will also be spared the lasting injury produced by the artificial stimulus given to certain branches of industry, by an overgrown government expenditure drawn from foreign sources. *The solid foundation* of future prosperity will rest on a base which cannot easily be shaken; namely, *the genuine capabilities of the country*; and although in such a state of things, there will be few fortunes made with rapidity, and there will be less scope for mercantile speculations; yet there will be a steady advance, and no fear of retrogression.

The SECOND principle equally prudential and just (to mention no higher motives) in reference to the present and the future is, that an ample provision for the civilization and christianization of the neighbouring natives should form part of the pecuniary obligations imposed upon the new colony. The justice and policy of this must be evident to any one who seriously considers the position in which a large number of professed christians place themselves in the settlement of a new colony.*

It is their duty, as the most intelligent party, to devise plans by which the incidental evils of colonization to the nation should be avoided.† Peace and security to civilized

* The following extract from "Colonization," by Rev. J. Beecham, is as unanswerable in argument, as it is appropriate:—"There is another radical defect in our colonization system, deserving of very special notice. It is the want of a comprehensive and adequate provision for the religious instruction of the Aborigines. Of such moment is this subject, that a practical disregard of it would most certainly have led to the failure of any scheme of Colonization, however well-planned in other respects. Had our Colonization system been constructed on such principles that no lands should have been obtained from the natives but by fair and equitable purchase; and had it effectually provided for the introduction of a just and aumane policy, which, protecting the natives from oppression, should have proposed to secure to them all their rights and privileges;—had the system contemplated even all this, but stopped there, without affording religious instruction to the natives, it would not have prevented painful and injurious collisions between them and the Colonists.

"*The fact is, that barbarous nations require to be enlightened and elevated, before they can be brought to recognise and act according to the rules by which civilized communities are regulated*. They have to acquire a taste for social order, and need to be instructed as to the benefits which result from it. It is necessary that they should be taught to respect, from principle, the right of others; and to seek redress, when their own rights are invaded, from the operation of the laws, and not by resorting to violence and arms. *It is requisite that they should learn something of the decencies and proprieties of civilized life, before they can be mixed up with well-regulated society.* It must therefore be maintained, that, however just and proper may be the policy for regulating the intercourse of the Colonists and the Aborigines, the latter must be raised, in some good degree, from that state of ignorance, rudeness, and barbarity in which they are found, before they can be brought to enter into peaceful and decorous intercourse with the white strangers, and submit to the restrictions necessary for the maintenance of such intercourse."

†This can only be by the introduction of the teaching of christianity on a scale adapted so far as human means are concerned to produce a decided effect. In reference to the injurious results of the bad example of Europeans, &c. Mr. Beecham justly observes: "But the vicious example of white men, would never have effected so great an amount of mischief, had adequate religious instruction been provided for the natives. This would have fortified their minds against the bad white man's arts, and would have saved them from those diseases which are the consequences of sinful gratification. It

man in the vicinity of barbarians are best and most economically purchased through the instrumentality of moral influence. A number of active, zealous, and efficient missionaries, assisted by lay agents employed in schools, or in the practice of the more useful mechanical arts, would, under ordinary circumstances by the blessing of providence, produce a great change in the feelings and habits of a barbarous people, especially when their labours were not liable to interruption from capricious migrations and predatory and exterminating wars. *It is just that the expences of such a benevolent and christian enterprise should be borne by the colony, which eventually reaps its fair share of the temporal benefit arising from the civilization of its savage neighbours.* The means of the different religious societies are too limited, and the field they embrace already too extensive to admit of the application of so large a portion of their funds towards the accomplishment of an object which seems peculiarly imposed upon the colonies by their position and their interests. The terms on which such assistance could be rendered by the one party and received by the other, would not be of difficult arrangement. For even in the case of a Missionary Society being unable to accept such assistance from Government, towards the support of its Missionaries, in consequence of its principles forbidding the acceptance of pecuniary support to religious institutions; yet the Directors of a Society so circumstanced would probably not be unwilling to receive their portion of the amount appropriated for Missions; as they could apply it exclusively to the temporalities of the Missions, viz :—wagons, oxen, agricultural implements, buildings, schools, schoolmasters, and other lay agents: this would relieve them from an unavoidable branch of expenditure, which in South Africa, amounts on the whole to

can be triumphantly shown, that when the natives have been brought under the influence of Christian truth, communicated to them by Missionaries, they have then firmly resisted the solicitations to evil which formerly overcame them, and have become patterns of good conduct to the white men who previously had seduced them into sin."

nearly if not quite three-fourths of the annual cost of the Missions. The money should be granted to the Societies, and be regularly paid to their appointed agents, to be applied as the Directors of the several Societies may deem proper. The proportions among the several societies being adjusted on some equitable principle, founded on the number of stations established, and of missionaries and schoolmasters employed by each. The payment of these monies to the agents appointed by the several societies, would still secure the important advantage that each missionary would receive his salary from the society employing him, and not from the Government; and thus would be perfectly free from any imagined necessity of being subservient to the local authorities. A missionary must be the friend of good order, but he ought never to degenerate into a tool of Government.*

The THIRD principle of the *utmost importance in reference to the future security of the new colony, is that the rights of the natives be conscientiously respected.* We do them no injury by taking possession of waste and unoccupied lands; but in order to prevent future collision, the bounds of their territories should be accurately defined, and no inducement held out to them to sell lands *at present* occupied by them, or *even occasionally occupied* by them in seasons of drought. In settling their boundaries, let the utmost allowance be made for the increase of population, flocks and herds, in this and another generation or two, by which time we may

* It would be requisite that these *moral means* should be in active operation *before* or at least *as soon as* the colony commences. It will not do to wait until a *surplus* revenue enable the Colonial Government to be just or liberal. The expense of these *moral appliances* should form part of the estimated cost of the colony. Let there be *no mistake* in this matter. Something definite ought to be determined upon, before the colony is authorised. As Natal is first likely to be settled, I would observe that the revenue of that colony ought to be charged with the payment of the *temporalities* of at least two Missions among the Amapondos, one among the Mantatees, one among the natives dependant on the English at Natal, and two among the Zulus. At least £2,000 per annum would be requisite for many years to come, but this would be more than made up to the Government by the beneficial effect of the moral and intellectual cultivation of the neighbouring tribes.

hope that the introduction of new and improved modes of living may render their present possessions capable of supporting an almost indefinite increase of population. *The lands of the natives should be secured to them by a formal treaty with the British Government, beyond the power of any local authorities to alter.** Such tribes as place themselves under the Colonial Government, should receive titles and diagrams, thus their claims to the retention of their lands would stand on precisely the same legal footing as those of the European and other Colonists. *Want of accuracy in the definition of boundaries, or any other cause leaving an opening for the future indefinite extension of the Colonial territory, would defeat the ends of the present scheme of colonization,* which aims at preventing the serious evils arising from unauthorised emigration, by a plan which shall effectually guard against its possibility for the future.

The preceding principles being enforced and acted upon, it would be necessary to adopt a variety of preliminary measures, previous to the legal settlement of the Dutch emigrants, or the reception of other Colonists.

1st.—Commissioners should be appointed to arrange treaties with the native tribes bordering upon the lands about to be occupied. The principal parties concerned are the Griquas, Corannas, Bastards, Bechuanas under Maroco, and Abasutu under Moshesh; the Mantatees under Sinkonyela; the Tambookies under Mapassa and Vadanna; the Kaffers under Rili; and the Amapondos under Faku. As soon as possible similar arrangements should be made with the Zulus now under Matzilikatsi and Dingaan. The treaties should define boundaries, and settle a just system of international intercourse, founded on the principles of

---

* The plan of removing tribes of natives, on the plea of convenience, or even on the supposition of advantage, to result eventually to the natives themselves, must specially be guarded against. The process now going on in America is not only opposed to humanity, but is also equally impolitic in reference to the future peaceful relationships of the United States, and the Aborigines of that vast continent.

the treaties of Captain Stockenstrom, as modified by the recommendation contained in Notes III and IV. The missionaries would here render their valuable assistance.

2nd.—The Griquas should immediately be received as British subjects, under a modified arrangement suited to their present state.* The details of the plan to be adopted could soon be obtained from the leading men, and the missionaries residing amongst them.—(*See Bannister's Humane Policy, pp.* 229, 230; *Dr. Philip's Evidence Abor. Com., p.* 625.)

3rd.—The trade in gunpowder, lead, &c. should be placed completely out of the hands of private traders. This would render the tribes to the north of the Orange River entirely dependant on the Government authorities for supplies of this, to them, necessary article. To prevent illicit trade, grants of a limited quantity might be made quarterly to such Chiefs as can be depended upon, the allowance being immediately stopped on their ill behaviour or misuse of the article, in aggressive attacks on their neighbours. Unless *some* supply be made to them, it will be impossible to prevent the conveyance of large quantities across the boundary, as the temptations in the high prices offered would induce individuals to risk the danger of detection, and to dare the penalties of the law. By assuming

---

* The remark of Bannister (*Humane Policy, p.* 230) applies to all similar communities of coloured people, as well as to the Griquas, and it is a very important one. "A peculiar advantage seems likely to arise from forming the Orange River people into a community, separate from the present colony. *It will gradually raise the coloured man* in the estimation of the white inhabitants. Much communication in trade and otherwise, will still be carried on and be facilitated by it, inasmuch as the public peace will be better kept, and confidence improved. *But the assumed and real superiority of the white people, arising from the habits of their civilized ancestors, and from their greater present capital and abilities, will not crush the opening faculties of these people.*" This last observation explains the secret of the peculiar disadvantages to which the Aborigines of a country are exposed in their intercourse with Europeans, even when no positive injustice is committed. The only means of preventing the gradual wasting away of barbarous tribes when exposed to the effects of a civilivation too rapid in its advances for them to have any chance of reaching it, is the securing to them the undisturbed possession of their lands, by which means time is also secured for their gradual approximation in habits, tastes, &c., to the other classes of the community.

to itself the distribution of all the powder conveyed beyond the Orange River, the Colonial Government would acquire and preserve an almost unbounded influence in those regions.

4th.—Surveyors, together with *a few practical* Dutch and English farmers, should be sent to examine the sections of country proposed for immediate settlement. The one should execute rough surveys, marking out the principal rivers, mountains, relative elevations of the flats in their rise from the sea towards the interior, the timber forests, broken or level country, facility of communication, &c.; the other should report upon the nature of the soil, and the sort of pasturage, whether sweet, sour, or mixed; whether grass or karoo, the nature of the water in the rivers and springs, whether *brack* or *sweet*, and all such other topics as would naturally occur to *practical* farmers experienced in the various species of farming in the colony. Men should be sent from the sour-grass districts, from the sweet-grass and karoo farms, and from those which are chiefly agricultural; the observations of such men would place in the hands of the Colonial authorities the most genuine and valuable information.

5th.—A fixed and invariable rule to be established in reference to the disposal of lands, to be applied to the *first emigrants*, as well as to future settlers. Nothing has proved so great an injury to the Cape colony as the dispersion of the population, stimulated by the easiness with which grants of land were obtained, until within the last few years. From all accounts the greater part of the land proposed to be settled is calculated to support a much denser population than the average of the Cape colony; there is, therefore, less excuse should the same error be committed. Let the Government determine upon a section of country to be settled; this being surveyed and apportioned into lots, each suitable for a farm, varying in extent from 2 to 6,000 acres, according to their capabilities, supply of water, &c.

should be sold by auction to the highest bidder, a minimum price of one shilling and six-pence per acre being fixed. Suitable sites for villages, with extensive common lands attached to them, and small fields for cultivation should be chosen; grants in such villages, with a right of commonage, might be made to the poorer boers, widows, orphans, &c., and thus the claims of the destitute would be met, without beginning the evil practice of making grants of extensive farms. Near a sea port, or any site chosen as the seat of Government, the minimum price of land should be higher than in other less favoured situations, and considerable reserves kept back for sale at a future period; and these reserves might be occupied at a moderate quit-rent by such as had no means at present of purchasing land. Perhaps it might be considered prudent, in order to allure the population to reside in villages, to establish such villages on some of the most suitable sites, with extensive pasturage, lands attached to them, and to grant the right of pasturage to a certain number of individuals, on condition of building and residence. It would be desirable if all the emigrants, could be settled in parties of no less than ten families on one spot, with their farms distinct as to cultivation, with a common right as to grazing; but it is to be feared that the habits of the Dutch population would oppose serious obstacles. However, the attempt should be made, and a judicious functionary might accomplish much. It might also be desirable to permit such of the boers as had no means of purchasing land to continue grazing on the unsettled portions of the territory, they clearly understanding that this was on sufferance; and that they would have to leave when the arrival of fresh purchasers rendered a fresh supply of land requisite to be thrown into the market. *That this measure would occasion much discontent, is no reason why it should not be adopted; the Government must make a stand in the beginning against the ruinous practice of grants of land.* The credit allowed, and the amount of the instalments might be arranged so as to enable almost the poorest to purchase *to a given extent,* say 3,000 acres;

for such purchase ten years' credit might be given, one-tenth being paid off each year; allowing one year to elapse before the first year of credit commenced; for purchase of above 3,000 acres, the money of the additional quantity purchased should be paid at one, or at the farthest two, years' credit.*

In proceeding to the actual settlement of these lands, on the principle here advocated, it would perhaps be prudent to commence in three different quarters; beyond the Orange River, near the Griquas, where many boers are already settled; between Kafferland and the Orange River, where a few boers are now living; and at Natal, where the bulk of the emigrants design to remain.

The situations of the first two tracts of country (described in pp. 160-170) No. 1, 2, 3, being so near the colony, two districts might be formed and appended to the eastern province, under the Government of which they would naturally fall. The tracts No. 1 and 2, would furnish noble sites for a portion of the Hottentot and slave population, to whom *grants* of land for villages, should *be given*, as an inducement to settle. The settlement of the country described as No. 4 and 6, could not take place at present, or for years to come, until other sections of the unoccupied country were filled up. Our main concern is therefore with the country No. 5, extending from the Tugala river, nearly as far as the Zimvubu, and from the Sea to the Quathlamba or Draakenberg range. This district is pretty well known, a party of Europeans having long resided within its limits. It has also been described by Captain Gardiner and Mr. Isaacs. Its extent is somewhere about 20,000 square miles or 12,800,000 acres, and if peopled in the same degree as Albany, it would support 100,000 inhabitants, and no doubt

* I have entered thus minutely into the arrangements as to the disposal of lands, because this is one of the most vital questions, and a mistake here would prevent the realization of revenue, as well as the safety and civilization of the new colony.

is capable of a much greater population.—(*See Parliamentary Papers relative to the Cape, part* 2, *pp.* 94—102).*

The country dependent on Port Natal, extending from

* The following extract from the Graham's Town Journal, (9th Aug. 1838) exhibits a sober statement of the advantages resulting from the occupation of Natal.

"Natal is unquestionably a dependency of the colony, and must soon be formally recognized as a British Settlement. To those who know the value of this country, the apathy of the Government in not having taken this step long ago is inexplicable. As a maritime station it is of great importance; for let it become the rendezvous of British cruisers, and the illicit slave trade now carried on at Inhambane, and at other ports along the east coast, must cease; whilst for commercial purposes in general no situation can be conceived more advantageous. On this point Mr. Isaacs, in his work recently published, makes the following remarks:—

"The whole of the Eastern coast of Africa, from Point Natal to the northern extremity at Cape Guardafin, at the mouth of the Red Sea, has been but little frequented (with the exception of the Mozambique) by any nation except the Americans. Occssionally an English whaler may put in not for any direct commercial purposes, but merely to refresh with water and provisions in case of her requiring them. The whole of this large extent of country, and the western coast of Madagascar, with the islands in the Mosambique channel, are, therefore, but little known as possessing commercial advantages by any but Americans, and they doubtless enjoy all those beneficial returns which adventuring thither justly gives. * * * For a settlement, therefore, aiming at embracing an intercourse with the tribes in the several countries to which my details refer, Port Natal seems to me the most eligible spot for a settlement. Its contiguity to Mosambiqne, to Madagascar, and to the Comoro and other islands, undoubtedly manifests its peculiar advantages over any other part of the coast for the purposes of a factory. It is, if I may be permitted to use the term, the *point d' appui*, from which commercial adventurers may take their departure to the north-east, and even to the Red Sea, in vessels of such draught of water as may be able to get to anchorage; and I have often been convinced of the truth of what the American ship-masters have declared to me. " that with a few small craft, drawing but little water, we might enjoy most of the coasting trade from Natal to the Straits of Babelmandel." Natal also lying so immediately in the course for the Mauritius, all the accumulated produce would find its way to England, without any variation of the course of such vessels, which might, on the voyages out and home, be disposed to touch to obtain homeward freight, or to land outward supplies. * * * That a most lucrative commerce might be carried on, I think I have now sufficiently shewn; and that Natal offers the most convenient spot, from which communications may be held with the interior; *but it still requires a protection,—the adventurer and the capitalist, before they seek to invest their property in countries where no constituted authority exists, and where no protection against casualties is afforded them,* usually look round to see what security they have for their capital, and if they can adventure with any chance of success; *but if they find that their own country affords the protection needed, then their speculations are commenced with vigor, and they prosecute them with all that fervour and industry, so peculiarly the character of a British merchant.*"

"Let these advantages be duly estimated, and then add thereto, the fact that by the occupation of Natal, you give to the incursions of the Kaffers and other tribes occupying the country between that station and the colony, the most powerful and effectual check, and the result must convince all, that the true interests of the country require that Natal should be formally recognized, and taken possession of, without any further delay."

the Tugala to the Umzimkulu, called by the English settlers VICTORIA, has been repeatedly ceded by the Zulu Chief Chaka and Dingaan to British subjects, and for the last 14 years has been solely inhabited by a few English and their native dependants, about 2,000 in number. Recently it has been partly occupied by the emigrant Boers (640 men 3,200 women and children, and 1,260 coloured people, who have with them 300,000 sheep, 40,000 head of cattle, and 3,000 horses, with 1,000 wagons). From the testimony of all travellers and residents down to Mr. Boshoff, whose account is found in the preceding Note, there can be no doubt that this country is far superior to any part of the Cape colony. The agricultural capabilities of the soil, and the regularity and quantity of the rains falling, seem to increase gradually as we advance in an easterly direction along the coast from the Cape colony. I have travelled some distance beyond the Zimvubu, and can speak as to the immense forests, rich alluvial flats, and luxuriant vegetation, and which I am informed continues to Natal, and from thence half way to Delagoa Bay. The interior country towards the mountains is partly short sweet grass and karoo, and is well adapted to sheep; there is reason to suspect the existence of strata of coal, since considerable quantities have been found; water abounds in all directions, and there can be no doubt but that in the hands of industrious Europeans, this country would support a very dense population. As a site for a colony, none could be more suitable. Being near the Cape, and within four days' sail by steam, it could be easily governed without any expensive establishment, quite as easily and more so than many of the remote districts of the Cape colony itself. It is a compact piece of country, of not too large extent, and its natural boundaries the Drackenberg on the west, the Amapondos on one side, and the Zulus on the other, would induce a concentration of the settlers, favourable to civilization and good government. Port Natal, as a port for trade, is nearly equal to Table Bay, and its situation points it out as the future emporium of the Bechuana and interior trade. The duties on imports and exports would help the revenue of the new colony, as well as the direct taxes on land and stock ; and there is already the nucleus of a settlement in the boers and few English now in the country. The task of the Government is therefore a comparatively easy one. By taking possession of this port by a few military, the whole country is effectually placed under their controul : and from all we can learn, the emigrants are anxious to come under the rule of an authorized Government. After settling the present emigrants according to the plan previously proposed, *it would be highly inexpedient to force sales of more land. Let time be allowed for European capitalists, whether from England or the Cape, to receive correct information of the capabilities of the country, especially in reference to sheep ; and there can be no doubt but that a number of respectable Colonists from Europe and the Cape, would soon purchase lands, and form valuable farming establishments.** A small population gradually extending itself on a sound and healthy system, is far preferable to a widely-spread settlement, occupied by a lethargic horde of Colonial Boers, at least two centuries in civilization behind the rest of the European world. In a political point of view, the value of an influx of English inhabitants is of no small importance.*

---

* If European capitalists were aware of the advantages of sheep-farming in South Africa, their attention would soon be directed to the Cape colony, and to Natal when settled. It is a positive fact, proved by the experience of years, and attested by some of the most respectable individuals in the Cape, that a flock of sheep on a suitable farm, will after deducting all expenses of management, pay the capitalists 30 per cent, with an annual increase of capital besides. The country is at *least* equal to Australia, and in the opinion of some of the Australian farmers, is superior for sheep. When so many wild schemes are every day put forth, it is a wonder that a few capitalists do not unite, and send out one or two sensible men to view the the capabilities of the colony and Natal, and then act on their recommendation. Such men would have the advantage of the result of the experience of men of high character and property in the colony to assist them. The exports of wool from the Cape colony in 1837, amounted to 373,203 lbs., valued at £26,169, or one fourteenth of the total exports of the colony. The quantity is equal to that exported from New South Wales in 1825 : and the Cape farmers are only *just beginning.* With security, what would their exports of wool amount to 10 years hence ?

* The Home Government has now a good opportunity of acquiring information on the subject discussed in this Note. Captain Stockenstrom is in

In order to enable the Government to take up the new colony, without burdening the finances of the mother country, as well as to render assistance to Missionary agency among the neighbouring tribes, (a point of the utmost importance whether as regards justice to the natives or security to the colony) it would be necessary for a loan to be raised on the security of the British Government, the interest of this loan to be paid by the revenue of the new colony, and its principal discharged from the sale of lands.* This latter source of revenue would produce a large sum of money if properly regulated, and *providing the lands were not brought too hastily into market*. Sufficient might also be raised from this source to enable the Government to assist emigration of young married people on a plan similar to that adopted in New South Wales. If land in Australia be sold at a minimum price of five Shillings per acre, the land at Natal

England, and the Rev. J. Archbell who has seen more of South Africa than any other man, and possessed no small influence North-East of the Orange River, is also on a visit home, and would be able to furnish much valuable additional information.

* The true principles of colonization appear to be beginning to be understood at home, and the recent discussions on the new colonies in Australia, carried on through the press, have thrown much light on this interesting question. Even in South Africa we are beginning to have a few glimpses of light; emigration begins to be discussed, and sound principles advocated. Witness the following extract from the *Graham's Town Journal:*

"We find by the late arrivals, that a prospectus is now in circulation in London, suggesting a scheme for establishing another new colony in Australasia. It sets forth that, a few naval and military officers, and other gentlemen, bent upon emigrating with their families to some British colony, have formed themselves into an association, with the intention of adding to their number, and that should the scheme succeed, their removal to a distant colony might be accomplished without the feeling of expatriation usually consequent on settling in a foreign country.

"We find, however, by this prospectus, that the following are viewed as fixed principles in every undertaking of this sort:—

" 1st.—That no colony can fully develope its resources, whatever its natural capabilities may be, unless it be permitted *to manage its own local affairs,* in the same manner that a corporate city is privileged to do in the mother country.

" 2d.—That a due regard be paid to the establishment of an *uniform system in the disposal of the waste lands;* and which is stated to be best secured by affixing a *sufficient* price per acre, &c.

"We need scarcely say, that we perfectly agree with this writer. *Give us the management of our local affairs*; abolish the ruinous system of squandering away the waste lands on adventurers and favourites, and the Eastern Province of the Cape of Good Hope would soon vie in importance with any dependency of the British crown."

should not be sold *eventually* for much less. After the *present* emigrants are supplied with land *in proportion to their stock, at prices not lower than prices in the Cape colony, the rest of the land should be reserved for European capitalists.* By this means emigration from the colony would be checked, since the emigrants would not have the inducement of obtaining land for nothing. Those who are likely to improve land and prove valuable Colonists, are able to pay a fair price for it.

That the system of colonization here advocated, combined with a just regard to native rights, and the operation of efficient instrumentality for their spiritual and temporal benefit, would occasion the Government, whether of the Cape or of Natal, much trouble, may be readily admitted. Duties of a complex nature, differing considerably from the ordinary routine of official life, are the result of our position on a vast continent, with powerful and barbarous nations in our vicinity. We are *to them and their future interests*, a power, mighty *for good* or *for evil, for their conservation* or *their destruction.* Were we *now* merely contemplating a scheme of colonization *in a new country*, conscientious and timid men might be expected to shrink from the undertaking, the benefits of which were encumbered with so tremendous a responsibility.* But in South Africa we are

---

* Why should schemes for colonies in regions where as yet we have no Colonial establishment be entertained? New Zealand or the Sandwich Islands for instance. We cannot help the extension of our Colonial system in North America, Australia, and South Africa; and there is ample room in these extensive regions for millions of settlers, as well as abundant scope for the exercise of the benevolent endeavours of philanthropists for the welfare of the Aborigines by means of settlements founded on real or fancied improved plans of colonization. In New Holland, in North America, and at the Cape, the settlers *will* spread, there being no *sea boundaries* betwixt the present Colonists and large tracts of unoccupied land, they *will* advance, and there is no remedy within the power of man; *therefore, we must regulate the march of colonization by going before it* and thus provide against the recurrence of evils which past experience leads us to anticipate. The great principle of making a colony pay for itself, and of *rendering its revenue available for the benefit of the neighbouring natives,* should be insisted upon as a *sine qua non* without which no colony should be established. The carrying these principles into effect is *perfectly practicable.* If the new colony be worth colonizing, *it can pay* for its own expenses by the sale of its lands. Of course, this fund is not available all at once, and the young settlement must

already committed. We cannot recede. Our power *will* advance, and that within a few years, as far as the tropics. It rests in part upon our present measures, whether this power in its triumphant march, exercise a malign and withering influence, or whether it shall dispense in its train, the blessings of christianity and civilization, which are for "the healing of the nations." To adopt the powerful language of Doctor Philip *(Evidence Abor. Com., p.* 631), as just as it is eloquent, in reference to this very subject:—" *An able Governor of the Cape, might in twelve years influence the continent of Africa as far as the tropic; influence it for good, make every tribe to know its limits, to be content with its own, to respect its neighbours, and to drink with eagerness from the fountains of our religion, civil policy and science.* The Missionaries have already done enough to prove, that all this is not only possible but easy; much easier for a wise man to accomplish, than it is for a fool to render the whole of this part of the continent not only more barbarous than it

borrow money to defray its current expenses, until by an *economical* use of its resources as they gradually develope themselves, it can pay off its debts. Some will think five shillings too large for a minimum price of lands in South Africa; perhaps it might within the Cape colony; but from all accounts, the land at Natal is much more valuable for grazing and cultivation, and is well watered; the seasons are also more regular. Now in Albany land is seldom sold at less than one shilling and six-pence per acre, and there are valuable farms sold at a much higher price. It must also be remembered, that until the best lands were all purchased, no one would choose to buy inferior lands, so that the very choice of the country would be for the first purchasers, and a long credit would remove many difficulties arising from the want of capital. Besides, the application of the money paid for land to the general benefit of the community in paying the expenses of the civil and military government, the claims of the nation department, emigration, &c., would enhance the value of all property in proportion as the general security and comfort were increased by a wise and good government. I am aware that these views will be very unpopular with a certain class of unthinking Colonists, whose *beau ideal* of a new colony, is that of a settlement founded on extensive grants to settlers; an expensive military force paid by the British government, and for the supply of whose wants 30, or £40,000 would be spent; thus accustoming the first two or three generations of colonists to look to the British Commissariat, rather than to the resources of the colony itself for their support. It is to be hoped that the British government in taking up Natal, will guard against the granting or underselling of lands, with as much care as they would against an actual theft from the treasury. Shall we not signalize the year 1839 by the commencement of a colony which shall not cost the mother country a farthing, and *which shall conscientiously apply part of its resources to the benefit of the Aborigines in its neighbourhood*?

is at present, but hostile to us, and ever ready to combine for our destruction, and the destruction for a time of their own chance of civilization. What a responsibility then rests upon the British Government, even in the management of this apparently insignificant colony, and how anxious and persevering ought the friends of religion and humanity to be in saving us from the perils that threaten us."*

* Since writing the above, the Port of Natal has been "*seized*" by General Napier, by proclamation, dated November 14, 1838, of which the following is an extract:—

"I do therefore hereby proclaim and declare my determination to *seize* the said harbour of Port Natal, and to erect a fort therein, and to *seize* so much of the territory surrounding the said harbour, in whose hands soever the said fort and territory adjacent thereto shall happen to be at the time of such seizure, as shall be necessary for the proper occupation, maintenance, and defence of the said fort; and to keep possession of the same, in Her said Majesty's name, until otherwise directed by Her Majesty's Government.

"And I do further proclaim and declare, that the sole object of Her Majesty's Government in the proposed occupation of Port Natal is to prevent its being held by any of the hostile party, and to secure by such occupation the power of effectual interference in maintaining the peace of Southern Africa by such means and to such extent as shall hereafter appear to be necessary; and that, for such end, the said occupation shall be purely military, and of temporary nature, and not partaking in any degree of the nature of colonization or annexure to the crown of Great Britain; either as a colony or a colonial dependency; wherefore the said fort shall be, and the same is hereby declared to be, closed against all trade, except such as shall be carried on under special licence and permission of the government of this colony, any clearance or permission granted by any British, Colonial, or Foreign Custom House to the contrary notwithstanding."

NOTE IX.

CASE AND CLAIMS OF THE BRITISH COLONISTS OF ALBANY.

The claims of the British Colonists of Albany upon the paternal consideration of the Home Government, are undeniable. Their case of itself (apart from the general claims of the Eastern Province Colonists) is so clear, that no attempt has ever been made to reply to the arguments on which they ground their request for compensation and adequate protection. It is best stated in the language of their petition addressed in 1836, "*To the Honorable the Commons of the United Kingdom of Great Britain and Ireland, in Parliament assembled.*"

" The petition of the undersigned Inhabitants of the British Settlement of Albany, South Africa, *humbly sheweth,*—

"That on the 12th July, 1819, the Right Honorable Mr. Vansittart, Chancellor of His Majesty's Exchequer, submitted a motion to your honorable House, and which was agreed to, that a sum of fifty thousand pounds sterling should be applied to the purpose of conveying emigrants from Great Britain to the Cape of Good Hope, informing your honorable House, that this colony " was suited to most of the productions both of temperate and warm climates, to the olive, the mulberry, and the vine, as well as to most sorts of calmiferous and leguminous plants, and that the persons emigrating to this settlement, would soon find themselves comfortable."

" That in consequence of this flattering representation, and in firm reliance on the good faith, protection, and paternal regard of the British Government, petitioners were induced to quit the land of their birth, and to take up their abode in this part of His Majesty's dominions.

"That petitioners are bound to state to your honorable House, *that the expectations* held out to them by His Majesty's Government, as alluded to, *have not been realised, and that the hopes raised, and the promises made, in this instance, betray either great disregard of the live*s *and welfare of His Majesty's subjects, or an unacquaintance with the history or actual circumstances of the country to which they were thus invited to proceed.*

" That petitioners beg to represent to your honorable House that the country beyond the eastern boundary of this colony, is inhabited by a barbarous but numerous and warlike people, called Kaffers, whose dispositions and predatory habits, lead them to make continual inroads into the colony, sometimes murdering the inhabitants, burning and pillaging their houses, and almost invariably carrying off much live stock, consisting of horses and cattle, into their own territory.

" That during the period this has been a British settlement, viz.— thirty years, the frontier inhabitants have been repeatedly driven from their homes by these barbarous and restless people, and the whole of the country now forming the eastern province of this colony, and consisting of the districts of Albany, Uitenhage, Somerset, and Graaff-Reinet, laid waste, and reduced to a desert state."

After a reference to the frontier history, in proof of the previously disturbed state of the eastern province, the document proceeds to state a point of some importance in reference to the claims of these Colonists for compensation.

" That petitioners beg leave humbly to direct the especial attention of your honorable House, to the foregoing epitome of frontier history; inasmuch as upon a right understanding of these various incidents will depend their own case being clearly comprehended, and their difficulties fully appreciated. But if these be duly considered, in connection with the fact that under such specious and flattering representations, *they were invited to expatriate themselves from the land of their birth, that they might occupy the stations of the Military, and act as a defence to the colony against the barbarian hordes,* they feel convinced they shall receive that sympathy which has been hitherto denied them. Thus, on Lord Charles Henry Somerset receiving information of the intentions of the Government in respect to them, he unfolds his views in a communication addressed by the Colonial Secretary to the Landdrost of Uitenhage, in the following terms :—" From your intimate knowledge of the frontier, you will almost anticipate His Excellency's views for the sertlement of the persons who may first arrive, and His Excellency is sure that you will be aware that *the old line of military posts, now given up, between Graham's Town and the Great Fish River,* presents a country of great fertility and promise and capable of maintaining, with industry, a large population, and you will at once see the advantage, which *the colony,* as well as the individuals themselves, will derive from this portion of ground being early settled. His Excellency would wish to see the abandoned farms nearest Graham's Town first occupied, and in these occupations that it should be borne in mind, that the settlers are to be encouraged in their *agricultural pursuits, rather than in the maintenance of large herds of cattle.**

" In the month of April, 1820, the first party of emigrants were landed at Algoa Bay, and they then were informed that the lands upon which they were to be located, were immediately bordering on the Kaffer country, at a distance of one hundred miles further to the eastward. It is due, however, to the local Government to state that every thing was done which circumstances would permit, to ensure the comfort of the immigrants, and their safe and speedy conveyance to the place of their destination. And petitioners take this opportunity of stating to your honorable House, *that they landed on the shores of Africa with an anxious desire and a firm resolve to conduct all their operations in accordance with British views and feelings, and to base their intercourse, whether with the natives, or with other colonists, on British principles.* They also beg leave firmly to state, that no departure from this, on their part, has ever taken place; and though averments have been

* Vide communication from the Colonial Secretary to the Landdrost of Uitenhage, made to the contrary, they challenge their accusers, in the face of the world, to produce tangible proof in support of any such allegation.

" That your petitioners, with all their prejudices, enlisted on the side of the colored classes, whether foreigners or Colonists, and with the firmest reliance on the regard and protection of their own Government, commenced with cheerfulness to occupy and improve the lands on which they had been placed. Some, indeed, of their number, foreseeing the danger which awaited them, or from other causes, resolved upon removal, but were sternly prohibited from doing so,—the local magistrate being instructed by the Colonial Government that " he was not to feel himself, for the present, authorised to grant any permission of removal, without specific authority from the Colonial office,—*it being of the utmost importance with reference to the views of His Majesty's Government, that positive establishment should take place on the lands assigned.** It cannot escape the observation of your honorable House, *that the views of His Majesty's Government here referred to, were the future defence of the colony, by establishing a British settlement along the most exposed part of the Colonial frontier, and thus exposing the population to the future incursions of the barbarous hordes.* Still the immigrants, with few exceptions, were unconscious of danger, and though the whole of the country allotted them displayed in every part the most striking and painful mementos of savage warfare, which had for so many years prevailed among the neighbouring Kaffers and the border Colonists, they proceeded to construct their dwellings—many of them actually on the blackened ruins of the farm-houses of former residents,—and to establish themselves firmly on the soil.

" Your petitioners must here state that *the system adopted in the formation of this settlement was extremely faulty, and not founded on any practical kuowledge of the capabilities of the country,* or with a due regard to local circumstances, and the relations existing between the colony and the native tribes on its border. A sufficient illustration of this may be seen in the par-

---

* Vide letter from the acting Colonial Secretary, Mr. Ellis, to the provisional magistrate, Captain Traps, dated May 23d, 1820.

simony with which lands were allotted to the settlers, and in the principle that they were to be encouraged in agricultural, rather than pastoral pursuits; thus losing sight of the fact, that the country is alone suited to the latter,—many years experience having fully shewn that agriculture cannot to any great extent be successfully prosecuted;—nor were it otherwise would there be a market for the disposal, at a remunerating price, of the surplus produce. There are few inhabited parts of the colony of equal extent, so unsuited to agriculture as the settlement of Albany; and hence the immigrants, on the failure of successive crops, either from rust, locusts, drought, or flood, were *compelled* to have recourse to pastoral pursuits for the maintenance of their respective families. But here again they found themselves in a false position. The lands assigned to them only amounted in general to from 200 to 500 acres,—an extent which in this country is perfectly inadequate to the wants of a cattle farmer; a fact so generally known and admitted in all previous cases, that it appears from official data, that between the year 1814 and 1821, when four hundred and ten quit-rent places were granted by the Colonial Government principally to the Dutch inhabitants, that the average extent of each place amounted to nearly 4,000 acres.

" Your honorable House will not fail to anticipate that petitioners could not long remain in such close proximity with the Kaffers, without coming into collision with them; but as they entertained towards them no other feelings but those of benevolence and goodwill, the meeting took place, on the part of the settlers, not only without fear, but without distrust. The small military force on the frontier being, however, quite insufficient to check the inroads of the numerous predatory bands infesting the colony, as the cattle of the settlement increased, plunder became more frequent, and in several instances defenceless individuals were wantonly, and without the slightest provocation, slain by the treacherous barbarians. Those who were most exposed to these incursions, adopted the most conciliatory conduct to propitiate the savages,—engaged in a friendly traffic with them,—although from a mistake and dangerous policy forbidden by the Colonial Government,—and endeavoured, by every possible means, to avert those evils which ultimately overwhelmed the whole settlement.

" After stating the above, it will be readily inferred that petitioners could not remain long unconscious of the perils which awaited them; on the one hand from the inroads of the Kaffers, and on the other by the disadvantages under which they laboured, from other causes already referred to. Accordingly it was proposed, early in the year 1822, by several of the inhabitants of the settlement, to hold a general meeting, in order to decide upon the best means to be adopted of making known their difficulties and their actual position to the Imperial Government; but your peititioners were prohibited by the Governor of the colony from thus assembling.* As, however, their situation continued to be insupportably irksome, and as murder and pillage, by predatory bands of Kaffers, were of more frequent occurrence than ever, a memorial was drawn up, and addressed to the Right Honorable Earl Bathurst,† in which, amongst other details of existing grievances, are the following passages:—

"That the most pressing and insupportable of their grievances arise from the constant depredations of the Kaffers, who have, within a few months, committed several murders, and deprived the settlement of the greater part of its cattle; that these depredations are in a great measure produced by relinquishing that line of policy which held out to those tribes a hope of procuring, by friendly barter, such commodities as their acquired wants have rendered necessary, and which they are now obliged to procure by theft or force; by discountenancing and withdrawing the military force from the new settlement of Fredericksburg, and permitting the Kaffers to return, and ultimately to burn it to the ground; by withdrawing from the Fish River a line of posts which had previously effectually protected the settlers; by refusing aid to the more advanced farmers, plundering parties have been encouraged to drive those in, and afterwards to extend their incursions to all parts of the settlement, and even beyond it; and by withholding from the local military authorities that discretionary power with which they were formerly invested, which, by enabling them to enforce summary restitution, shewed the Kaffers that the offence must instantly be followed by the punishment: whereas, by waiting the decision of the Commander-in-chief, 600 miles distant, in every emergency, offences are allowed to accumulate to an alarming amount; and the slender means of de-

* Vide proclamation by Lord C. H. Somerset, dated 24th May, 1822.
† Dated 20th March 1823.

fence the settlement possesses, deprived of the power of acting with promptitude, is forced to present to the Kaffers at once the appearance of enmity aud weakness. That thus it appears to the Colonists, instead of the new settlement ever deriving any advantage from the civilization of these savages, that the existing measures can only lead to a war of mutual extermination."

"In directing the attention of your honorable House to this Memorial, petitioners will not, it is presumed, be deemed presumptuous in expressing their surprise that a detail of such serious grievance should have been left without immediate redress. It is due, however, to the then existing administration of government to state, that some time afterward commissioners were appointed to enquire into the condition of this and other of His Majesty's colonial possessions, on which occasion this settlement received a considerable share of attention, and the result was, that many important alterations were subsequently made, which tended greatly to abate those grievance of which they so frequently had been forced to complain.

"That petitioners have also to state, that on the formation of the settlement of Albany, the eastern province of this colony enjoyed no trade beyond the very limited demands of the widely dispersed inhabitants; but that it was not long before the British settlers, amidst all the unfavourable circumstances by which they were surrounded, created a profitable but rapidly growing traffic both with the natives of the interior and with the more distant parts of the colony. By the custom-house register at Port Elizabeth it appears that in the year 1828 the amount of exports and imports at Algoa Bay was £96,591, whilst for 1834 it had increased to £236,563. Such great improvements had also taken place in wool-bearing sheep, that it appears from the latest accounts from London, that the wool exported from this district is but little inferior, if not equal, to any offered for sale in the London market, either from Germany or from any British Colonial possession.

"But not only have the British settlers of Albany exerted themselves to improve the resources of the country and enhance the value of its native productions, but they have been equally sedulous to disseminate abroad, and to hand down to their posterity those great moral principles which are so justly the boast and glory of their native land. Numerous edifices have been erected by them for

Divine Worship, and schools established for the instruction of youth in the principles of religion; nor have they ever relaxed in their endeavours to promote all those institutions whose professed object is the amelioration of the condition of mankind at large.

"*Your petitioners are aware that their character and conduct have been represented to their country, by wicked and designing persons, as dishonest and cruel,—as oppressive to the native tribes, and as factious to the Government;* and they feel but too sensibly that they have allowed such slanderous accusations to pass unheeded, until they have fixed themselves but too firmly in the minds of their countrymen, suppressing that sympathy which they claim as their just due, and restraining the hand which would otherwise have been stretched out promptly in their succour and defence. *A sufficient refutation of all such calumnies may, however, be found in the fact that although the settlement of Albany has suffered so severely from the depredations of the Kaffer hordes, still until the late general irruption, no commando from this settlement ever entered the Kaffer territory, either to make reprisals or otherwise, with the exception of one solitary instance where a party of its young men proceeded to the succour of the Kaffers, at the very moment when destruction awaited them at the hands of the dreaded 'Fetcani.'* In vain, however, have your petitioners put forth a denial of accusations equally cruel and unjust,—the charges have been reiterated, and although they have petitioned His most Gracious Majesty the King in Council,* and also the Right Honorable the Secretary of State for the Colonies,† urgently praying for inquiry on the Spot into those charges which have been preferred against them, so manifestly to their injury, their prayers have not been acceded to, and they are still suffering under the withering effects of that calumny which has been so industriously circulated, and so generally credited, in every part of the British dominions.

"That petitioners having, as they trust, clearly proved to your Honorable House the injustice with which they have been treated both by the native tribes adjacent and by their own government;—having also clearly shewn from official records and admitted facts that ever since this colony has been a British possession the Eastern

---

* Dated 17th June, 1835.
† Dated 23rd January, 1836.

Province has been repeatedly depopulated by the formidable inroads of the Kaffers, and that their more petty incursions have been alike incessant, disastrous, and irritating. It now becoms the painful duty of petitioners to advert to the late destructive irruption, when without the least warning, and at a time to all appearance of profound peace, the barbarian hordes suddenly burst into the colony, demolished in one short week the entire labours of fifteen years, wantonly murdered upwards of forty of the peaceful inhabitants, destroyed by fire 455 farm houses, and 58 wagons, carried off 5,438 horses, 111,418 cattle, and 156,878 sheep and goats, scattered and destroyed nearly the entire harvest of the preceding year, and committed other ravages; altogether amounting to the total estimated value of £288,625 4s. 9d.*

"The result of this barbarous and unprovoked inroad is that great numbers of the frontier colonists are reduced from comparative comfort to a state of such abject poverty and want, that it must be seen to be fully understood, and it will scarcely occasion surprise to your honorable House, after the details which your petitioners have felt it their duty to lay before you, to add that the poignancy of their sufferings is immeasurably increased by the fact that the right honorable Secretary of State for the colonists, in a despatch† to His Excellency Sir Benjaman D'Urban, has stated his conviction, that in the conduct which was pursued towards the Kaffers by the colonists, and the public authorities of the colony, through a long series of years, the Kaffers had an ample justification of the late war, and that they had a perfect right to hazard the experiment."

"That petitioners take this opportunity of disclaiming most unequivocally any participation in conduct which could warrant or dictate the bitter reproach cast upon the colonists in this instance; and hence they are induced to appeal to your honorable House for that justice which they have repeatedly and urgently prayed for in vain, at the hands of His Majesty's government; and they now most humbly pray that your honorable House will be pleased to take their case into its most serious consideration, and that such measures may be adopted thereon, as shall seem to your honorable House best calculated to ensure them—

* Vide report of the Government Commissioner.
† Dated 26th December, 1835.

" 1.—*The appointment of a Commission of Inquiry to investigate on the spot into those charges which have been so injuriously made against them.*

" 2.—That they may receive pecuniary compensation for those ruinous losses which have recently befallen them, and which may justly be attributed to inattention to their repeated petitions, and most urgent remonstrances.

" 3.—For such adequate protection in future against the aggressive inroads of the native tribes, as shall stimulate the plundered inhabitants to re-establish themselves on their ruined and deserted farms; as shall check that extensive abandonment of the colony which is now in course of progress; and as shall restore that confidence in the justice and paternal regard of the British government, which had been forfeited, to a considerable extent, by the adoption of impolitic measures, and by lending a too credulous ear to the reprehensible calumnies which have been cast upon a community of British subjects, whose humanity and loyalty they do not hesitate to declare are alike unimpeachable."

In reference to the vague and rhetorical charge made against the Colonists of the eastern frontier, of having been guilty of continual aggressions on the Kaffers, the local journal makes the following striking statements, which cannot be contradicted.

" 1. That 85 years ago the boundary of Kafferland was the Keiskamma River, but that the Kaffers have at various times, within that period advanced westward from the Keiskamma River to the District of Swellendam.

" 2. *That during that time they have been continually plundering the colonists;* their inroads being frequently marked by the most wanton cruelties and bloodshed"

" 3.—*That the frontier districts of this colony have been repeatedly depopulated by them*, of which abundant evidence remains to this day in those numerous ruins of extensive buildings which have been fired and destroyed by them in their various inroads.

" 4.—*That it has been the constant aim of the Government,*

not to hinder the colonial farmers from pressing forward, as has been confidently affirmed, but to prevent their retreat from, and abandonment of the frontier districts. That to induce them to remain, promises of protection have been held out to them, together with offers of land in the most favourable situations,— and that where these have failed, retreat has been declared criminal, and the power of the Government exerted to prevent it.

"5.—*That in repelling the numerous inroads of these tribes, mild and conciliatory measures have been invariably tried until found utterly unavailing—and that at last the whole strength of the colony has been required to effect their expulsion, on which occasions the colonial farmers have been obliged to take the field without pay, to leave their familes in exposed and dangerous situations, and to endure the greatest hardships and privations in the general defence.*"

The British inhabitants of Albany, feel particularly injured by the evidence of Captain Stockenstrom, (see p. 98) in which it is stated that they have " *very often* served on commandos against the Kaffers, an assertion which must have slipped from that gentleman unawares, since it is quite contrary to fact, (the only commando in which they engaged being one sent to defend the Kaffers from the Fetcani). At a meeting held at Graham's Town, 6th September, 1836, the following resolution bearing on this subject was passed.

" The inhabitants of Albany most unequivocally DENY THE FACT STATED BY CAPTAIN STOCKENSTROM, in his evidence before a Committee of the House of Commons, that the British Settlers of Albany have "*very often*" served on commandoes, *or that they have in any way participated in those atrocities which he has described as being of frequent occurrence on such expeditions,— atrocities which are utterly disclaimed and abhorred by them,—* and with reference to which THEY NOW CHALLENGE IN THE FACE OF THE WORLD, THE PRODUCTION OF A SINGLE CASE IN PROOF OF ANY SUCH ALLEGATION."

In the congratulatory address sent to Her Majesty the Queen, from Graham's Town, October 1837, the grievances of the Colonists are again briefly adverted to :—

"*We cannot conceal from Your Majesty that the measures*

hitherto adopted have not afforded to the exposed inhabitants of this portion of Your Majesty's dominions any amelioration of their painful circumstances: nor can we refrain from expressing our poignant sorrow that *a line of policy should now be pursued which is based on the principle, that all those misfortunes which have heretofore been experienced by the incursions of the native hordes have been caused by their aggressive inroads upon the Aboriginal tribes in the first instance.* Feeling, therefore, that we stand degraded in the esteem of our country, we deem it incumbent upon us to declare to Your Majesty, with the firmness inspired by conscious rectitude, that such imputations are not founded on fact; but that, on the contrary, the inhabitants of this settlement have, ever since its establishment in the year 1820, exerted themselves sedulously to maintain amity with that people, and to promote to the utmost their temporal and eternal interests.

"It is our paramount duty also to state to Your Majesty that since the subversion of those benevolent measures which were adopted by Your Majesty's Governor, Sir Benjamin D'Urban, several *thousands* of Your Majesty's valuable and loyal subjects have abandoned the colony,—the land of their birth,—impelled thereto by *a painful sense of insecurity, and the absence of that public confidence* without which people can neither enjoy contentment nor arrive at prospesity.

"But while we make this humble appeal *for justice and for rigid enquiry into our case and circumstances,* we rely with implicit dependance on Your Majesty for redress of those grievances under which we labour; assured that Your Majesty's generosity will graciously pardon that importunity which nothing but the deep importance of those vital interests that are involved in the questions at issue would warrant our using."

The British Colonists forming by far the most intelligent portion of the population of the Cape, feel peculiarly aggrieved at the late alteration in the constitution of the Legislative Council, which appeared to them as placing the probability of a fair representative Government at a greater distance than ever. The local journal in April 1838, makes the following remarks on this change, and it is impossible to deny their propriety. It is difficult to understand how the clamorous advocates for the increase of the democratic branch of the British constitution, can coolly disregard the claim of the Cape Colonists, for at least a fair share in the management of their own affairs.

" We regret most deeply that it should have devolved upon His Excellency Sir G. NAPIER, at the commencement of his administration of this colony, to have made so inauspicious an announcement,—upon one whose family is distinguished for its love of liberty, and for its avowed attachment to popular rights, and to liberal principles.

"The alterations which are made in the constitution of the Legislative Council are, we understand, these :—

" 1st.—*No question is in future to be debated in the Council, unless the same be proposed for that purpose, by the Governor.* Hence the members are in this respect mere puppets, and can only speak at the bidding of the Governor.

" 2d.—*The appointment of members is on longer for life, but during pleasure.*

" 3d.—*None but the Governor himself can introduce a Bill into the Council.*

" Need we ask whether any *independent* man will submit to hold office on these terms,—will be content to sit in the council chamber gagged as well as fettered,—and after all expose himself to the degradation of *dismissal*, should he vote contrary to the wishes of those who have selected him as his passive instrument ? Why, the title of "HONORABLE," when unconnected with office will in future be equivalent in this colony to that of " servile tool of the Colonial Minister !"*

---

* The Colonists have reason to suspect that this deduction from the measure of freedom enjoyed by the Legislative Council, as well as the withholding from them any share in the management of the general affairs of the colony, is attributable to the effect of certain insinuations on the minds of the Home Government. The following is an extract from a letter of Dr. Philip to Sir Benjamin D'Urban, (dated Kat River, 22d September, 1834, published in returns Kaffer War, ordered to be published by House of Commons, 12th July, 1837, page 168.) In allusion to something which had taken place at George, arising out of the proposed vagrant act, the writer observes:—"It will, I hope, relieve your Excellency of your Legislative Council,

It is difficult to understand the views of the British Government respecting the character and conduct of the British Colonists in Albany. In reply to an address sent, January 1836, from Graham's Town, praying for inquiry, the following answer was received by the committee appointed to represent the petitioners:—

"Colonial Office, Cape Town, 7th October, 1836.

"GENTLEMEN,—I am directed by His Excellency the Governor to acquaint you, for the information of those concerned, that he has received a despatch from the Right Honorable the Secretary of State for the Colonies, acknowledging the memorial of the inhabitants of the Eastern Province, praying that a commission be appointed and sent to the colony, for the purpose of enquiring into certain statements which have been circulated in regard to the general conduct of the Colonists towards the native tribes.

and cure my friend Fairbairn of his predeliction for a legislative assembly. The influential people among our Colonists have but one idea of liberty, and that is the liberty of oppressing all beneath them : and till they are more enlightened and liberal on this subject, I must deprecate a legislative assembly as one of the greatest curses that could come upon the country."
"The idea of liberty" entertained according to Dr. P. by the Colonists is unfortunately too much the general idea of even respectable and popular assemblies of the highest character, and it is best checked by giving "*those below them*" a legal means of opposing such aggressions on their liberty by a fair representation of all classes of the community. Besides, Dr. P. forgets that the Governor of a colony, as the representative of the British Sovereign, has a *veto* in all acts of the colonial legislature, and that, therefore, by the appointment of a liberal and enlightened Governor, something would be done to *enlighten* and *liberalize* the views of the Colonists, supposing them to be so tyrannically disposed as Dr. P. imagines them to be. With the previous security of free and unlimited religious freedom, the liberty of the press, and a British Governor, I should not fear the acts of the most bigotted legislative assembly of any colony under the sun. On the contrary, nothing would tend more to bring *illiberal, ignorant,* and *prejudiced* notions into discredit, than their being fully elicited and promulgated through so public a medium as the debates of the legislature : the intelligent minority would acquire daily accessions, and would in a few years become a majority. A legislative assembly would prevent the Colonist being condemned *unheard;* they would obtain, *at least, a fair hearing for their case*; and THIS, ABOVE ALL THINGS, IS WHAT A CERTAIN FACTION DREADS. The happy adjustment of the Slavery question has removed every ground of objection to the formation of a legislative assembly or assemblies in the Cape colony. Since writing the above, it appears from a recent arrival from England, that the limiting of the power of the legislative council originated in a *mistake*; but whether this was the *mistake* of the Colonial Office at home, or the executive of the Cape, we are not informed. The Colonists have learnt one lesson from this transaction, namely, that what has been considered the *liberal* portion of the Cape press is quite prepared to defend any curtailment of *their* liberties. Witness the defence of the limitations of the power of the legislative council, April 1838, by the editor of the *South African Commercial Advertiser*.

"Deeply regretting, as he does, the promulgation of any statements which have given so much pain *to these loyal and meritorious subjects of His Majesty—the inhabitants of the eastern province*—Lord Glenelg has expressed his desire that memorialists should be informed that *His Majesty's Government disclaim all participation in the sentiments which have dictated the reproaches cast on the character of the Colonists.* He appreciates, and cannot but applaud, the solicitude of the memorialists to relieve themselves from the effects of the statements in question; but he has felt it, however, impossible to concur in the expediency of appointing a commission of inquiry. Such a measure would not, in His Lordship's judgment, answer any useful purpose, inasmuch as the report of a commission, and the evidence resulting from an inquiry, would be too voluminous for general circulation; nor does Lord Glenelg regard the proposed commission as a proper mode of repelling imputations on a whole people. He conceives there are other and much more convenient channels through which the memorialists, without incurring the delay, the expense, and the prejudice, which would attend an enquiry by commission, might effectually promulgate their defence against accusation; and to those methods of vindication, the parties concerned will probably, he imagines, think it expedient to resort.

"I have the honour to be, Gentlemen,
"Your most obedient servant,
(Signed) JOHN BELL."

"To W. R. Thompson, E. Norton, G. Jarvis, A. Anderson, and R. Godlonton, Esquires.

This disclaimer on the part of the authorities at home is so far satisfactory,* but what are we to understand by cer-

---

* The following is an extract from a respectable and independent London paper, the *Watchman*, August 30, 1838.
"We readily give insertion in another column, to a letter from the Rev. WILLIAM SHAW to a friend in this country. We shall not at present comment upon it further than to remark, that if the recent British settlers in the frontier district of the Cape colony are to be abandoned to ruin, *it will avail them but little that Lord* GLENELG *has disclaimed, on the part of the Home Government, all participation in the sentiments which dictated the injurious accusations which their enemies have preferred against them.*"
The following is an extract of a letter of the Rev. W. SHAW referred to in the above:—
"I have already seen enough to be fully convinced of the ruinous consequences, to great numbers of the settlers and country people, by the late

tain passages in Sir G. Grey's speech, in reply to Mr. Gladstone's remarks on presenting the petition of the Albany settlers, 10th July, 1838?

"The case before them had already been sufficiently gone into by means of the enquiry instituted, and the document submitted in consequence of the inquiry to the consideration of the House. It was a lamentable fact, that the state of that part of the Colony could hardly be worse than it notoriously had been for some years, *owing in the great degree to the aggression of British subjects* on the *Aboriginal* Inhabitants, *and their endeavours to extend their territory in this quarter for selfish and interested purposes*.

"The pretexts for these enlargement of territory, from year to year,

Kaffer irruption. I am aware that well-informed persons in England never doubted this; and it could not require any corroborative testimony, if it were not that interested persons have sought to mislead the public mind on this subject. I can assure you that the effects of this fearful disaster will be felt for years to come, both as it respects the *temporal* and *spiritual* interests of the settlers; and I hope you will not hesitate to publish it as my most decided opinion, that if *adequate compensation* be not granted to the sufferers, it will be a most flagrant breach of faith on the part of the British Government, *who sent the settlers to the lands which they now occupy*; and it will always be justly quoted as a lamentable instance of neglect of British interests, by those who should have fostered and protected them, at the same time that they practically cared for the native tribes. I find that many of the ruined people are despairing of help, but I have endeavoured to console them with the belief that the Government will not abandon them; and I never will believe (unless compelled by facts) that any administration will refuse to recognize their just claims to compensation. You know my views on this subject generally, and they have undergone no change. The border policy of this colony, for years previously to the irruption of the Kaffers, had been very bad, and therefore was very injurious both to Colonists and Kaffers; but for this the settlers were not to blame; they complained several times of the border system, and very earnestly entreated for the substitution of some other plan. They now very naturally think, that it is a great hardship that any class of persons in England should hold themselves responsible for the *effects of a system* which they *always deprecated*; and that to exhibit charges, which *have not been*, and *never can be proved*, against an innocent and well-meaning people, because the system of which *they were not the contrivers*, but *the victims*, has produced bad consequences, is only to offer *insult* instead of *commisseration* to the sufferers.

"My utmost efforts shall be used in every way consistent with my office and character as a minister of the gospel, to calm the tumult of our people's minds. In common with the rest of the community, they have been *greatly* and *injuriously excited* by recent events;—and, considering the ungenerous treatment which they and their ministers have received from a party who affect to be friends of the Kaffers, but who, *in fact, have as yet done next to nothing for that people*,—I cannot wonder at the idnignation which is every where manifest, although I am bound, by a thousand motives, to exhort them "to forgive their enemies,", and to "pray for them who have despitefully used them."

had been the presumed necessity of increasing the security of the Colonists, by placing our intermediate territory between them and the Kaffer Tribes; the result was aggression on the part of the Colonists, often causeless and unprovoked, and on the part of the Aborigines irruption and massacre. Bloodshed had been the feature of this attempt at acquiring that which the aggressors had no right to, and it was not till within the last two years that measures could be taken by the Colonial Government there, with a chance of success, to put a stop to this sanguinary contest. Having said thus much, he might also confess he could not see that any advantage could be derived from substituting a fresh inquiry into the causes of these transactions, *so disgraceful to the British name, and prejudicial to British interests.* A full investigation had already taken place; the report was before the House, and the Colonial Government had taken steps which encouraged Lord Glenelg to hope that there must be a speedy end to a state of things so much to be regretted. Where then was the necessity for the Governmet to incur heavy expense by consenting to a fresh Commission of Inquiry? For his part, he must express the most perfect confidence, that no measure in the Colony would be left untried to carry into effect the recommendations of the Colonial Government, for establishing a system of broad policy in this Colony, which might prevent a recurrence of the evils which had taken place by a departure from such a line of policy hitherto. General Napier had been sent out to this portion of our territories, with full instruction and ample powers, to restore the affairs of the colony to a wholesome condition. He now trusted he had made out a case to convince the House, *that this was not an occasion upon which the British Parliament could be induced to sanction, under pretext, the application of persons who had placed themselves in trouble and peril by means of their aggressions. (Hear)" !!*

There must surely be some mistake in the report of this speech, so contradictory to the disclaimer of Lord Glenelg of any " *participation in the sentiments which have dictated the reproaches cast on the character of the Colonists,*"—who are by His Lordship described as *loyal and meritorious subjects of His Majesty.*" It is needless to state that the charge of " aggression on the Aboriginal inhabitants," which are stated to be " so disgraceful to the British name," are totally unfounded. Whatever opinion may be formed of the policy of the Colonial Executive, the British settlers are just as innocent in reference to the effects of that policy upon their native neighbours, as the people of England themselves.

It forms no part of my plan to enter upon the discussion of the Colonial policy of the British Government. Something faulty there must be, in a system which taxes the British nation to about three millions sterling per annum, for the purpose either of defending the colonies from foreign aggression, or of repressing the out-breaks of a general discontent.* Here we may learn a lesson from an enemy and profit by the wisdom of Napoleon, whose opinion on Colonial matters are thus quoted in Allison's history of Europe,

* The following extract is from a respectable liberal paper, and afford matter for much reflection:—

Canada,	£219,718
Nova Scotia and New Brunswick,	139,664
Newfoundland,	17,317
Bermuda,	48,734
Bahamas,	32,330
West Indies,	286,972
Jamaica,	423,231
Honduras.	16,910
Gibralter,	116,958
Malta,	167,671
Ionian Islands,	132,104
Cape of Good Hope,	313,410
Mauritius,	97,410
Sierra Leone,	46,209
Gambia,	10,161
Ceylon,	94,184
New South Wales,	328,318
Van Diemen's Land,	167,607
Western Australia,	17,122
St. Helena,	51,893
	£2,727,923
Estimated amount of payments at Western Australia, quarter ending March 31, 1837,	5,704
Total payments,	£2,733,627

"Another million at the very least, probably a million and a half, must be added to the Canadian expenditure during the present year. That may be considered as "extraordinary," but henceforth we may be prepared for a regular advance in the cost of ruling Canada; and it is pretty certain that the military payments for the colonies, if kept up on the present scale, will amount to at least three millions per annum."—*Spectator.*

Vol. IV, pp. 697—700, a work of deservedly high repute and authority.

"Doubtless" said he "you must govern the colonies by force; but there can be no force without justice. Government must be informed as to the real situation of the colonies, and for this purpose, IT MUST PATIENTLY HEAR THE PARTIES INTERESTED: for it is not sufficient to acquire the character of justice, that the ruling power does what is right. It is also necessary that the most distant subjects of the empire should be convinced that this is the case, and this they will never be, *unless they are sensible that they have been fully heard.* Were the council of state composed of Angels or Gods, who could perceive at a glance every thing that should be done, it would not be sufficient, *unless the Colonists had the conviction that they had been fully and impartially heard.* All power must be founded on opinion; it is in order to form it, that an institution similar to that proposed, (Chamber of Agriculture in the colonies) is indispensable. At present there is no constitutional channel of communication between France and the colonies; the most absurd reports are in circulation there as to the intentions of the central government, and it is as little informed as to the real wants and necessities of its distant possessions. If the Government had on the other hand, a Colonial representative to refer to, it would become acquainted with the truth, it would proclaim it, and transmit it in despatches to its Colonial subjects."—The observations of the author of the work from which the above extract is taken, are worthy of due consideration by all who wish well to the continued amicable union of the British colonies with the mother country.

"It is observed by Mr. Hume, that the most remote provinces and Colonial possessions of a despotic empire, are always better administered than those of a popular Government, and that the reason is, that an uncontrolled monarch being equally elevated above all his subjects, and not more dependant on one class than on another, views them all, comparatively speaking, with equal eyes; whereas a free state is ruled by one body of citizens who have obtained the mastery of another, and govern exclusively the more distant settlements of the empire; and are consequently actuated by personal jealousy or patrimonial interests, in their endeavours to prevent them from obtaining the advantages of uniform and equal legislation.

" *England will ultimately lose her splendid Colonial empire*, from the same cause which proved fatal to that of Athens, Carthage, and Venice, viz :—*the selfish system of legislation*, exclusively adapted to the interest, or *directed by the prejudices of the holders of political power in the centre of the state*, and *the general neglect of the wishes of its remote and unrepresented Colonial dependencies*."—*(pp*. 699—700.)

FINIS.

APPENDIX.

No. I.

Remarks on certain attacks made upon the Wesleyan Missionaries in South Africa, with reference to their conduct and opinions, relative to the Kaffer war.

ADDRESS TO SIR BENJAMIN D'URBAN.

In the month of June 1835, the Wesleyan Missionaries presented an address to Sir Benjamin D'Urban, containing the following paragraph, which has been the subject of so much misrepresentation:—

"Lamentable and distressing as the events of the Kaffer war have been, as well towards the Kaffers themselves as the Colonists, we are yet consoled with the reflection, that so far as the Colonial Government is concerned, it has been conducted in accordance with the principles of justice and mercy. We know in common with our countrymen, that the Kaffers were themselves the aggressors, and that they most wantonly, cruelly, and ungratefully commenced this war, with a people who sought and desired their welfare and prosperity."

The explanation drawn from the Missionaries, in consequence of the unfair attacks to which they were subjected in England, will prove satisfactory to every *candid* reader: and it is here given as a cool and dispassionate reiteration of their past and present opinions on a point which, when the *furor* of party subsides, will cease to be a controverted one:—

"The undersigned Wesleyan Missionaries, who were present at the Meeting in which an address to His Excellency Sir Benjamin D'Urban, was agreed upon, and officially signed 'W. J. Shrewsbury, *Chairman*, and W. B. Boyce, *Secretary*,' 2d June, 1835;— deem it necessary to place on record their explanation of the opinions which that document was intended to convey, and which they believe it does clearly and unequivocally express, when fairly interpreted, apart from party influences and prepossessions.

"They are impelled to this step from the unfair advantage which has been taken of the evident misconception of their meaning, which appears in the following paragraph, extracted from a despatch of Sir Benjamin D'Urban, dated 19th June, 1835, addressed to Lord Glenelg, and *now for the first time* brought under their notice.

"His Excellency says:—

'I am not aware that I can usefully add anything in the way of detail of what has passed; as however I have reason to believe that the important measure of extension will be assailed by Doctor Philip, and of course by the London Mission, on the ground of injustice in itself, and very probably (since it is a party peculiarly liable to exaggeration in statement, where an object or theory is to be supported), of severity in its execution, I think it may be right to inclose an address (that otherwise I should not have done) which I have received from the whole body of the Mission here, seven in number, all well versed in the subject by long residence in Kafferland, and all intimately acquainted with the passing events of the period, since they were residing in various parts of it, or on the immediate frontier, when the Kaffer coalition attacked the Colony, and have continued so ever since; and I consider the unqualified opinion which this address gives on the subject of no little value, since, collectively, and individually, the characters, doctrine, and proceedings of this Missionary body, will bear the strictest scrutiny, and since their information is derived from close and personal observation.'

'That opinion, your Lordship will perceive, states, their conviction of the wantonness, cruelty, and ingratitude of the Kaffer aggression,—of the consequent justice of the course which it has been my indispensable duty to avenge,—and that this duty has been discharged in accordance with the principles of mercy.'

"From the above passages in the Governor's despatch, it has been inferred, that the Wesleyan Missionaries committed themselves by their Address, in a public and official approval of the extension of the Colony to the Kei river, and of every other measure, adopted by His Excellency up to that period.

"The Undersigned feel convinced that the language of their address warrants no such interpretation, than which nothing was more distant from their intentions, or more opposed to their well known views of the inexpediency of Missionary interference in questions of a purely political nature.

"The Address was intended principally to express their grateful sense of His Excellency's general kindness, and to acknowledge the important services he had rendered in providing for the safety of four Missionaries with their families, and their return through a country involved in war, from beyond the Kei river to the Colony. But as erroneous impressions prevailed in a distant part of the Colony, and would of course be communicated to our native country, respecting the origin of the war, and the manner in which it had been conducted by the forces under the command of His Excellency; and as, under the influence of such false impressions, *the character of a large number of the members of the societies under our pastoral care had been publicly and violently assailed, and consequently our ministerial fidelity impugned ;*—We felt it to be our bounden duty in justice to all parties concerned,—to the Governor,—to the public at home and in the colony,—to our societies,—and to ourselves, to state,—not as a matter of doubtful opinion, *but from our certain knowledge, that the Kaffers were in this war the aggressors, and that the war was just on the part of the colony ; because a war of self-defence and of absolute necessity ;—and further, that this war was carried on by His Evcellency in strict accordance with the principles of justice and mercy.*

"Our competence, from local knowledge, to form a correct opinion on the subject cannot be questioned;—and, not to plead that the same opinions have been expressed in much stronger language than we ever used, by some of the Scottish missionaries of the Glasgow Society, in speeches at a public meeting, a report of which was furnished by themselves to the editor of a colonial journal;—yet we may remark, that our prejudices in favour of a people among whom we trust to spend no small portion of our lives,—together with our complete independence of colonial support and control, are sufficient guarantees to all impartial persons, that we could be under no temptation of yielding to the influence of local prejudices or temporary excitement. Connected as we are with England, and fully aware of the generous impulses of popular feeling, (although in this case misdirected,) the temptation, if any, was calculated to bias us, on the side, which in our native country is deemed to be, exclusively that of justice and humanity.

"The *facts* of the case, obliged us to contradict prejudices and impressions, some of which have been of long standing, others of more recent origin, and all of them heightened and enlivened by *ex-parte* statements, made by respectable and influential individuals *residing far from the scene of action*, and *quite ignorant of the real state of affairs*. We counted the cost of what in a worldly point of view may be deemed our " imprudent" honesty, and are content to suffer for a while in the opinion of the great and good,—the *élite* of our native land; being confident of this, that a full investigation and careful consideration of the case in all its bearings, will assuredly convince those who for a time have blamed us, that men who have been willing to sacrifice on the shrine of *truth*, that which to such a class of men, must be dearer than life itself,—the sympathies and attachment of the religious public,—may be depended upon as men, who, under no circumstances, will lend themselves to misrepresent or to deceive.

" *We made no allusion in our address to the frontier system pursued previous to the war, either by way of approval or the contrary ; neither did we in the slightest degree allude to the plans of his Excellency for the future* ; subjects entirely irrelevant to the main purpose of our address, and upon the latter of which at that time it would have been quite premature to have hazarded an opinion.

APPENDIX. V

"The Undersigned claim to be judged from their recorded sentiments, and not from the erroneous deductions of others; from their actions, and not from *ex-parte* statements of misinformed persons. In appealing to this certain test, by which they desire to be tried, they refer to two documents contained in the Parliamentary evidence published by the Aborigines' Committee;—the first is a letter addressed by Mr. Boyce, March, 1834, to Sir **B** D'Urban, illustrative of their well-known views on the subject of the old border policy;—the second, is the evidence of the Rev. John Beecham, in which is detailed, the conduct pursued by them in July, 1835, when, in endeavouring to save the Kaffers from the certain ruin which must have followed the prosecution of the war, they successfully pleaded with His Excellency the Governor, to forego his original condition of expatriating the hostile tribes beyond the Kei river, and obtained permission to communicate with the Chiefs then at war with the Colony, with a view to the restoration of peace. In the furtherance of this object, some of their number risked their lives, and thus give a practical proof of their devotion to the real interests of the Kaffer tribes.

"In conclusion, the Undersigned appeal to the fact of their resumption of their original stations in Kafferland with the full consent, and at the earnest and special request of the chiefs and people,—as a proof that the parties *mainly interested*, and best able to judge, deem the line of conduct pursued by them, to have been calculated to serve their best interests.

"After a full consideration of the opinions which they have avowed, they see no reason for retraction or regret. Believing that much of the clamour which has been excited in England against them, has originated in a misapprehension of their sentiments; they now submit the foregoing statement to the consideration of candid and dispassionate persons, and trust that all further explanation will be deemed unnecessary."

Signed,
R. HADDY,   W. B. BOYCE,
SAMUEL PALMER,   WM. J. DAVIS,
JOHN AYLIFF,   HENRY H. DUGMORE,
WM. SHEPSTONE.

"The above document, copied from the original in my possession,

was drawn up by the Rev. W. B. Boyce, and having been attentively considered by the missionaries present at a special District Meeting, held at Morley, Kaffraria, 13th May, 1837,—was signed by *all* the parties concerned, who were present at the Meeting
As witness my hand,
W. SHAW, Chairman.

TESTIMONIES OF OTHER MISSIONARIES CORROBORATIVE OF THE STATEMENTS OF THE ADDRESS.

For proof that in this war the Kaffers were " the aggressors," and that it was on their part a premeditated attack; I would refer to the documents appended to the Court of Inquiry respecting Hinza's death, since re-printed in " Returns, Kaffer war," (ordered by the House of Commons to be printed, 12th July 1837), and also to the evidence of the Glasgow Society's Missionaries, and others contained in the above " Return." It was quite a *mistake* into which the Colonial Secretary, Lord Glenelg, was led, when he supposed that the Wesleyan Missionaries *alone* deemed the attack of the Kaffers upon the colony, to be on their part unjust. *By whom he was so grossly deceived, is a question which the Wesleyan Missionaries have a right to propose*, and some apology is due to them from His Lordship on account of the prejudicial impressions excited against them, however unintentionally, by the misstatement in the despatch dated 26th Dec. 1835. It is to be hoped that the candour of the noble lord, will readily grant that redress which is justly due, *and thus preclude the necessity of further reference to this painful subject.*

In the opinions expressed by the Wesleyan Missionaries, the Ministers of the Established Church of England,—the Missionaries of the Glasgow, London, Baptist, and Moravian Societies *coincided.*

1st.—CHURCH OF ENGLAND:—

The Rev. Mr. M'CLELAND, Colonial Chaplain, Port Elizabeth;

Rev. Mr. HEAVYSIDE, Colonial Chaplain, Graham's Town, have not hesitated to express openly their views of the injustice of the Kaffer aggressions, and of the injurious consequences resulting from the injudicious interference of Dr. Philip, &c.; and for this testimony they have received their fair share of abuse from the *liberal* press.

2nd.—MISSIONARIES OF THE GLASGOW SOCIETY.

REV. MR. LAING, in his speech at the Wesleyan Missionary Society, Graham's Town, May 22, 1835, speaks of the war as "an infatuated and cruel attack on the colony," and describes the Kaffers as "covetous and blood-thirsty natives." In a letter to Sir B. D'Urban, dated February 4, 1835, he speaks of the "blindness and wickedness of the Kaffers who have invaded the colony;" and such is his conviction of their guilt, that it appears to him requisite "that the country of the invading Kaffers must be taken from them, to indemnify the colony for the losses it has sustained;" and in the anticipation of this being the case, he requests reserves to be made for the peaceable Kaffers.—(*See Returns Kaffer War*, *p.* 177.)

REV. MR. CHALMERS, in his speech at the Baptist Missionary Meeting, at Graham's Town, Angust 30, 1835, speaks of the "peaceable and unoffending Colonists, left destitute not by any misconduct of their own, but effected solely by the wicked and relentless arm of the cruel and daring invader."—(*See also the letters of the Glasgow Missionaries in Returns Kaffer War, printed August* 12, 1837.

3rd.—MISSIONARY OF THE LONDON SOCIETY.

REV. MR. BROWNLEE seems to have had no scruple as to the injustice of the aggression on the colony, since in a letter to Sir Benjamin D'Urban, dated Beka, March 7, 1835, he gratuitously "drops a few hints that may be of service at the present moment." These *hints* are respecting the positions of the belligerent Kaffers, and the best means of "scattering the Kaffer forces, and preventing their escape with cattle to the ravines of the Kye."—(*See Returns, Kaffer War, p.* 180.)

4th.—Missionary of the Baptist Society.

The late Rev. J. Davies thus observes in his memoirs of Mrs. Davies:—

"I understand, that in our native land christian sympathy is turned almost exclusively towards the Kaffers. Every instance of suffering amongst *them*, is repeated in doleful accents in the parlour, in the pulpit, and on the missionary platform. But nothing is said about the poor settlers, only "*that they are wicked christians*;"—nothing is said about the houses burnt,—nothing is said about our wives and our children driven to the bush in the dead of night to hide themselves from the point of the blood-stained assegai,—nothing is said of our widowed wives and fatherless children,—nothing is said of mothers butchered, with their babes in arms,—nothing is said of the affectionate wife drawing with her own hand the quivering spear from the bosom of her husband,—nothing is said of our gallant sons contending for their lives, till all their ammunition is expended; then surrounded, and finally slaughtered one by one,—nothing is said of the greyheaded father, robbed of every head of cattle of which he was possessed, in one night, and deprived, with one fatal sweep, of all the comforts for which he had been toiling under an African sun for fourteen or fifteen long years,—nothing is said of the venerable matron reduced amidst the failings and decrepitude of old age to beggary and want,—nothing is said of our missionaries with their wives and their children, driven from their homes, to seek an asylum in Graham's Town; whilst their books, and their furniture, and their houses, are reduced to ashes by the reckless barbarians, for whose good they had been toiling year after year;—nothing, in one word, is said of the tide of desolation, which has been poured over our land from one end to the other; nor of our boers, who after enduring with their constitutional long suffering the perpetual and reckless depredations of the Kaffers year after year, till at last, unable to contend with their galling vexations any longer, have voluntarily expatriated themselves by hundreds, with their wives and their children, and have sought for that peace in the solitudes of the wildermess, which they could not find whilst sheltering themselves under the wings of our Colonial Government. No sympathy is exercised, and no condolence is expressed; *no*, on the contrary *displeasure* is manifested, and strong indignation is expressed, against the supposed outrages, which the settlers have committed against the Kaffers. You perceive I call them '*supposed outrages*;' and so they are. We, who live on the frontiers KNOW, that they have no REAL EXISTENCE. The plain truth is this:—Now and then, solitary acts of impropriety and injustice might have been committed. By an opposing party, these have been coloured and magnified, and made a handle of, and the settlers, as a *body*, have been blamed, yea, branded with infamy, as cruel, and blood-thirsty oppressors. But such they are not: *as a body, I confidently affirm it, they are as industrious, as honorable, as free from being guilty of rapine, plunder, and outrage against their neighbours, whether white or black, as any given number of men in England or any where else.* The grand secret lies here : NO DISCRIMINATION HAS BEEN MADE. The innocent has been condemned with the guilty. As is often the case, the *great body* has been branded with infamy, *because* a few *solitary individuals have acted* dishonorably. This is the TRUTH, THE WHOLE TRUTH, and NOTHING BUT THE TRUTH. This I write more especially for the instruction of my friends in England.

"I am perfectly unconnected with politics. From first to last, I have kept myself in the shades. In public I have said nothing,—I have written nothing,—I have done nothing. And what I have now written, I have written simply and alone, for the sake of TRUTH and RIGHTEOUSNESS; hoping that it will in some small degree rectify the *mistakes* into which our friends at home *have been* LED, respecting the character of their industrious and hard-labouring brethren in this colony."

5th.—MISSIONARY OF THE MORAVIAN SOCIETY.

REV. MR. BONATZ. This gentleman's opinion is to be found in the *Missionary Register*, January 1837, of which the following is an extract :—

"One of the Missionaries of the United Brethren, Br. Adolph Bonatz, placed at Shiloh, among the Tambookies, while he escaped the immediate effects of the War, was in a situation which enabled him to form an impartial judgment : and he seems, in the following extract from one of his communications, though with pain, to fix the greater portion of the blame of aggression on the Natives:—

'It is not easy for me to give a decisive answer to your inquiries as to the true origin of the Kaffer War, and the probable duration of the peace concluded in September last. Though I am a zealous advocate for the Tambookies and Kaffers, I cannot but ascribe the chief part of the blame to them. The Colonists on the border-line have, doubtless, been guilty of frequent provocations, which have contributed to the rupture; but these are not to be compared with the numerous thefts and rapines committed by the Kaffers, for which no redress could ever be obtained from them. It is the prime maxim of a Kaffer to steal when and where he can; and if he is pursued and deprived of his prey, this alone is sufficient to enkindle a deadly hatred in his breast. *Rarely does it happen that hostilities commence with the Colonists. The last war was by no means a hasty outburst, for I had heard of the design three years before; and the only cause which I can assign for it, is the irreconcileable enmity which the Kaffers cherish against our Government for repressing their depredations.*'

The agreement of the Missionaries of so many societies, is sufficiently corroborative of the views entertained by the Wesleyan Missionaries, and fully justifies the expressions used in their address to Sir Benjamin D'Urban: and I would recommend to our censors the following just and charitable remarks of the Editor of the *Missionary Register*, January, February, 1837):—

"It was to be expected, under such circumstances, that the conduct of the Missionaries and Representatives of the Societies labouring in these parts, should be brought under discussion. In forming a judgment of the opinions and proceedings of men of undoubted piety and zeal under such trying circumstances, the utmost candour and a thorough knowledge of the case, are absolutely necessary to sound conclusions."

THE KAFFERS NOT DESCRIBED AS "WOLVES" BY THE
WESLEYAN MISSIONARIES.

The following document explanatory of an absurd statement, criminatory of the Wesleyan Missionaries, (originating in some misapprehension of Sir Benjamin D'Urban), but which served as the text of sundry eloquent appeals to popular feeling in England, is inserted, not from any importance attached to the charge, but as a specimen of the *animus* of a certain party against us, when such childish twaddle could be made the subject of editorial articles, and Missionary speeches :—

[EXTRACT.]

From Minutes of a special District Meeting, held at Morley, Kaffraria, May 11, 1838.

" His Excellency Sir Benjamin D'Urban, in a despatch addressed to Lord Glenelg, dated June 19, 1835, and published in the Parliamentary Papers relating to the Kaffer war, (*see p.* 17), having stated that our Missionaries residing beyond the Kei river, had admitted that their labours had become (at the period to which he adverts) utterly useless ; that they had succeeded in no instance with reference to the conversion of the Kaffers, and that they had compared the Kaffers, for the intractability of their disposition, to wolves ;—What is the opinion of this meeting, on this statement of the Governor ?

" Answer 1.—The brethren concerned disclaim having made any such statement as that to which the question refers, and after making every allowance for the misconception of casual allusions in private and desultory conversations, held between the Missionaries and His Excellency, or any part of his suite ;—we agree in their own opinion of the extreme improbability, that they could have made statements, so utterly irreconcilable with the existing and well known facts connected with the progress of christianity on these several stations ;—facts which are flatly contradictory of the alleged statement.

2.—The brethren also decidedly disclaim having compared the Kaffers to wolves; and they protest against such a construction of any expressions used by them, in conversation with any person whatever. The Wesleyan Missionaries in this district, at that time, having never concurred in the opinion, that the Kaffers are ' irreclaimable savages.'

" A true extract.

   (Signed)   " W. SHAW, Chairman of the district."

APPENDIX.

"MORNING CHRONICLE" AND MR. BOYCE.

The EDITOR OF THE "MORNING CHRONICLE," in his zeal to vilify a *Wesleyan* Missionary, has fallen into an odd mistake. (See *Morning Chronicle*, 5th August, 1836):—

"The inclosures Nos. 14, 15, are singular documents, and will be the subject of much comment. In the latter (Remarks by W. B. Boyce, Wesleyan Missionary), *by way of justification of the harsh measures he recommends*, he states a fact, which all experience hitherto proves, that Colonists from Europe always destroy native tribes." Then follows a garbled extract from my letter to Sir Benjamin D'Urban, making it neither grammar nor sense; in lieu of which I beg leave to refer the reader to the actual letter on which the editor founds his statement. It will be seen that instead of recommending *harsh measures*, I was there advocating an improved system of border policy, the treating the Kaffers on the principles of their own law, and all this *to prevent the Kaffers sharing the fate of most uncivilized people when in contact with Europeans*. (*See Parliamentary Papers, Kaffer war, p. 45.*) So much for the accuracy and justice of gentlemen of the press, where *party* is concerned.

THE LATE MR. PRINGLE AND MR. BOYCE.

The late Mr. PRINGLE, in his *African Sketches*, has inserted a note which requires comment. In the text a Boer is introduced, giving his opinion of the commando of 1828, in defence of the Kaffers against the Fetcani.—"Here we had massacre in all its horrors, &c. But this I hear your English missionaries defend, or wink at, because it was done by Englishmen in authority." The note of Mr. Pringle is as follows:—"This refers, *I presume*, to a letter by Mr. Boyce, Wesleyan missionary, inserted in the *South African Advertiser*, March 13, 1833, defending the justice and expediency of destroying the Fetcani." (Page 367.)

When the *Sketches* reached the Cape colony, it was

clearly proved by the editor of the *Graham's Town Journal,* that the letter which was *presumed* to be alluded to, *was not written at the period referred to in the text!!!* *(See Introductory Remarks to History of Kaffer War, pp.* 18, 19.)

"In illustration of the manner in which charges are got up against the frontier Colonists, a notable instance may be adduced from the work of Mr. Pringle; at page 367, of his *African Sketches*, he quotes from a letter which he states he had received a few weeks before from a Colonist, whom he describes as a most '*respectable*' and trustworthy person, but whose name he does not publish, lest ' it should expose him to bitter colonial persecution.' This respectable person was travelling in company with a field-cornet. ' He was commenting on the measures then in progress for establishing a sort of *cordon sanitaire,* in order to cut off all intercourse with those parts of the interior where the small pox was raging destructively among the native tribes.' In the course of conversation, the field-cornet digresses from the delinquencies of himself and neighbours, to the Fetcani commando, and observes,—' *But all this I hear your English missionaries defend ;*' and lest this covert attack, for which the whole episode appears to be introduced, should not be understood, it is explained in a note that the allusion is to Mr. Boyce's letter in the *South African Commercial Advertiser,* 13th March, 1833. Now if the reader will bear in mind that this conversation is said to have taken place when the small pox raged among the natives beyond the northern boundary, viz.—at the close of 1831, and will then refer to the date of Mr. Boyce's letter, he will find that it was not written till 15 or 16 months subsequently. It is by such acts as these that the frontier inhabitants are injured and traduced ; by such means, that the public mind has been poisoned, and the sympathy of Government for their situation almost, if not altogether, suppressed."

When this exposure was first made in the *Graham's Town Journal*, the editor of the *South African Commercial Advertiser* adroitly attempted to explain the matter so far as my name was concerned, as a mistake of Mr. Pringle's, and to fix the censure upon my esteemed brother Shrewsbury. See the following paragraph, (June 24, 1835).

" We are requested to state that the phrase ' But all this I hear your English Missionaries defend,' in the speech of the Field-cornet, inserted in Pringle's 'African Sketches,' does not refer to Mr. Boyce's letter published in the *Commercial Advertiser*, of March 13, 1838, as Mr. Pringle in a note on the passage, '*presumed*' to be the case; but to a letter written by the Rev. Mr. Shrewsbury, dated ' Butterworth, September 30, 1828,' in which among other observations respecting the 'Attack on the Fitcani,' we have the following words:—

' And the British army, supposing (as, indeed, they had every reason to suppose) that they were engaging Chaka's warriors, till after the battle was over, when they *learned that they had been fighting with another tribe !* Thus, by a most *extraordinary concurrence of circumstances*, Hinza has been saved from the expected assault of an enemy he dreaded, and from the desolation of an enemy, of *whose vicinity he had not the most distant idea !* THUS HAS GOD SAVED THE MISSION; GLORY BE TO HIS HOLY NAME !'

" This letter was published in the Report of the Wesleyan Missionary Society in 1828."

By this miserable attempt at *explaining* the matter, I am convinced that the allusion to the English Missionaries attributed to the Boer, is a mere fabrication imposed upon Mr. Pringle, and inserted on the authority of the " respectable" Colonist, for the mere purpose of exhibiting a Wesleyan Missionary as a *truckling, bloody* monster. It is very improbable, nay all but impossible, for a Boer in a distant part of the colony, to have read or heard of the letter of Mr. Shrewsbury; besides, the letter itself does not say one word in defence of the commando against the Fitcani, but simply speaks of the result as having *providentially* proved favourable to the tribe of Hinza and the Mission.

The letter respecting the Fitcani commando was in reply to an *anonymous* slanderer in the *South African Commercial Advertiser*, January 1833. The commando in question, was an expedition sent by orders of General Bourke, the Lieutenant-Governor of the colony in 1828, for the purpose of *defending* the Kaffers and Tambookies against the marauding tribes of the interior. This *act of mercy* on the part of the Colonial Government *towards its Kaffer neighbours*, has been *insidiously* confounded with the commandos sent to punish the Kaffers, and has been most pertinaciously described as one of the most glaring instances of Colonial aggression on the lives and property of the native tribes!! Although I was not in Africa until 18 months after the commando had taken place, yet having resided nearly four years, part of 1830, 1831, 1832, and again in 1837, in the Amapondo country, near the scene of action, in a village chiefly composed of families belonging to the Fetcani refugees, who had fled from the battle, and had been received as *serfs* by the Chief Faku, I have had the best possible opportunity of acquiring correct information. *I am convinced that the interference of the British Government saved the Kaffers from extermination*, for had not the Fetcani marauders experienced a check, the still more formidable Zulus would in the next year have commenced upon the Tambookies and Kaffers, and reduced them to a state of distress similar to that which the Amapondos experienced in 1827—1829. For defending the justice, policy, and humanity, of thus interfering *to save the Kaffers*, I have been accused of "*defending Colonel Somerset's bloody Commandos!!!* It is impossible to imagine a more glaring instance of wilful misrepresentation.—*(See Colonel Wade's Evidence, pp.* 409—411, *Evidence Abor. Com.: also p.* 91, *Report Evidence Abor. Com).*

No. II.

Exertions of the Wesleyan Missionaries in procuring peace for the Kaffers.

Mention has been made in a preceding page (32) of the

interference of the Wesleyan Missionaries, in procuring peace for the Kaffers, Sept. 1835. The following extracts from the Parliamentary papers, contain the particulars of this negotiation, which has been so strangely *overlooked* by certain *soi disant* philanthropists; although in their anxiety to vilify the Wesleyan Missionaries, every other page of the documentary evidence seems to have been most diligently scrutinized.

1st.—Extract from the evidence of the Rev. J. Beecham. —(*Evidence Aborigines' Committee, pp.* 495, 496.

" We have evidence that our Missionaries did, in the first place, most decidedly object to the proposed banishment of Makoma and Tyali across the Kei. In a letter, dated Graham's Town, August 1, 1835, the Rev. W Boyce gives an account of an interview which he had with the Governor a few days previously, in which he freely expressed his opinions on the painful state of things resulting from the continuance of the Kaffer war. Mr. Boyce says, he felt it to be his duty to state wherein he thought His Excellency's policy was objectionable, and might be misrepresented; he decidedly objected to the expulsion of the tribes of Makoma and Tyali beyond the Kei,—he argued that the thing was impossible,— that Hinza's son would not allow them to pass the Kei,—and that should it be attempted to enforce the measure, the result must be the extermination of about 50,000 people, partly by our troops,— partly by famine, and partly by Hinza's son. He shewed that, as a matter of mere policy, the measure, if it could possibly be carried into effect, was questionable; that so many people, all acquainted with the localities of the colony, and exasperated into enmity, and concentrated in all their strength just beyond the Kei river, and close to a weak frontier, without any check from English influence among them, would prove very serious enemies to the colony; whereas, if taken under Colonial protection and British law and checked by British influence, and watched by a judicious resident, they might not only have their active enmity neutralized, but be converted into our good friends. He moreover respectfully submitted that the insisting upon the expulsion of so many people, involving as it did the loss of so many lives, and perhaps the extermination of the major part of them, would tend to injure His Excellency's measures in the opinon of the public at home, and would, perhaps, prevent the confimation of even the most judicious and beneficial of his plans by His Majesty's government; he, therefore, begged His Excellency not to insist upon the Kaffers going beyond the Kei; especially as the fact that Hinza's son Crili would not permit them to cross into his territory, afforded him a favourable opportunity for modifying his conditions to meet the altered circumstances of the case. The result of this conversation was, that Mr. Boyce offered his services to undertake a journey into Kafferland, for the purpose of attempting to induce the hostile chiefs to enter into a negotiation for the termination of hostilities. He afterwards consulted with his brethren, the other Wesleyan Missionaries, at Graham's Town, as to the best measures for accomplishing their object; and having arranged a plan, it was submitted for the consideration of the Governor in a written communication, dated Graham's Town, July 28, 1835. The plan was as follows:— Mr. Boyce proposed to take Mr. Shepstone along with him, and proceed on the following Monday for Kaffer Drift Post, for the purpose of visiting Kama, and Umkye, in the hope of procuring from them women to carry their message. As Kama's wife and Pato's wife are both sisters of Makoma, they were of opinion that one or both of them, would undertake to carry a message to Makoma and Tyali in the Amatola Mountains. Some of Umkye's women they judged would easily be found to carry a message to Umhala, Zetu, and the other chiefs, who were supposed to be in some part of the country between the Gunube and Kei rivers. The message to be conveyed was to this effect:—Mr. Shepstone it was proposed, should send to Makoma and Tyali, thanking them for giving orders to spare his life, and advising them as their friend to make offers of submission to His Excellency, and stating it as his opinion that should he do this, their expulsion beyond the Kei might be avoided; and Mr. Boyce was to send a similar message to Umhala and Zetu, the sons of Slambie, backed with, the additional authority of his office as missionary to their fathers tribe; reminding them of the last advice of Slambie to his sons, namely, that in all cases of difficulty, the advice of the missionary was to be followed. This message was to be accompanied with a promise that the missionaries would plead with the Governor in their behalf. The plan thus marked out was approved of by His Excellency, and the two missionaries immediately commenced their journey, and successfully accomplished the object for which it was undertaken. The hostile chiefs at once made overtures of peace, and shortly after a treaty was concluded, which annulled the sentence of banishment that had been previously pronounced against Makoma and Tyali."

2nd Extract.—*(Kaffer War. Return printed by order of House of Commons, July* 12, 1837, *pp.* 253, 254.*)*

[*Enclosure* 17, *in No.* 23.]
Copy of a letter from Mr. W. B. Boyce to Governor Sir B. D'Urban.

"Graham's Town, 28th July 1835, Tuesday evening.

" May it please your Excellency,

" This afternoon I consulted with my brethren on the best means of communicating with the chiefs in the Amatola Mountains secretly, so as to excite no suspicions, and at the same time to send such a message as would answer the desired end without in the least committing your Excellency.

" If the following plan be approved of, we think of leaving Graham's Town on Monday for Kafferdrift Post, on our way to visit Kama and Kye, and from them to procure women to carry our message.

First, Kama's wife, and Pato's last wife are sisters of Makomo; we think that they personally, one or both of them, will undertake to convey a message to Makomo and Tyali in the Amatola Mountains. Some of Kye's women will easily be found to carry a message to Umhala, Zetu, &c., who are probably in some part of the country between the Goonoobe and the Kei Rivers.

"Secondly, To prevent the necessity of using your Excellency's name, which might possibly lead the chiefs to form extravagant hopes as to the terms they might expect to obtain, we purpose to act as follows;—

1. Mr. Shepstone will send to Makomo and Tyali, thanking them for their orders to spare his life, and by way of recompensing them for this kindness, will commiserate their present distressed condition, and as their friend who wishes them well, and as a missionary whose duty it is to seek the establishment of peace, will

advise them strongly to send to your Excellency to ask for mercy, stating as a matter of private opinion, that in such case their expulsion beyond the Kei would perhaps be avoided, and other conditions less destructive to them be imposed, such as the giving up stolen cattle, horses, guns, murderers, &c ; and further advising them to ask from your Excellency a place to sit in, *i. e.* a country, there to live under English law. This advice will be enforced by the intelligence sent them at the same time of the determination of your Excellency to carry on the war with increased vigour as soon as the ploughing season is over in the colony, and the consequent certainty of their speedy destruction.

" 2. I shall send a similar message to Umhala and Zetu, the sons of Slambie, backed with the additional authority of my character as the missionary of their father's tribe, reminding them of the last advice of Slambie to his sons, viz. that in all cases of difficulty the advice of the missionary was to be followed.

" 3. We can also state to these chiefs, that although their conduct has made us ashamed of them for a long time past, yet that now, in their distress, and in the certainty of their destruction if peace be delayed until the boors return from ploughing, we will venture to intercede for them, provided they send first to ask for mercy from your Excellency, and thus embolden us to speak in their behalf before they are completely ruined.

" By this means we shall avoid using your Excellency's name, and thus prevent the chiefs from imagining that the colonists are tired of the war. Should the chiefs send to ask for mercy, then your Excellency can negotiate unfettered by any promises, &c., and can impose such terms as the circumstances at the time may render desirable. If the chiefs remain obstinate, then the Colonial Government cannot be charged with inhumanity, as Your Excellency will have made every effort to save them from impending ruin. But we are almost certain that at least some of the chiefs will gladly embrace the opportunity of throwing themselves upon Your Excellency's mercy, and that immediately ; as the Kaffer time for cultivation is quickly approaching, and they will be anxious to obtain a place in which to settle in peace previous to its commencement; otherwise, even if the sword spare them this year, they must die of famine the next.

"I have thought it better to write a few lines to your Excellency rather than to seek another interview. If your Excellency would prefer giving me a verbal approval or disapproval rather than to write, I can wait on Your Excellency at any time that may be appointed.

Trusting Your Excellency will excuse this hasty scrawl at this late hour, I remain, &c.

(Signed) W. B. BOYCE."

Journal of Messrs. William Shepstone, Samuel Palmer, and William B. Boyce, during a short visit to the kraals of Pato and Kye, on this side the Keiskamma River.

"3d August 1835. Left Graham's Town, and slept at Cawood's Post.

"4th August. Left Cawood's post with an escort of six mounted Hottentots, which we dismissed on our arrival at the kraal of Kobus Congo, on the Gwalana River. Under the care of Kobus we proceeded to the kraal of Pato, on the Beka River, having sent a message to the chief Kama to meet us there.

"5th August. Kama arrived about noon, and we immediately stated our business to the three chiefs, Pato, Kama, and Congo. They answered, 'The object of your visit is worthy of the children of God, and one the most desirable in which good men can wish to be engaged: it is good, very good—yea, so good, that it is not good; it is a wonder you never thought upon it before,' Kobus Congo observed, 'War never did and never can make a country right. The chiefs who have made war are only children; they knew nothing of war. They were in a slippery place; they slipped, and in slipping they have fallen. We thank, we thank greatly; we have not words to thank.' We determined to send four women, one of whom was a woman of rank and influence of their own family, who had been married into Gaika's tribe, but had returned home a few days before: this woman was sent for at sunset, and with the others arrived in the course of the night.

"6th August. In the presence of Pato, Kama, and Kobus Congo, we delivered the following message to the four women about to proceed to seek an interview with Makomo, Tyali, &c.: 'Sunjika (Mr. Shepstone) recollects the message sent by Makomo to Pato's tribe at the beginning of the war, viz. that they were to take care that no evil should befall him; he now thanks and has not forgotten Makomo's kindness, so that when in the colony he heard of Makomo's difficulties, he wished to send him a word. The Missionaries also thank Tyali for his word that none of the missionaries should be injured; they think upon that word, and now seek to repay the good intentions of the chiefs by informing them of the storm that is collecting on the other side, which must soon overwhelm them. They saw there was no time to be lost, as already one large body of troops had arrived, and another is expected every day. The boors also, having finished ploughing, were about to reassemble and again enter Kafferland. We had also heard that the Governor had said, that if he entered Kafferland again, he would sweep the country clean; but although this was his determination, yet we knew he was very merciful, as within the last few days he had given proof of his releasing Buku; and having seen this, and being aware of the preparations being made for a second commando, we, namely, Mr. Shepstone, Mr. Palmer and Mr. Boyce, had taken this journey for the sole purpose of sending our advice to Makoma, Tyali, &c. Our word is this: Ask for mercy; say, 'Mercy, great chief!' Say you are tired of war. Ask for a place in which you may sit and plough, as your time for ploughing has arrived, and if you do not now obtain mercy, then such of you as survive the war must die of hunger the next year. Remember that your father Gaika did not entirely reject the advice of his missionary, but often listened to him. If you do not make a trial of our advice, we are clear of your blood. We do not desire to know where the chiefs are, and shall ask no questions of the women, on their return, as to where they saw the chiefs. You must send women to Colonel Smith, and he will send to the Governor, and when we here this, we will entreat for you of the Governor. This same advice which we now send to you we shall send to Slambie's children through Umkye."

"At 1 P. M. we left Pato's kraal and rode to Umkye's place, at which we arrived in less than two hours. Kye appeared more than ordinarily pleased: he said, " I thank heartily; your object well becomes such men as you are, but I fear there can be but little mercy for the sons of Slambie, for even since they first asked mercy, they had, on the not receiving a favourable answer, attacked

Fort Wellington; I will, however, immediately send a message to them. Umhala, Isiyolo, Um Fundi and Zetu are over the Kei, but Zetu has returned lately to collect the scattered people together who are out plundering,' It appeared to us that the chiefs were over the Kei to ensure their personal safety, but that the great bulk of the people were on this side of the river, as they are constantly plundering, or attempting to do so. On our return to Pato's kraal we met the four women, who were proceeding towards the mountains.

"17 August 1835. In the preceding night the four women, Nomabulu, Notonto, Meso, and Deliene, returned from the mission on which they had been sent. After detailing their various marching and countermarching to avoid the troops, they stated that 'they first found Macomo, to whom they delivered our message, who said, 'I thank truly, truly, truly; is this really the word of the missionaries?' Tyəli was sent for, and the message was again repeated to both the chiefs, and both thanked most heartily. Tyali said, 'In my thirst for news, I thank; we have been separated by war from our missionaries, and we have had no one through whom we could send to the Governor; we have sent thrice, but have had no reply. We thought that when the Governor passed by and made peace with Hinza, that all would be peace, and since then we have merely defended ourselves in the mountains; when things came upon us, we only just pushed them off. Many things have transpired between us and the Colonists, and we did say, when Gaika's cattle were taken, we would resist; but we should never have fought, had not the Hottentots said to us, 'Fight you; let us fight.' Is this a fast word the missionaries give us? may we depend upon it? We will take your advice; we will say, mercy, great chief; but we will not at first ask for a place to sit in, neither will we mention our not going over the Kei; we will merely ask for mercy; afterwards when we obtain a hearing, then we can ask. We thank the three missionaries; they must not tire, now the path is open, and they can send news to us at any time.'

"We left Pato's kraal on the Beka about noon, and slept at Cawood's post: the next day, 18th August 1835. we arrived in Graham's Town.

(Signed) For WILLIAM SHEPSTONE, SAMUEL PALMER, and self.
WILLIAM B. BOYCE.

Graham's Town, 21st August 1835.

The perusal of the preceding extracts will show the share which the Wesleyan Missionaries had in bringing the war to a termination. Although generally speaking, it is not right to make comparisons of one class of men with another, to the disadvantage of either party; yet on this occasion, the contrast between the conduct of the Wesleyan Missionaries, and that of Doctor Philip, is forced upon our notice by the injudicious friends of that gentleman. Through the medium of the press, and in popular meetings in England, he has been represented by others, as well as by himself, as THE FRIEND *of the Kaffer tribes*, with whom in fact, he is but slightly acquainted, and possesses very little influence, while he has as yet, done nothing for them. What steps for instance, did Doctor P. take on the spot, to save the Kaffers from the consequences of their own folly? It is notorious that Sir B. D'Urban left Cape Town highly prepossessed in his favour, and that they had been for some time previous, on terms of intimacy. When Sir Benjamin D'Urban came to Graham's Town, and was exposed to the influence of "interested Colonists," did Doctor P. ever avail himself of his previous intimacy to suggest the necessity of caution, &c.? Was it friendly or christian in Doctor P., to cease at that critical period all communication with Sir Benjamin, at the very time he would in his opinion most need the counteracting influence of his counsels? Was it honourable in Doctor P., thus totally to neglect epistolary or personal communication, or remonstrance, with Sir Benjamin, in reference to measures deemed by him objectionable; and yet all the time be diligently employed in attacking his measures, by letters addressed to influential persons at home? Meanwhile through Doctor P.'s carelessness, or want of moral courage, to interfere in a suitable manner on the spot, the Kaffers were left to experience *famine* and the *sword;* and the interposition of the British Government would have arrived too late for any good to them, had not the abused and maligned Wesleyan Missionaries interfered. The man whom Doctor P. described as

xxiv   APPENDIX.

having "*talents alike suited for the cabinet and the field*," would certainly have comprehended the value of such advice, as Dr. P. was capable of giving; and he who "*although a Governor, could afford to have a conscience*," could not have remained insensible to the soul-stirring appeals which Dr. P. is in the habit of inditing. The Wesleyan missionaries, with no advantages arising from Sir Benjamin's personal favour, but on the contrary, *labouring under the disadvantage of having been grossly misrepresented by Dr. Philip to him*, were yet able to produce an impression, and to procure the non-execution of the most objectionable part of Sir Benjamin's intentions. Unless the reason of Dr. P.'s supineness be satisfactorily explained, he must be content to be considered as verily guilty, of so much of the blood and misery, which his interference at an *early* period of the war might have prevented.

No. III.

"*Wrongs of the Kaffer Nation,*" by Justus.

Very recently this work was put into my hands. As a specimen of unblushing impudence it is unequalled in the whole range of contemporary literature. The writer presuming upon the ignorance of the major part of the reading public, has so mixed up the grossest exaggerations, and falsehoods, with a small portion of undoubted truth; that it would require a minute analysis of the work, and a comment upon almost every sentence to do justice to its shameful and unparelleled mendacity. Had it come into my hands sooner, I should have noticed some of the more glaring and insidious misrepresentations it contains, although in such a case, a selection of topics would have been difficult, where almost all are equally censurable. It will be seen however, that though not controversially alluded to, the main positions or assumptions of "Justus" are completely disproved by the plain statement of facts, in the Notes I to VI. The publisher's name on the title-page of *Justus*, is the only respectable thing in the book. How the firm in question were induced to lend the sanction of *their names*, to cover the disguise of a cowardly libeller, *ashamed to discover his own*, we have yet to learn. Some apology is due by them to the religious public, for the circulation of so much anonymous slander. That they have "ignorantly" offended, is but a poor excuse. Did it never occur to them, that no *honest reason* could possibly exist, for the assumption of a fictitious signature? and that where *private character* was so unscrupulously maligned, malice on the part of the concealed libeller, might naturally be supposed to exist? By the very issue of *such* a work, under a feigned name, the publishers have rendered themselves morally responsible, and they can only justify themselves to the world, by compelling the *cowardly unknown* to discover himself, and to stand forth in his own person the defender or apologist, of his own conduct.

Anonymous criticism is at best an unmanly screen, even when opinions are discussed apart from all personalities. It gives to the mysterious unknown, whether he be the periodical critic, or the mere pamphleteer, a weight of influence, frequently unwarranted by the extent of his attainments, or the force of his character. The concealment of the writer's name, precludes the necessity of the exercise of that self-respect and regard to character, which impose a check upon the language, and conduct, of open and avowed partizans. A feigned signature is an effectual shield against all counter criticism, and the writer sits secure behind the veil he has chosen to draw between himself, and the critical curiosity of his opposers or worshippers. Were the veil withdrawn, our ignorant conceptions of the conductors of the press would seldom be realized. The parties interested, conceal from the public eye, the individuals who claim through the medium of the press to exercise dominion over their opinions. The public are thus placed in the situation of those ancient heathens, who ignorantly worshipped in a certain temple, when lo! and behold, instead of *Jupiter tonans*, the deity of the place proved to be a reptile or a monkey.

By some, the authorship of " Justus" is attributed to Doctor Philip. This is not my opinion. Doctor P. gives a colouring, a power, and a point to his writings, which whether we agree or differ from him, cannot fail to interest us; there is therefore, *internal evidence*, that he is guiltless of writing and publishing 300 pages of matter, which never by chance rises above mediocrity either of expression or sentiment. Whether Doctor P. or some of his colleagues *were assenting* to the compilation of *Justus*, and whether they furnished the materials,—arranged the plan, and pointed out the individuals to be *victimized* ; are questions which Doctor P. should fairly meet. It is very singular, that the parties particularly obnoxious to the Rev. gentleman are singled out for special abuse, and exposed to all the venom and spite of what Dr. Johnson calls "*a good hater*." Most probably the actual compiler or amanuensis, is some aspiring *trading* adventurer in philanthropy, trying his "'prentice hand" on Colonial delinquencies. If so his party may be congratulated on the acquisition of a scribe, who, if he bring but a small degree of talent to his work, yet amply atones for his deficiency in that respect, by his thorough familiarity with the whole compass of Billingsgate abuse, and by his magnanimous disregard of the claims of truth, and of the ordinary courtesies and decencies of civilized and *christian* society.

No. IV.

Colonel Somerset and the old Border Policy.

The conduct of this gentleman has been referred to in a

APPENDIX.

preceeding page (7). It is but bare justice to him, to call attention to the following extract from a memorandum addressed by him to Colonel England, July 1832, when the latter officer was about to assume the commandantship of the frontier, during Colonel Somerset's temporary absence in England. The extracts show the admirable temper of the writer, and afford an additional proof of his kindly feeling towards the Kaffer tribes, of whom it has been the fashion in certain quarters to represent him as the ruthless oppressor.

"The general feeling of these tribes is a desire to remain upon friendly terms with the colony, and undisturbed in their present position. Notwithstanding this feeling, small marauding parties from those tribes will be constantly in the colony. The only remedy for this is to adopt the measures laid down for the guidance of patrols; these, however, will not always be successful, and frequent applications will be made to the Commandant by individual farmers for assistance and redress. Upon these occasions all that the Commandant can do upon failure of the usual means, will be to call upon the chief amongst whose tribes the depredation may have been traced, to restore the cattle or to pay an equivalent. Upon tracing stolen cattle to a kraal, nothing can be done but to seize the cattle at once; firmness upon these occasions being the principal dependance for success.

"If it becomes necessary in consequence of failure in tracing the spoor, or for other reasons, to apply to the Chief, it will be necessary after explaining the circumstances, to *hear fully his explanations;* weighing well as to the amount of credit to be given to the probability and truth of his statements. A Chief, however much he may be anxious to prevent the depredations of his people, (fearing the consequences) will never readily admit his people to be in fault, and will turn the point at issue into fifty different positions, in order to throw off the blame or responsibility: not so much to save his people, as from a feeling they have that cattle once in their possession are *bona fide* their property, and they will part with them as they would with drops of blood.

"In cases of depredation, expedition is the great secret; if the Kaffer gets twelve hours' start of your patrol, the chances are you hear no more of your cattle.

"It frequently, however, happens that the depredators (particularly in the case of horse stealing) do not belong to our border Kaffers, but that they come from tribes on the Buffalo and Kei Rivers. This makes the utmost expedition the more necessary, as if they once contrive to get through the border tribes, all pursuit is fruitless.

"The Kaffers are great beggars, always wanting some little favour granted, and it will be found good policy to give way in small matters, that you may succeed and command upon more important points.

"One thing I find it necessary particularly to attend to, namely, that where a complaint is made either of harshness or injustice to hear the statement myself, and to investigate every point, and give my decision upon the matter; the Commandant will do more with the Kaffers in this way than can be imagined. Let them know, and let them feel that you will be firm, that you will punish depredations, *but that you will allow no injustice to be done, and that you are yourself always to be appealed to whenever they have a grievance.*" [See also *Parliamentary Papers*, especially *Return Kaffer War*, for other letters of Colonel Somerset, which shew that he was generally opposed to the depriving the Kaffers of the Neutral Territory.]

No. V.

Claims of the Wesleyan Missionary Society upon the British Government for compensation on account of losses sustained by the Kaffer war.

The following extract from the *Watchman*, (London weekly paper) will serve as an introduction to this subject, which ought not to be lost sight of by the Wesleyan Society, and the real friends of the aborigines of South Africa.

"It would afford us gratification to learn, that the Missionary Societies, at least, are to have compensation for the losses which they sustained in the Kaffer war. *The Wesleyan Society, which occupies the principal field of labour among the Kaffer tribes, experienced, as we have understood, a loss in mission property amounting to several thousands of pounds; and is no compensation to be made for this?* Is the Society to have inflicted upon it a two-fold injury? Its Missionaries, notwithstanding their successful endeavours. in many years of toil and privation, to promote the welfare of the Kaffers—*notwithstanding that their influence was so beneficially exerted in the first instance to restrain many of the Kaffers from joining in the invasion of the colony, and afterwards in bringing about a peace between the contending parties,*—although it has appeared on the testimony of Kaffer Chiefs themselves, *that these missionaries had, for ten years previously. to the war, preserved them and their people from the operation of the Commando system ;*—the Missionaries of the Wesleyan Society we say, who can furnish such practical proofs of their zeal for the real interests of the native tribes, have been artfully and villainously misrepresented as the enemies of the Kaffers, because they opposed themselves to the designs of a party, which sought to accomplish its own purposes under the guise of a pretended philanthrophy— a philanthropy which could palliate, even eulogise, greater atrocities than any committed in the Kaffer war, when the interests of the party rendered it necessary to adopt such a course. Is not this enough? *Has not the Wesleyan Society suffered a sufficient amount of injury in the treatment which its Missionaries have experienced, without being left to meet out of its own funds the great expense of rebuilding the mission premises, and restoring the various property which had been destroyed during the war?* We have admired the patience and forbearance of the Wesleyan Missionary Society in this whole affair; but is this latter injury to be quietedly submitted to? *Will not redress be sought in some other quarter?*"

The expense incurred by the Wesleyan Missionary Society by the destruction of the Mission Stations, loss of cattle, furniture, &c., additional charges arising from the detention of their Missionaries in the colony, cannot be estimated at less than £6,000. They have peculiar claims on the justice of the British Government, arising from the fact *that their stations were destroyed by the enemy in consequence of the open and avowed opposition of the Wesleyan Missionaries, and their Kaffer converts and friends to the war.* It is the grand principle of the Wesleyan Missionaries by which they are guided in their civil relationship in the countries of their "captivity," where "the Lord their God hath brought them," *to seek the peace,* both of the communities among which they dwell, and of those also to which they stand related by national ties. Whatever his private opinion may be as to party politics, a Wesleyan Missionary is bound by his religious principles, neither to connive at domestic treason, nor foreign invasion, whether it occur in Canada, the West Indies, or South Africa.

Another ground of peculiar claim which the Wesleyan Missionary Society possesses for compensation, arises from the fact that *the Missionaries of that Society by their timely interference in assisting in concluding the war, saved the British Government an expenditure of many thousands.* Had the war continued six months longer, what would have been the additional cost to the British Government? Would £50,000 have covered it? Wesleyville Mission Station was abandoned at the request of the Colonial Government, in order that the faithful portion of the Kaffers under Pato and Kama, might be concentrated between the Fish and Keiskamma rivers near the sea, and thus assist in securing Lower Albany.

The Wesleyan Missionary Society may also urge its claims for compensation, on account of its losses in the late war, on the ground of the exertions it has made, and is yet making for the promotion of the religious and educational interests of the inhabitants on the eastern frontier, both within and beyond the Colonial boundary. Not to refer at present to its efforts among the Kaffers themselves; in Albany the friends of this Society have erected by their voluntary contributions, a number of places of worship;

several of which in the more scattered settlements, are the *only* places to which the inhabitants, black or white, can conveniently resort for the worship of Almighty God. This society has also established schools in connection with its various places of worship, and there are now (1838) no less than 1,100 pupils, comprising children of European Settlers and Aborigines of various tribes, who are receiving elementary and religious instruction in these institutions, to which the Colonial Government has never thought proper to grant a single farthing; although they provide the only means of instruction at present afforded to a large proportion of the rising generation in the British Settlement of Albany. Now it cannot be too much to expect that a society which has accomplished so much for the benefit of the settlement, should receive some assistance from the Government, at least towards meeting the serious losses it has sustained by the late unhappy war.

The following tabular view of the Missions of the Wesleyan Society, in South Africa, will serve to shew that this Society is not behind any other religious body in the extent and success of its efforts to promote the welfare of the various native tribes inhabiting this portion of the African Continent; and that while its Missionaries have been enduring calumnies and reproaches the most bitter, for an alleged want of regard to the best interests of the Aborigines; their labours (perhaps the best answer to their accusers) shew them to have done at least as much for the natives, as those whose fame has been trumpetted forth, to the four winds of heaven, as "the friends," and "the saviours" of the Aborigines of Southern Africa.

APPENDIX.

TABULAR VIEW OF THE WESLEYAN MISSIONS IN SOUTH AFRICA.

STATIONS.	Missionaries.	Salaried Agents.	Gratuitous Teachers.	Pupils in the Schools.	Attendants on the Ministry.	Members or Communicants.	Population within limits of the Mission.	REMARKS.
ALBANY.								These Congregations and Societies consist of British Settlers and Natives, the latter comprising Mosambiques, Emancipated Slaves, Hottentots, Kaffers, Fingoes, Bechuanas, &c. &c.
Graham's Town & Settlements in its vicinity,	2	1	60	787	1,490	472	....	
Salem, and ditto.	1	..	6	110	300	86	....	
Bathurst and ditto,	..	1	10	143	340	121	....	
Fort Beaufort, and ditto,	1	1	7	58	170	47	....	
Total in Albany,	4	3	83	1,098	2,300	726	15,000	
KAFFRARIA.								
Newtondale & Kama's tribe	1	1	2	40	100	10	10,000	This tribe has established the observance of the Christian Sabbath, by law; it has also entered into a treaty of *alliance* with the British Government.
Beka, and Pato's tribe,	1	1	2	90	200	12		
Wesleyville & Imidanke	1	1	2	70	150	12		
Fort Peddie and Fingoes,	..	1	4	108	250	20	1,000	The *Fingoes* at the close of the war amounted to about 14,000, but the greater part of these being poor people, are at present engaged in service with the Colonists. About 1,000 reside in the territory allotted them, and they will be joined by others, as soon as by their service, they have accumulated a stock of cattle.
Mt. Coke & Slambie's tribe	1	2	1	50	150	6	15,000	
Butterworth & Hinza's tribe	1	1	2	79	300	24	50,000	
Clarkebury & Tambookies,	..	2	1	86	200	28	75,000	
Morley, and ditto,	1	3	2	430	550	36		
Buntingville & Amapondos	1	2	2	113	420	17	50,000	
Total in Kaffraria,	7	14	18	1,066	2,320	165	201,000	Amongst this population, none but Wesleyan Missions at present exist. The stations of the other Missionary Societies in Kaffraria, are amongst tribes not enumerated in this Table.
ALBANY,	4	3	83	1,098	2,300	726	15,000	
KAFFRARIA,	7	14	18	1,066	2,320	165	201,000	
BECHUANA COUNTRY,	4	7	10	400	2,250	250	35,000	Barolongs, Mantatees, Korannas, Griquas, Newlanders
CAPE DISTRICT, including NAMAQUALAND,	6	5	60	1,002	2,050	217	40,000	Population of Cape Town and District, part of Stellenbosch, and say 3,000 for Namaqualand.
Total,	21	29	171	3,566	8,920	1,358	291,000	

APPENDIX. xxxiii

It may be necessary to remark, that in the Tabular View, it is not professed that perfect accuracy has been attained as to the population and the attendants upon the Ministry; but it is believed the numbers given are very nearly correct. The column headed, "Attendants on the Ministry," is meant to include all persons who have formed the *habit* of attending divine service at the Wesleyan Chapels with more or less regularity, and who regard these chapels as their usual places of worship, whether they are "Members" (Communicants) or not.

All the other numbers quoted in the Tabular View may be perfectly relied upon, being drawn from the latest and most accurate returns, (December 1838.)

The Society employs two printing presses, one for Kaffraria, and the other for the Bechuana country. Grammars of the Bechuana and Kaffer languages have been compiled by two of its Missionaries; and by the joint labours of several of them, the four Gospels and Acts of Apostles, with other portions of Scripture have been translated and printed in the Kaffer language.

Some persons appear to be under an impression that the Wesleyan Missionaries have received no small patronage from the Colonial Government; and this is insinuated by that partizan writer, "Justus," as being the price for which they have bartered the integrity of their Missionary character. But it is enough to say, that this is a calumny which has not even a shred of evidence to give it plausibility. As a Society, the Colonial Government has done nothing for the Wesleyans in South Africa; nay, it has not even done them justice; Episcopalians, Presbyterians, and Roman Catholics, have respectively received, and still receive support for their religious and educational institutions; and even the Independents, represented by the London Missionary Society have obtained at various periods, *large grants of land*, amounting in the whole to more than 20,000 acres, besides an exercise of patronage in the distribution of about *one-half* the valuable lands, forming the Kat River Settlement; but the Wesleyans have received no such grants for their Missionary Settlements, nay, in some instances, the Colonial Government has exacted the Transfer Dues, (a heavy tax, amounting to four per cent. on the purchase money) of the land bought by them, on which to erect their Chapels,—Schools,—and Missionary establishments within the Colony.

It is true that a sum of £75 per annum is paid towards the support of the Wesleyan Minister at Salem; even for this pittance, however, the Wesleyans are not indebted to the local Government, but to a wise and liberal arrangement made by the British Government in 1819, in connexion with the plan for colonizing South Africa, by British Settlers, by which it was stipulated that parties of one hundred families emigrating to the Cape colony, should receive support from the Government for a minister of whatever denomination they might prefer. On this principle a party, of whom the majority were Wesleyans, chose to have a minister of their own denomination; and the Colonial Government was directed by the Right Honorable Henry Goulburn, then Under Secretary of State for the Colonies, to allow such a salary for the Wesleyan minister as might be " adequate to his decent maintenance." But so far from the Wesleyans being smiled upon by the Government of the colony, the kind intentions of the Home Government were partially thwarted, when the Colonial Authorities fixed £75 per annum as being a sum adequate to the " decent maintenance" of a Wesleyan minister; creating thereby, something like an insulting distinction betwixt them, and the ministers of the other denominations in the colony, who receive Government support, and whose salaries are fixed at £200 per annum and upwards.

As to the Wesleyan schools, it has been already stated that the Colonial Government has done nothing whatever for them. This, however, should be understood to refer to the *existing* schools of the society. The Colonial Government did allow £22 10s. per annum towards the salary of a Schoolmaster at Salem, for a few years; but this was afterwards withdrawn, and more than twice the amount was paid for the salary of Schoolmasters, in other parts of the District, where the population was not equal in amount, and where the Schools did not generally include more than half the number of pupils who were accustomed to receive tuition in the Salem school. An application has been very recently made by the Wesleyans for an annual grant towards the salary of a schoolmaster at Clumber, where a school is already in existence; but this application has been unsuccessful, on the ground that a "general system of education for the colony is already recommended to the Home Government." But how this can be a reason for refusing support to a country school in a most destitute neighbourhood, it is hard to understand; especially when at another place of similar destitution, in the same district, but where the population is less numerous, and where a school including the same number of pupils as at Clumber cannot be collected, a minister of another denomination has obtained a promise from the Governor that a schoolmaster shall be supported. Add to this that although the Wesleyans are the most numerous religious body in the Albany district, and they probably pay in this district, the largest amount of general taxes, from which the Government makes its grants to the public schools; yet their ministers and members have ever been most studiously excluded from the district School Commission; which controls the only Government schools in the district. The only remedy for these grievances would be for the Government to grant to the religious bodies which actually establish schools, some annual assistance towards their support, upon some just and well-defined principle referring either to the number of pupils actually instructed, or to the sums raised by voluntary subscription, and actually expended in the education of youth; leaving each denomination to the management of its own schools.

There might be some difficulty in adopting this principle in the United Kingdom, but there can be none in this colony, where in point of fact there is no exclusively established Church, but all the leading denominations are receiving more or less towards the support of their Clergy and Ministers.

It will be seen from the above observations, that so far from the Wesleyan Missionaries having been the objects of any special and distinguishing kindness displayed by the Government, the very reverse is the fact. They have too often experienced in that quarter, a coldness bordering on contempt,—a kind of treatment, which, judging from what has happened in other cases, seems to have arisen from their having never given the Government any trouble. Had they thought it quite consistent with their office and character, to avail themselves of the press, and the platform, for the purpose of magnifying their grievances, and of agitating and clamouring, there is reason to believe that a little more attention would have been given to their wants and claims. But it is surely time for them to speak out, on these points, when their very forbearance is referred to as a proof of their venality, and when the kind and handsome terms in which some gentlemen high in office in the Colony, have occasionally thought proper to speak of their conduct and character, are quoted as evidence that there has been collusion betwixt them and the Cape Government. The Wesleyan Missionaries feel themselves as free from sinister influences, as any men can be. They fear not the frowns of Government, neither are they unduly elated by its smiles. They know how to "Honour" the Queen, and to shew due respect and deference to Her Majesty's representatives, but they "Fear God" *only.*

ERRATA.

The reader will be pleased to correct the following errors of the press:—

INTRODUCTION, page iv, line 14; for 1834, read 1824.
,,   — ,, 31; for 1834, ,, 1830.
NOTE I.   ,, 15, ,, 9; for *these*, read *the*.
,,   16, ,, 12; for *combined*, read *continued*.
,,   19, ,, 7 of the note; for *party*, read *hasty*.
NOTE II. ,, 52, ,, 18   do.   after *frontier policy*, insert *of the Colonial Government*.
,,   54, ,, 18; for *them*, read *thieves*.
NOTE III. ,, 83, ,, 13; for *and*, read *any*.
,,   95, leave out the top line, which has been printed by mistake twice.
,,   — ,, 22; for *partial*, read *practical*.
,,   101, ,, 12; for *opertion*, read *operation*.
,,   — ,, 19; for *parcipate*, read *participate*.
NOTE IV. ,, 114, ,, 4; for *from*, read *for*.
,,   116, ,, 9; insert *be* at the end.
,,   117, note, line 10 from the bottom; for *obeyance*, read *abeyance*.
NOTE V.   ,, 130, line 3 from the bottom; for *desolate* read *dissolute*.
NOTE VII. ,, 170, No. 4: for *immence*, read *immense*.
NOTE IX. ,, 209, foot note, line 21 from the bottom; dele "*free and*"
,,   211, ,, ,, 16 ,,   for "*hold themselves*," read "*hold them*."

INDEX

A

Abasuto tribe (*see* Basuto tribe)
Aberdeen, Earl of: Notes, 6, 11, 50
Aborigines Protection Society: Notes, 146, 177
Aborigines, Select Committee on:
 Intro., v, viii, xi
 Notes, 1, 3, 5–7, 9, 11, 18, 20, 24, 32, 51, 72, 165, 185, 194–5
 App., v, xv, xvi
African Sketches, by Thos. Pringle:
 Intro., iv
 App., xii–xiv
Agents, English: Notes, 33–4, 46, 76, 85, 88, 90, 99, 100, 112–3, 140
Albany:
 Intro, viii, xv
 Notes, 3, 72, 97, 188, 194, 196–215
 App., xxx
Alexander River: Notes, 170
Algoa Bay:
 Intro., xvi
 Notes, 8, 18, 198, 202
Allison: Notes, 213
Alliterative Concord (*see* Euphonic Concord)
Amapakati: Notes, 61–2, 76, 78, 84–90, 112
Amapondo Tribe:
 Intro., x
 Notes, 115, 174, 183–4, 190
 App., xv
Amatola Mountains:
 Foreword, 10, 32
 App., xvii, xviii
American Missionary Society: Notes, 146–7, 164
Ameva River: Notes, 19, 20, 91
Anderson, A.: Notes, 210
Anti-Slavery Society, 21
Appleyard, Rev. John Whittle: Foreword, 13–14
Archbell, Rev. J.: Notes, 192
Armstrong, Capt., 88–9
Arrowsmith: Notes, 169
Atlas: Intro., xvi
Ayliff, Rev. John:
 Notes, 139
 App., v

B

Badenhorst: Notes, 161
Balfour Mission Station: Notes, 8
Bannister, —:
 Intro., x
 Notes, 8, 10–11, 164, 177, 185

Baptist Missionary Society: App., vi–viii
Barrow, J.: Intro., ii, iii–v
Bashee River: Notes, 115
Bastard tribe: Notes, 145, 170, 184
Basuto tribe: Notes, 145, 174, 184
Bathurst, Earl: Notes, 201
Bear, —.: Notes, 89–90
Bechuanas:
 Notes, 14, 121, 126, 145–7, 174, 184, 190
 App., xxxii
Beecham, Rev. John:
 Notes, 1–2, 26, 178, 181
 App., v, xvi
Beka River:
 Notes, 3
 App., vii, xx, xxii, xxx
Bell, Col.: Notes, 8, 58
Bergenaar tribe: Notes, 174
Berg River: Notes, 159
Beresford, Capt.: Notes, 18
Bethelsdorp: Notes, 8
Bigger, Junior: Notes, 164
Birmingham Reformer: Intro., iv
Blaauwkrans River: Notes, 148, 150–1, 160
Block Drift: Notes, 139
Bonatz, Rev. Adolph:
 Notes, 19
 App., ix
Boors (*see* Colonists, Dutch)
Boshoff, 147, 155–63, 170, 190
Botha, Field Cornet T.: Intro., vii
Botman, Chief: Notes, 12, 19, 35, 45, 96, 99
Boundary Wall: Notes, 114–5
Bourke, Genl.: App., xiv
Bowker, Robert: Intro., xii
Boyce, Rev. William Bennington:
 Foreword, 9–13
 App., ii, v, vi, xii–xxii
Breede River: Notes, 159
Brink, J. G.: Notes, 58
Brink, P. J.: Notes, 58
British and Foreign Bible Society:
 Foreword, 13
Brownlee, Rev.:
 Notes, 65
 App., vii
Buffalo Mountains: Intro., xii
Buffalo River: App., xxviii
Buku, Chief: App., xxi
Buntingville Mission Station:
 Foreword, 9, 11

Notes, 115, 171
App., xxxii
Burnly, Mrs.: Notes, 35
Burton, C.: Notes, 97
Bushman's River: Notes, 3, 148, 150–1, 159
Bushmen:
  Intro., ix
  Notes: 75, 111, 157, 166, 170
Butler, Ensign: Notes, 74
Butterworth Mission Station:
  Notes, 20
  App., xiv, xxxii
Buxton, T. F.: Notes, 18

C

Caledon River: Notes, 145, 170
Camdeboo: Notes, 158
Cane, John: Notes, 164
Capai, Chief: Notes, 115, 171, 174
Cape Mounted Rifles: Notes, 34
Cape of Good Hope Papers: Notes, 54
Cape Town:
  Foreword, 13
  Intro., i
  Notes, 8, 21, 35, 116, 123
Cawood's Post: App., xx, xxii
Celliers, Charl: Notes, 162
Chaka, Chief:
  Notes, 3, 171, 190
  App., xiv
Chalmers, Rev.:
  Notes, 20, 36
  App., vii
Chase, J. C.: Notes, 97
Chumi River: Notes, 44, 139
Church Missionary Society: Notes, 152
Church of England: App., vi
Clarkebury Mission Station:
  Notes, 115
  App., xxxii
Cloete, H., 58–60
Clumber: App., xxxv
Cole, Sir Lowry:
  Intro., vii
  Notes, 7–8, 11
Colesberg: Notes, 157
Collett, James: Notes, 81–2, 88
Collins, Col.: Notes, 2
Colonial Records: Intro., viii
Colonists:
  Intro, i–ix, xii–xvii
  Notes, 1–2, 5–6, 14, 20–1, 26–7, 49, 60, 95, 101–3, 176–8, 196
  App., xxii

Colonists, British:
  Intro, iv, viii, ix
  Notes, 27, 72–4, 190–1, 196–215
  App., xxxii
Colonists, Dutch:
  Intro: iv, vi–ix
  Notes: 27, 141, 160–3, 165–6, 168–75, 184–91, 198
Colonists, Emigrant: Notes, 160–91
Colonization, by Rev. J. Beecham:
  Notes, 2, 26, 178, 181
Commando Law: Intro., vii
Commando System:
  Intro., iii, v–viii, xiii
  Notes, 79, 173
  App., xxix
Commissioners: Notes, 33, 35
Congo, Chief Kobus:
  Notes, 20, 35, 43, 53, 75, 96
  App., xx
Congregational Magazine: Notes, 23
Convict Labour: Notes, 114, 125
Corunna tribe: Notes, 157, 166, 174, 184
Court of Inquiry, 1836:
  Intro., xiv
  Notes, 13, 19
Creili, Chief (*see* Kreli, Chief)

D

Davies, Rev. J.: App., viii–ix
Davis, Rev. William J.: App., v
Delagoa Bay: Notes, 51, 145, 174, 190
Deliene: App., xxii
Dingaan, Chief: Notes, 147–8, 151–4, 162, 164, 171, 184, 190
Dinisi, Chief: Notes, 91
Doke, Dr. C. M.: Foreword, 12
Donkin River: Notes, 170
Donkin, Sir Rufane: Notes, 7
Draakberg Mountains (*see* Drakensberg Mountains)
Drakensberg Mountains: Notes, 147, 155, 158–9, 160, 171, 188, 190
Dugmore, Rev. Henry H:
  Foreword, 12
  App., v
Dundas, Major: Notes, 8
Durban Mission, Wesleyan: Foreword, 13
D'Urban, Sir Benjamin:
  Foreword, 9, 10
  Intro., xi, xiii, xiv
  Notes, 3, 9, 16–18, 20–5, 30–1, 48, 51–5, 60, 76, 103, 204, 207–8
  App., i–xxiv
Dushani tribe: Notes, 33, 35

E

Ebden, J. B.: Notes, 58
Eiland's River: Notes, 158
Elephant River: Notes, 170
Ellis, ..: Notes, 199
England, Col.: App., xxvii–xxviii
English East India Company: Notes, 146
Eno, Chief: Notes, 12, 15, 19, 35, 42, 45, 96, 115
Euphonic Concord in Xhosa: Foreword, 10–12

F

Fairbairn, John:
  Intro, iv, vi
  Notes, 12, 14, 24, 209
Faku, Chief:
  Notes, 100–1, 115, 171, 174, 184
  App., xv
Field Cornets:
  Intro, vi, vii
  Notes, 15, 34, 39, 42, 45, 123–4, 129
50th Ordinance: Notes, 126–7
Fingoes:
  Notes, 35, 61, 75–6, 91, 95, 99, 100, 108, 110, 121, 126,·137, 139, 140
  App., xxxii
Fish River:
  Intro: ix, x, xvi
  Notes, 2, 3, 5, 13–14, 74–6, 137–8, 198, 201
  App., xxx
Fitcani tribe:
  Intro, viii, x, xvi
  Notes, 170, 174, 203, 206
  App., xii–xv
Fort Beaufort: Notes, 88–90
Fort Peddie: Notes, 75, 140
Fort Wellington: App., xxii
Fort Willshire:
  Intro., xiv
  Notes, 19
Frazer's Camp: Notes, 138–9
Fredericksburg: Notes, 201

G

Gaika, Chief:
  Intro, xi
  Notes, 6, 14, 20, 31–5, 40, 44–5, 75, 88, 91
  App., xxi–xxii
Gaika tribe:
  Intro, xi
  Notes, 20
  App., xx
Ganya, Chief: Notes, 19

Gardiner, Capt. H. F.: Notes, 164, 188
Gazelle, Chief: Notes, 35, 44
George: Notes, 159, 208
Gladstone, W. E.: Notes, 211
Glasgow Missionary Society:
  Notes, 12, 14, 20, 23–4
  App., vi, vii
Glenelg, Lord:
  Intro, v, viii, x, xiii, xiv
  Notes, 17–18, 23–4, 210–11
  App., ii, vi, xi
Godlonton, R: Notes, 210
Gonaqua Hottentots:
  Intro, ix
  Notes, 3
Gonokwabie tribe: Notes, 12, 52, 64, 75, 88, 93, 95–6, 108–9, 110, 139
Gonubie River: App., xvii
Goonoobie River (*see* Gonubie River)
Goulburn, Henry: App., xxxiv
Graaff Reinet: Notes, 7, 197
Grahamstown:
  Foreword, 9, 12
  Intro., ii, xvi
  Notes, 19, 60, 72, 106, 116, 125–6, 133, 198, 206, 209
  App., vii–viii, xvi–xviii, xx, xxii, xxiii
Grahamstown Journal:
  Notes, 58–9, 142–5, 177, 189, 192
  App., xiii
Grammar of the Kaffir Language, by W. B. Boyce: Foreword, 12
Great Fish River: Notes, 3
Grey, Sir George: Notes, 211
Griquas: Notes, 14, 141, 145, 155–6, 157, 166, 169, 170, 184–5, 188
Guanga River: Notes, 93
Gwalana River: App., xx

H

Haddy, Rev. R.: App., v
Halstead, Thomas: Notes, 153
Hare, Col.: Notes, 106
Harris, Capt.: Notes, 146
Hart, —: Notes, 86–7
Heavyside, Rev.: App., vii
Herschel, Sir John: Notes, 146
Hex River, 158, 159
Hintza, Chief:
  Intro., xii, xiv–xv
  Notes, 13, 16, 17, 19, 20, 115
  App., vi, xiv, xvi, xxii
History of Europe, by Allison: Notes, 213–15
Hodgkin, Dr.: Notes, 146
Hottentots:
  Intro, ix, x

Notes, 3, 6, 8–10, 13, 15, 19, 24, 74–5, 111, 119, 121, 126–32, 135, 137–8, 173, 188
App., xxii
Humane Policy, by Bannister:
Intro, xi
Notes, 10, 11, 164, 177, 185

I

Infant School, Cape Town: Notes, 21
Introduction to the Narrative of the Kaffir War, by R. Godlonton: Notes, 164
Isaacs, N.: Notes, 164, 188–9

J

Jarvis, J.: Notes, 210
Joubert, —: Notes, 156
Journey to the Zoolu Country, by H. F. Gardiner: Notes, 164
Justus: App., xxiv–vi, xxxiii

K

Kafferland:
Intro, i, vii, x–xii, xiv, xvii
Notes, 3, 5, 12, 14, 16–17, 19, 22–3, 27, 48, 50, 56, 61, 71
Kaffer Law: Notes, 110, 112
Kaffer's Drift Old Post:
Notes, 138
App., xvii, xviii
Kaffraria (*see* Kafferland)
Kama, Chief William:
Notes, 35, 46, 52, 75, 96, 108, 139
App., xvii, xviii, xx, xxx
Kat River:
Intro, xi
Notes, 5–9, 14, 18, 74, 77, 88, 208
Kat River Settlement:
Notes, 6, 8–10, 12, 19, 99, 129
App., xxxiv
Kay, Rev. S.: Intro., viii
Kayser, Rev. —: Notes, 44, 70
Kei River:
Intro., ix, xiii
Notes, 30–2, 48, 51, 94, 141
App., iii, v, xi, xvi–xix, xxii, xxviii
Keiskamma River:
Notes, 5, 42, 51, 74, 77, 115, 205
App., xx, xxx
King William's Town: Notes, 34, 59, 65
Kok, Chief Adam: Notes, 155–6
Koonap: Notes, 81
Kraai River: Notes, 75
Kreli, Chief:
Notes, 48
App., xvi, xvii

Kurrichane: Notes, 146
Kye, Chief (*see* Umkye, Chief)
Ky Gariep River: Notes, 170

L

Landman, —: Notes, 147
Langa, Chief: Notes, 3
Laing, Rev.: App., vii
Letter to Colonial Secretary, by Capt. Stockenstrom: Notes, 165–8
Letter to the Earl of Aberdeen, by Rev. W. Shaw: Notes, 6, 11, 50
Letter from Piet Retief to Governor: Notes, 142–3
Letter to Sir B. D'Urban, by Rev. W. B. Boyce: Notes, 76–9
Letter to Sir B. D'Urban, by Dr. J. Philip: Notes, 51
London Missionary Society:
Intro., xi
Notes, 8–10, 12, 14, 17, 23–4, 65, 128–30, 137
App., ii, vi, vii, xxxiii
London and Westminster Review: Notes, 108
Louw, Piet: Notes, 139

M

M'Clelland, Rev.: App., vi–vii
Makomo, Chief:
Foreword, 10
Notes, 5–9, 11–12, 14, 18–19, 34–5, 38, 44–5, 56, 70, 75, 91, 96
App., xvi–xviii, xx–xxii
Mancazana River: Notes, 15, 91
Mantatee tribe: Notes, 145, 147, 174, 183–4
Mapassa, Chief: Notes, 75, 91, 170, 184
Map of South Africa, by Arrowsmith: Notes, 169
Mapoota River: Notes, 170
Magomo, Chief (*see* Makomo, Chief)
Maritz, P.: Notes, 147–8, 150, 152, 160–1
Maritz, Stephanus: Notes, 162, 164
Massilekatse, Chief (*see* Moselekatse, Chief)
Matwa: Notes, 35, 45, 91
Matzilikatze, Chief (*see* Moselekatse, Chief)
Memoir of Rev. William Shaw, by Rev. W. B. Boyce: Foreword, 11
Meso: App., xxii
Mildenhall, —: Notes, 88–9
Militia of the Colony (*see* Commando System)

Missionaries:
  Intro., i
  Notes, 7, 11–14, 17, 23, 33, 35, 48, 53, 63, 66, 131, 174–5, 182–3, 192, 194
Missionaries, Wesleyan:
  Foreword, 9
  Intro., xvii
  Notes, 6, 12–14, 18, 23–4, 32, 53, 79, 95, 115, 139
  App., i-xxiv, xxviii-xxxvi
Missionary Register:
  Intro., xi
  Notes, 19
  App., ix, x
Mission Presses:
  Foreword, 12–13
  App., xxiii
Modder River: Notes, 156, 170
Molesworth, Sir W.: Notes, 29
Moodie, D.: Intro., vii
Moravian Missionary Society:
  Notes, 19
  App., vi, ix
Morley Mission Station:
  Notes: 115, 171
  App., vi, xi, xxxii
Morning Chronicle: App., xii
Moroko, Chief: Notes, 156–8, 184
Moselekatse, Chief: Notes, 143, 146–8, 151, 170, 184
Moshesh, Chief: Notes, 174, 184
Mount Coke Mission Station:
  Foreword, 9
  Notes, 12, 18

N

Napier, Sir George: Notes, 65, 97, 99, 107–8, 115–6, 140, 195, 208, 211
Narrative of the Kaffir War, by T. Pringle: Notes, 7, 164
Natal: Notes, 115, 155, 158–9, 163–4, 171, 179, 183, 188–91
Neutral Territory:
  Notes: 6, 8, 12, 15, 139
  App., xxviii
Newgate Calendar: Intro., v
Newland: Notes, 157
Newtondale Mission Station:
  Foreword, 9, 13
  App., xxxii
Nielson, William: Notes, 155–6
Nieuw Hantam: Notes, 155, 158
Nomabulu: App., xxii
Nonibe, Chieftainess: Notes, 31, 35, 45–6
Norton, E.: Notes, 210
Notonto: App., xxii

O

Oliphant, A.: Notes, 58
Orange River: Notes, 131, 141, 145, 155–6, 170, 185–6, 188, 192
Orphan Chamber, Cape Town:
  Notes, 97
Owen, Rev. F.: Notes, 148, 152, 155

P

Pagati, Chief: Notes, 46
Palmer, Rev. Samuel:
  Foreword, 10
  Notes, 115
  App., v, xx-xxii
Parliamentary Papers re Kaffer War:
  Notes, 17, 23, 25, 77, 116, 147, 189
  App., xi-xii, xvi, xxviii
Pato, Chief:
  Notes, 35, 46, 53, 70, 75, 88, 96, 108, 139
  App., xvii, xviii, xx-xxii, xxx
Peddie: Foreword, 13
Perciner, Tonjes: Notes, 138
Peula Stream: Notes, 42
Philip, Rev. Dr. John:
  Notes, 9, 12–14, 17–18, 21, 24, 51, 185, 194–5, 208–9
  App., ii, vii, xxiii-xxiv, xxvi
Phillips, Sir Richard: Intro, xvi
Pillans, C. G.: Notes, 58
Police-Kaffer (*see* Treaties)
Police, local: Notes, 123–4
Pondoland: Foreword, 9, 11
Population, Cape Colony *circa* 1838:
  Notes, 119
Port Elizabeth:
  Intro., xvi
  Notes, 19, 202
  App., vi
Port Natal: Notes, 141, 145–6, 153, 155, 158–9, 162, 164, 171, 188, 190, 195
Potgieter, ..: Notes, 147
Pretorius family: Notes, 151
Pringle, Thomas:
  Intro., iii–iv
  Notes, 7, 10, 15
  App., xii-xiv
Printing Presses (*see* Mission Presses)

Q

Quathlamba Mountains (*see* Drakensberg Mountains)
Queen Adelaide Province: Notes, 34, 56, 61

R

Read, Rev. ..:
  Intro., xi
  Notes, 8–10, 12, 14
Rensburg family: Notes, 151
Retief, Piet: Notes, 141, 147–8, 152–5, 160, 162
Returns, Kaffer War: App., vi–vii, xviii
Riet River: Notes, 156, 158, 170
Rili, Chief: Notes, 91, 115, 184
Roman Dutch Law: Notes, 161
Ross, H.: Notes, 58
Rudolph, ..: Notes, 147
Ruiter, Chief: Notes, 3

S

Salem Mission Station: App., xxxii, xxxiv, xxxv
Sandili, Chief: Notes, 31, 35, 45
Sand River: Notes, 143, 158, 160
Select Committee on Aborigines (*see* Aborigines, Select Committee on)
Self Government, Cape Colony: Notes, 116–7
Settlers, British (*see* Colonists, British)
75th Regiment: Notes, 34
72nd Regiment: Notes, 34
Shaw, Rev. William:
  Foreword, 9, 11–13
  Notes, 6, 10–11, 50, 53, 133, 210–11
  App., vi, xi
Shepstone, Theophilus:
  Foreword, 11
  Notes. 37, 48, 70
  App., xvii
Shepstone, Rev. William:
  Foreword, 10
  App., v, xviii, xx–xxii
Shiloh Mission Station:
  Notes, 19
  App., ix
Shrewsbury, Rev. W. J.: App., ii, xiii, xiv
Sikonyella, Chief: Notes, 147, 152, 189
Siwane, Chief: Notes, 31, 35, 45
6th Kaffer War: Foreword, 9
Siyolo, Chief: Notes, 99
Slambie, Chief:
  Intro, xii
  Notes, 3, 6, 20, 31, 45
  App., xvii, xix, xxi
Slambie's tribe:
  Intro., xi–xii
  Notes, 12, 20, 35, 48, 75, 93

Smit, ..: Notes, 162–3
Smith, Dr. Andrew: Notes, 147
Smith, Sir Harry:
  Foreword, 10
  Intro., i, xiii
  Notes, 33, 35, 37–48, 56–7, 58–60, 65–71, 103
  App., xxi
Sneeuwberg Mountains: Notes, 158
Somerset, Col. Henry:
  Notes, 89
  App., xv, xxvi–xxviii
Somerset district: Notes, 197
Somerset, Lord Charles: Notes., 198, 201
Sonto, Chief: Notes, 35
South African Commercial Advertiser:
  Intro., iv–v
  Notes, 24, 58, 99, 102–5, 145, 208–9
  App., xii–xiv
Sparks, Ensign: Notes, 20
Spectator, The London:
  Intro., iv, x
  Notes, 213
State Aid for Missions: App., xxxiii–xxxvi
Steedman, ..: Intro., vi–vii
Stinkhoutberg: Notes, 158
Stock, Chief: Notes, 35
Stockenstrom, Capt. Andries:
  Intro., vii
  Notes, 3, 7–10, 65–6, 69, 71–5, 79, 93–5, 97, 99–104, 106, 108, 113, 137, 139–40, 145, 165–8, 185, 191–2, 206
Stockenstrom's River: Notes, 170
Stock theft in Colony: Notes, 119–20
Stormberg Mountains: Notes, 169–70
Stormberg River: Notes, 170
Stormberg Spruits: Notes, 75
Sunday River: Intro., ix
Sunyika (*see* Shepstone, Rev. William)
Sutton, Lieut.: Notes 20
Suta, Chieftainess: Notes, 31, 35, 45
Swellendam: Notes, 159, 205

T

Taaibosch Berg: Notes, 169
Table Bay: Notes., 199
Tambookie tribe:
  Intro., x
  Notes, 7, 19, 75, 91, 115, 131, 169, 170–1, 174, 181
  App., ix–x, xiv–xv
Tarka district: Notes, 7

Thaba Nchu: Notes, 157
Thompson, W. R.: Notes, 210
Tinta: Notes, 35
Traders: Intro., i
Traps, Capt.: Notes, 199
Travels in South Africa, by J. Barrow: Intro., v
Travels in South East Africa, by Isaacs: Notes, 164
Treaties with Chiefs: Notes, 75–94, 98–9, 108–11, 184–5
Treckard, ..: Notes, 19, 145
Tugela River: Notes, 147, 150–1, 154, 159–60, 171, 188–90
Tyali, Chief:
  Foreword, 10
  Notes, 12–14, 17, 19, 31, 34–5, 38, 44–5, 75, 86–7, 96
  App., xvi–xviii, xx, xxi–xxii
Tzatzoe, Chief Jan: Notes, 17, 35, 46

U

Uitenhage: Notes, 8, 145, 197–8
Umbooti River: Notes, 159
Umfundi, Chief: App., xxii
Umgazi River: Notes, 171
Umgeni River: Notes, 159
Umhala, Chief:
  Notes, 44, 48, 75, 93
  App., xvii–xix, xxii
Umkye, Chief:
  Notes, 46, 75
  App., xvii, xviii, xxi
Umlaas River: Notes, 159
Umselikatsi, Chief (see Moselekatse, Chief)
Umtata River: Notes, 169, 171
Umzalak River: Notes, 159
Umzimkulu River: Notes, 147, 171, 190
Umzimvubu River: Notes, 14, 115, 150, 169, 188, 190
Uys, Piet: Notes, 147, 151, 160

V

Vadanna, Chief: Notes, 115, 184
Vagrancy: Notes, 119–37, 157
Van Aardt, ..: Notes, 89
Van Sittart, ..: Notes, 196
Vet River: Notes, 158
Victoria: Notes, 190
Voortrekkers (see Colonists, Dutch; see also Colonists, Emigrant)

W

Wade, Col.:
  Notes, 6, 8, 14, 16
  App., xv
Wanderings in South Africa, by Steedman: Intro., vi–vii
Warner, J. C.: Foreword, 11
War of the Axe: Foreword, 13
Watchman, London:
  Notes, 210
  App., xxviii–xxix
Wesleyan Magazine: Notes, 19
Wesleyan Missionary Society:
  Notes, 14, 23
  App., vii, xiv, xxviii–xxxvi
Wesleyan Mission Stations in South Africa: App., xxxii
Wesleyville Mission Station:
  Foreword, 9
  Notes, 11–12, 16, 18, 108, 139
  App., xxx, xxxii
Williams, ..: Notes, 9
Winterberg Mountains: Notes, 131, 169
Witchcraft: Notes, 36, 42, 47, 59, 60, 62–4, 66, 70
Wrongs of the Kaffer Nation, by Justus: App., xxiv–xxvi, xxxiii

X

Xhosa Euphonic Concord (see Euphonic Concord)
Xhosa language: Foreword, 10–11, 13
Xo-xo: Notes, 20

Y

Yo-Yo, Chief: Notes, 19
Young, Rev. S: Notes, 18, 20

Z

Zetu, Chief: App., xvii–xix, xxii
Zimkulu River (see Umzimkulu River)
Zimboobo River (see Umzimvubu River)
Zitzikamma: Notes, 137, 139
Zonderend River: Notes, 159
Zoolas (see Zulus)
Zulus:
  Intro., x
  Notes, 146–52, 169–74, 183–4, 190
  App., xv
Zuurveld (see Albany)